*The Reality of God
and the Problem of Evil*

D1596555

The Reality of God
and the
Problem of Evil

BRIAN DAVIES

continuum
LONDON • NEW YORK

BT
160
.D38
2006

Continuum International Publishing Group
The Tower Building, 11 York Road, London, SE1 7NX
80 Maiden Lane, Suite 704, New York, NY 10038

www.continuumbooks.com

First published 2006

British Library Cataloguing-in-Publication Data
A catalogue record for this book is available from the British Library.

ISBN: 0–8264–9241–X

Typeset by Kenneth Burnley, Wirral, Cheshire
Printed and bound in Great Britain by Antony Rowe Ltd, Chippenham, Wilts

Contents

In memory of Gareth Moore (1948–2002)

A fine thinker and a great friend

Introduction

As we all know very well, people act badly – sometimes even atrociously. They hurt each other in various ways. Some of them commit gruesome murders. Some of them succeed in acts of genocide. Some of them just pain other people by what they say to them. As we also know, there is (and for a long time has been) a great deal of physical pain and suffering, and a lot of psychological pain and suffering which is not the doing or intention of any human being. Before people came on the scene there were prehistoric animals, many of whom must have died in agony.[1] And there are human beings alive today who are congenitally depressed, who have terminal diseases, and who are victims of natural disasters which leave them disabled. Our world is now, and has long been, full of anguish. Let me put all this by saying that evil is something with which to reckon.[2]

'Evil', of course, is a strong word that people now employ fairly rarely. Nobody likes being given an injection by a dentist (a bad thing to have to endure), but hardly anyone would call the pain of that injection an 'evil'. Then again, we may not approve of people who lie to excuse their late arrival at a party (perhaps this is morally bad), but we would not normally refer to them as evil for doing so. We tend to employ the term 'evil' when referring to a great or horrendous deal of badness – like that present in genocide, ruthless serial killing, wanton cruelty, cancer, the deaths of thousands of people by virtue of an earthquake, and so on. But badness is badness, even if it admits of degrees (from slight to horrendous). Medieval thinkers had one word for it in all its forms – *malum* (which we can translate either as 'badness' or as 'evil'). *Malum*, they rightly concluded, is all-pervasive. And, with this thought in mind, I say, once again, that evil is something with which to reckon.[3]

Given this fact, we might be forgiven for concluding that life is pretty grim and makes very little sense on the whole even if we appreciate much of what it gives us – like our families (if we have families), our friends (if we have them), the taste of a good wine (if we can afford it, or get someone to buy it for us), and the music of Mozart (if we have been privileged to have been introduced to it and are not deaf). Yet there are those who believe that the world is created and governed by a God who is omnipotent, omniscient and good. These people tell us that everything we encounter is God's gift to us and is guided by providence or mind (God's providence and mind). They insist that what we deem to be bad or evil in the world is no good reason for abandoning belief in God.

Given how we find the world to be, however, how can these people be right? With this question we come to what is commonly called 'the problem of evil'. It is, of course, an intellectual problem. I might wonder how to protect my family from terrorists, or I might worry about how to avoid heart disease or hurricanes. Then again, I might ask myself how best to control my desire to kill people, or how I might reform compulsive rapists. The problem of evil, however, is usually taken to be a *theoretical* matter, not one where the focus is on how one might bring about some desirable goal (a *practical* matter). In much philosophical literature it is commonly regarded as a philosophical challenge to belief in the existence of God. Does the occurrence of evil in the world show that there certainly is no God, or that there probably is no God? In response to this question some say 'Yes' and some say 'No'. If we take sides with either party here, or are interested in their positions, we are engaged with what now goes by the name of 'the problem of evil'.

How should we approach this problem? My view is that the right way to do so is to proceed by attending to what I would call 'basics'. That is to say, in order profitably to think about God and evil we need to begin by asking 'Is there a God?' and 'What is God?' So in this book I approach the problem of evil by trying to attend to such basics. In the very first line of his *De Providentia*, Seneca (3 BC–AD 65) writes: 'You have asked me, Lucilius, why, if a providence rules the world, it still happens that many evils befall good men. This would be more fittingly answered in the course of a work in which we prove that a providence presides over the universe, and that god concerns himself with us.'[4] You might think of the present book as written by someone partly seeking to follow Seneca's advice.

To start with I offer an introduction to ways in which people have reflected on God and evil since the time of David Hume (1711–1776), whose writings on God and evil did much to influence subsequent discussions of the topic (Hume is almost required reading, or an essential starting point, for the modern debate on God and evil). The purpose of this introduction is to give you (should you need it) a sense of how people have approached the topic of God and evil in recent years (though I also briefly refer to some less-than-recent authors).

I then proceed to talk about God and evil by focusing on the basics to which I have just referred. What I shall be arguing is very much what has been defended by many classical Christian authors – especially Thomas Aquinas (1224/6–1274), to whom I am particularly indebted and to whom I refer frequently in what follows. It has been suggested to me that I refer *too frequently* to Aquinas in this book, and perhaps that is so. Yet, as well as being a major figure in the history of theology, Aquinas is a thinker whose stature is increasingly acknowledged by philosophers (especially analytical ones).[5] And he strikes me as especially illuminating when it comes to issues with which I am here concerned. Aquinas, I think, is someone with whom we may approach the topic of God and evil with renewed vigour and insight. It therefore seems to me appropriate often to bring him into my discussion and sometimes even to engage in expositions of him and in evaluations of what some of his critics have had to say against him. The fact that I do so should not, of course, be taken to imply that points made by Aquinas, ones that I deem valuable, are not also ably made by other authors. Nor should it be taken to imply that a view is right just because Aquinas held it.

I shall be arguing that once what I call 'basics' have been attended to in a certain way, much that has recently been written on God and evil (by both foes and friends of God) should be viewed as either beside the point, just plain wrong, or even morally dubious. But I also want to say something positive about God and evil – to comment on how we might actually think of evil given God's reality. My basic line, counter-intuitive though it might seem, is that we can take much evil to be positively desirable. I deny that the problem of evil shows God to be certainly or probably non-existent. When it comes to evil itself, I argue that, up to a point at least, sense can be made of it (or, at least, of God's goodness in relation to it) if we view it as belonging to a divinely created order, and especially if we view it in the light of some of the things that Christians (and *only* Christians) have said. Theologians sometimes suggest that evil is a mystery and that this is what one should stress with an eye on the problem of evil. My position, though, is that evil, as such, is not a mystery.[6] As we reflect on the problem of evil we should, I think, be ruminating not on the mystery (or problem) of evil but on the mystery (or problem) of good – our proper question being 'Why is there not more good than there is?'

It is easy to write on God and evil without going back to the basics of which I speak above. By this I mean (and only mean) that one is spared a lot of work if one does not take it as part of one's brief to approach the topic of God and evil by starting with questions about the existence and nature of God. Yet I take it as part of my brief to do just this. So I have a major problem at the outset. Discussions concerning the existence and nature of God are legion, and they raise all sorts of questions which cannot be fully dealt with in a single volume. In this one I have tried to deal with many of these questions in what I hope is a cogent way. But I recognize that much that I say could be developed and that there are objections to it which, for reasons of space, I simply pass over in silence. As I have said, though, it seems to me impossible fruitfully to engage with the problem of evil without having some (relatively developed) understanding of God at the outset. Such understanding is what I shall try to present as part and parcel of what I have to say about God and evil (though, as you will see, I believe that our understanding of God is extremely limited).

For comments on various bits of what follows I am grateful (with the usual disclaimer) to Christopher Arroyo, Victor Austin, Michael Baur, David Burrell, Norris Clarke, Peter Geach, Paul Helm, Luke Timothy Johnson, Gyula Klima, D. Z. Phillips, James Ross, James Sadowsky, Charles Taliaferro, Margaret Walker and Charles Wrightington. T. W. Bartel, my copy-editor for this volume, helped me considerably, for he went about his task as a serious thinker and not just as someone able to note where a reference is missing or where a semicolon needs to be provided. I am also grateful to Fordham University for awarding me a Faculty Fellowship (2004/05) which gave me time to work on this book as well as on other things.

In conclusion I should note that all biblical quotations come from the New Revised Standard Version.

Notes

1. It has been suggested that non-human animals do not actually suffer. See, for example, Illtyd Trethowan, *Absolute Value* (George Allen & Unwin: London, 1970), pp. 153f. I think that most people, however, would take this to be a highly eccentric view. Those who do not might express their belief in their position by taking a knife to an unanaesthetized cat. I doubt, though, that many of them would be prepared to do this. In this book, anyway, I take it for granted that non-human animals can undergo suffering. They cannot, of course, suffer in what we might think of as a 'refined' (or 'human') way. They cannot, for example, be pained because their colleagues do not value them enough, or because they have been rejected by people with whom they have fallen in love, or because they endure deep remorse for something they did. But, I am assuming, they can suffer as sentient physical organisms and often give every evidence of doing so. Pain behaviour is a reason for ascribing pain to something – even a non-human animal. And I presume that things which undergo pain undergo suffering.

2. For a brief, albeit partisan, survey of humanly inflicted and other evils, see William Hart, *Evil: A Primer* (St Martin's Press: New York, 2004).

3. In 'The Concept of Evil' (*Philosophy* 79, 2004) Marcus G. Singer takes only people to be paradigmatically evil. And, he says, they are evil because of their evil acts, these being 'acts that are horrendously wrong, that cause immense suffering, and are done from an evil motive – the motive to do something horrendously wrong, causing immense suffering' (p. 193). I sympathize with Singer's discussion since it aims, with some reason, to distinguish evil from what is less than evil. We do, however, typically talk of the evils of various kinds of sickness and other natural occurrences.

4. I quote from Seneca, *Moral Essays*, vol. 1, tr. John W. Basore (Harvard University Press: Cambridge, Mass., 1928).

5. The following volumes (a representative sample only) all testify to the truth of this observation: Brian Davies (ed.), *Thomas Aquinas: Contemporary Philosophical Perspectives* (Oxford University Press: Oxford, 2002); Anthony Kenny (ed.), *Aquinas: A Collection of Critical Essays* (University of Notre Dame Press: Notre Dame, Ind., 1976); Anthony Kenny, *Aquinas on Mind* (Routledge: London, 1993); Anthony Kenny, *Aquinas on Being* (Clarendon Press: Oxford, 2002); Norman Kretzmann, *The Metaphysics of Theism: Aquinas's Natural Theology in 'Summa Contra Gentiles I'* (Clarendon Press: Oxford, 1997); Norman Kretzmann, *The Metaphysics of Creation: Aquinas's Natural Theology in 'Summa Contra Gentiles II'* (Clarendon Press: Oxford, 1999); Robert Pasnau, *Thomas Aquinas on Human Nature* (Cambridge University Press: Cambridge, 2002); Eleonore Stump, *Aquinas* (Routledge: London and New York, 2003).

6.   I mean by this that I do not think that evil is generally something that does not admit, at least in principle, of some kind of explanation. That there are numerous grounds for supposing that evil can be thought of as mysterious, however, is not something I wish to deny. If you think that I should, then you might benefit from reading Predrag Cicovacki (ed.), *Destined for Evil? The Twentieth Century Responses* (University of Rochester Press: Rochester, NY, 2005).

One

The Problem of Evil

In part 10 of David Hume's *Dialogues Concerning Natural Religion*, three characters (Demea, Philo, and Cleanthes) continue a discussion that has already been going on for some time.[1] The discussion, however, now enters a new phase. Cleanthes has previously been stressing the view that God is, in many ways, like human beings, and both Demea and Philo have resisted his way of talking.[2] As part 10 of the *Dialogues* gets under way they press their case against him by drawing attention to evil. 'The topic of human misery', says Philo, 'has been insisted on with the most pathetic eloquence, that sorrow and melancholy could inspire.'[3] According to Demea, 'the united testimony of mankind, founded on sense and consciousness' shows that our pain and suffering is something undeniable.[4]

What kinds of woe do Philo and Demea have in mind here? To begin with, Philo is thinking of damage things do to each other. He says:

The whole earth . . . is cursed and polluted. A perpetual war is kindled amongst all living creatures. Necessity, hunger, want stimulate the strong and courageous: Fear, anxiety, terror agitate the weak and infirm. The first entrance into life gives anguish to the new-born infant and to its wretched parent. Weakness, impotence, distress attend each stage of that life: And it is at last finished in agony and horror . . . The stronger prey upon the weaker, and keep them in perpetual terror and anxiety. The weaker too, in their turn, often prey upon the stronger, and vex and molest them without relaxation. Consider that innumerable race of insects, which either are bred on the body of each animal, or flying about infix their stings on him. These insects have others still less than themselves, which torment them. And thus on each hand, before and behind, above and below, every animal is surrounded by enemies, which incessantly seek his misery and destruction.[5]

Demea subsequently suggests that people tend to triumph over animals that threaten them, but Philo merely continues to drive home his point. He notes that we are prone to worry and fretfulness even when we have achieved certain states of well-being, and he adds that we oppress each other:

> This very society by which we surmount those wild beasts, our natural enemies; what new enemies does it not raise to us? What woe and misery does it not occasion? Man is the greatest enemy of man. Oppression, injustice, contempt, contumely, violence, sedition, war, calumny, treachery, fraud; by these they mutually torment each other. And they would soon dissolve that society which they had formed, were it not for the dread of still greater ills, which must attend their separation.[6]

Demea does not disagree with Philo here. Indeed, he goes on to enlarge on what Philo says by adding to his list of horrors. For, notes Demea, people are also the victims of their physical and psychological constitutions. We are, he observes, prone to disease; and we are subject to remorse, shame, anguish, rage, disappointment, anxiety, fear, dejection, and despair:

> Were a stranger to drop, on a sudden, into the world, I would show him a specimen of its ills, an hospital full of diseases, a prison crowded with malefactors and debtors, a field of battle strowed with carcasses, a fleet foundering in the ocean, a nation languishing under tyranny, famine, or pestilence. To turn the gay side of life to him, and give him a notion of its pleasures; whither should I conduct him? to a ball, to an opera, to court? He might justly think, that I was only showing him a diversity of distress and sorrow.[7]

In short, Philo and Demea have three kinds of woe in mind – (1) ills inflicted on things in the world by natural predators and the like, (2) ills inflicted by people on each other, and (3) ills that affect us because of ways in which our bodies and minds operate (or fail to operate). And Philo thinks that all of these misfortunes place a pretty hefty question mark over belief in God in so far as a likeness is pressed between God and human beings. He asserts:

> EPICURUS's old questions are yet unanswered. Is he [God] willing to prevent evil, but not able? then is he impotent. Is he able, but not willing? then is he malevolent. Is he both able and willing? whence then is evil?[8]

Cleanthes has been comparing God with people, especially morally good ones. Philo is now implying that badness in the world casts doubt on such a comparison. For good people alleviate or prevent ills in so far as they can. Given that many ills are not alleviated or prevented, the inference (so Philo is suggesting) is that God (if there be one) is either lacking in power or morally bad. And that is what others have concluded. In reply to Philo, one might suggest that there are ills of which God (though neither impotent nor malevolent) is simply ignorant. Yet God is commonly said to be all-knowing (omniscient), and with this thought in mind many have added to Philo's charge the codicil: 'Given the ills that there are, God (if there be one) is not omniscient, or not all-powerful, or not morally good; or he is some but not all of these; or he is none of them.' Yet, so it is often claimed, God is *all* of these things. So people thinking along Philo's lines (or thinking that they think along Philo's lines) have frequently insisted that theists are faced with a problem, one damaging to their position as theists – *the problem of evil*, as it is usually called, though, as we shall presently see, it makes sense to speak in this context of *problems* of evil (implying philosophically distinct problems) rather than of *the problem* of evil (implying only one).[9]

Problems of evil and some responses to them

(a) Critics of theism
(i) Hume
As we have seen, Hume (via Philo) appears to be suggesting that it seems hard to believe in God (on one understanding of 'God') given the existence of the evils that we encounter. But this is a very general point to make (and, arguably, not an especially damning one for the theist – after all, one can find it hard to believe in many things one knows to be real).[10] So one might wonder whether Hume wants a con-

clusion having more bite so as seriously to undermine theism. Scholars differ when it comes to interpreting the *Dialogues Concerning Natural Religion* (they differ as to which bits of the text represent Hume's own views), but it seems to me that Hume, in the end, wants to suggest that evil shows that there positively is no God (as Cleanthes conceives of him).

Once Philo has made his case (as reported above) Cleanthes responds by asserting that things in the world are nothing like as bad as Philo makes them out to be. He says:

> The only method of supporting divine benevolence (and it is what I willingly embrace) is to deny absolutely the misery and wickedness of man. Your representations are exaggerated: Your melancholy views mostly fictitious. Your inferences contrary to fact and experience. Health is more common than sickness: Pleasure than pain: Happiness than misery. And for one vexation, which we meet with, we attain, upon computation, a hundred enjoyments.[11]

Yet Hume does not give Cleanthes the last word at this point in his text. For, with Cleanthes having tied his version of theism to the belief that things are better than Philo depicts, Philo promptly insists that Cleanthes' claim is 'doubtful' and that pain is 'infinitely more violent and durable' than pleasure.[12] And Hume goes on to represent Philo as confidently resting his case against Cleanthes on this basis. Discussion of God and evil continues in the *Dialogues* beyond part 10, but nothing emerges to suggest that Hume is not himself happy with the conclusion that, if God is as Cleanthes takes him to be, then there is no God. He has Philo conceding that there *might* be a God even as Cleanthes conceives of him and even though the world is as Philo takes it to be. As the *Dialogues* as a whole makes pretty clear, however, Hume doubts that there is reason to believe in such a God.

So Hume's position on God and evil seems to be this:

(1) Evil in the world is evidence against the existence of God (on one understanding of 'God').
(2) On one understanding of God it might be possible for the evils in the world to be real and for God to be so as well.
(3) There is no reason to think that, in the sense of 'God' taken for granted in (1) and (2), there is a God.

Of course, the less than illuminating phrase in that summary of Hume is 'on one understanding of "God"'. Yet Hume is clearly thinking of God as portrayed by Cleanthes, according to whom God is only different from people when it comes to degree and allowing for the fact that he (unlike people) is ungenerated, incorporeal and everlasting. Philo's worries about God and evil focus on the notions of power, will and goodness. As is clear from many parts of the *Dialogues*, Cleanthes believes God to be powerful, able to act voluntarily, and good. As is also clear, however, he takes God to possess these attributes in much the way that people do – only more so. For him, God and I are both powerful, able to act voluntarily, and good, though God is all of these things to a much greater extent than I am. In particular, so he seems to think, God is much better than I am from the *moral* point of view, and it is this picture of God that Philo, thinking about evil, seeks to undermine.

Let us say that you and I are fairly powerful if we can lift a chair (something that a flea, for example, cannot do). Let us also say that we have the capacity to will if we can just choose to make a pie (something that a stove cannot do). Let us also say that we might be considered to be morally good if we befriend people in need and act, in general, as someone like Mother Teresa of Calcutta did.[13] According to Cleanthes, God is like us in these respects, but he is more powerful, has more options for willing and is much better behaved. Now, so Philo (and Hume) appear to be saying, that view of God is at odds with the facts of evil. There might, Hume seems to think, be both evil and the God in which Cleanthes believes. But it seems *prima facie* unlikely, and it cannot be proved that there is such a God as the one in which Cleanthes believes. Or as Philo says: 'There is no view of human life or of the conditions of mankind, from which, without the greatest violence, we can infer the moral attributes [of God], or learn that infinite benevolence, conjoined with infinite power and infinite wisdom.'[14] In short, Hume seems to be suggesting that, lacking a proof to the effect that there is a morally good and all-powerful God, the reality of evil should lead us to conclude that there is no such God.[15]

(ii) J. L. Mackie

Present-day attacks on belief in God based on evil derive much of their impetus from what Hume writes in the *Dialogues*. So it is not, perhaps, surprising that one of the most influential of recent critics of theism who focuses on evil should be a well-known commentator on Hume. Here I am referring to J. L. Mackie (1917–1981), whose famous paper 'Evil and Omnipotence' has had a considerable impact on philosophical discussion, though its position can be distinguished from that adopted by Hume.[16]

Mackie crisply asserts that evil shows that there *cannot* be a God. He writes:

> In its simplest form the problem is this: God is omnipotent; God is wholly good; and yet evil exists. There seems to be some contradiction between these three propositions, so that if any two of them were true the third would be false. But at the same time all three are essential parts of most theological positions: the theologian, it seems, at once *must* adhere and *cannot consistently* adhere to all three.[17]

But is it true that theists who acknowledge the reality of evil are somehow contradicting themselves? In the work from which I have quoted, Mackie supports the charge of contradiction in three ways.

(i) First, he explains why we should think that God and evil cannot both exist.

(ii) Then he explains how they might both be thought to exist, though only in a way which rejects traditional views about God.

(iii) Finally, he considers a range of solutions to 'the problem of evil', solutions which, so he argues, are misguided.

To begin with, Mackie concedes that 'God exists', 'God is omnipotent', 'God is wholly good', and 'Evil exists' do not, when affirmed together, obviously amount to the manifest self-contradiction of statements like 'One and the same assertion can be simultaneously both true and false' or 'There is something which is both entirely red and entirely green'. The contradiction, says Mackie, 'does not arise immediately; to show it we need some additional premises, or perhaps some quasi-logical rules connecting the terms "good", "evil", and "omnipotent"'.[18] Yet, so Mackie thinks, we can supply such premises or rules. As he puts it:

These additional principles are that good is opposed to evil, in such a way that a good thing always eliminates evil as far as it can, and that there are no limits to what an omnipotent thing can do.

From these principles, says Mackie, 'it follows that a good omnipotent thing eliminates evil completely, and then the propositions that a good omnipotent thing exists, and that evil exists, are incompatible'.[19]

Mackie's second move is to acknowledge that worries about the possible co-existence of God and evil can be set aside, but only at a cost. 'The problem [of evil]', he says, 'will not arise if one gives up at least one of the propositions that constitute it.'[20] So the problem does not arise if, for example, one denies the assertion that God is omnipotent. Nor does it arise if one denies that evil is real. As Mackie implies, however, most theists would not want to deny the assertions now in question. So, as Mackie also implies, giving up 'at least one of the propositions that constitute' the problem of evil is not a serious option for theists.

Some theists, however, without wishing to deny either divine omnipotence or the reality of evil, have tried to explain how the existence of evil can be reconciled with the omnipotence and goodness of God. In seeking to clinch his case against theism, Mackie mentions four such explanations – to each of which he offers counter-arguments:

(a) According to the first, good cannot exist without evil.

(b) According to the second, evil is necessary as a means to good.

(c) According to the third, the universe is better with some evil in it than it would be with no evil.

(d) According to the fourth, evil is due to human free will.

Mackie objects to the first claim by arguing that it effectively denies that God is omnipotent. For, Mackie suggests, good can exist without evil. An omnipotent God, he says, 'might have made everything good'.[21] In response to the second claim, Mackie sees no reason why an omnipotent God has to put up with evil as a means to good. It may, he says, be true that causal laws in the universe necessitate certain evils if certain goods are to arise. But, he adds, omnipotence can hardly be constrained by causal laws which obtain in the universe.

With respect to the third claim Mackie's main objection is that we are still left with a God who is prepared to allow for preventable evil. It has been argued that, even if good can, in principle, exist without evil, there are lots of particular goods which could never have arisen without certain evils. Take, for example, the goodness displayed in the lives of people who consistently care for people in trouble. Such goodness, it would seem, depends for its very being on the fact that people get into trouble. But, says Mackie, in willing a world in which goodness such as this exists, God is willing evil – evil which need never have been.

In turning to the fourth claim Mackie is addressing what is, perhaps, the most popular move made by theists in the face of evil. Commonly referred to as the 'Free Will Defence', this maintains:

(1) Much evil is the result of what people freely choose to do.
(2) It is good that there should be a world with agents able to act freely, and a world containing such agents would be better than a world of puppets controlled by God.
(3) Even an omnipotent God cannot ensure that free people act well (for, if they are free and not puppets controlled by God, what they do is up to them).
(4) Therefore, much evil is explicable in terms of God allowing for the possible consequences of him willing a great good.

However, and without denying the value of human freedom, Mackie finds fault with the Free Will Defence. For he does not see why God could not have made a world in which people always freely act well. He writes:

> If God has made men such that in their free choices they some-times prefer what is good and sometimes what is evil, why could he not have made men such that they always freely choose the good? If there is no logical impossibility in a man's freely choosing the good on one, or on several, occasions, there cannot be a logical impossibility in his freely choosing the good on every occasion. God was not, then, faced with a choice between making innocent automata and making beings who, in acting freely, would some-times go wrong: there was open to him the obviously better possi-bility of making beings who would act freely but always go right.

Clearly, his failure to avail himself of this possibility is inconsistent with his being both omnipotent and wholly good.[22]

(iii) William Rowe

We shall be seeing more of the Free Will Defence later. For now, however, let me turn to another anti-theistic approach to God and evil – the view that, though theists might not embrace contradictory beliefs in the way that Mackie thinks they do, the existence of evil is none the less *good evidence against* the existence of God.[23] Sometimes called the 'evidentialist argument from evil', this line of thinking (essentially a modern version of Hume's position) can be summarized by referring to William Rowe's much-discussed article 'The Problem of Evil and Some Varieties of Atheism'.[24]

In general, Rowe allows that evil (e.g. intense human and animal suffering) might be justifiable if it leads to some greater good, a good not obtainable without the evil in question. With this allowance made, Rowe's basic argument is that there is unjustifiable evil which is good evidence against God's existence. Or, in Rowe's own words:

1. There exist instances of intense suffering which an omnipotent being could have prevented without thereby losing some greater good or permitting some evil equally bad or worse.
2. An omniscient, wholly good being would prevent the occurrence of any intense suffering it could, unless it could not do so without thereby losing some greater good or permitting some evil equally bad or worse.
3. [Therefore] [t]here does not exist an omnipotent, omniscient, wholly good being.[25]

Since Rowe holds this argument to be logically valid, his main concern is to argue for the truth of the first and second premises.

The second premise, says Rowe, 'seems to express a belief that accords with our basic moral principles, principles shared by both theists and non-theists'.[26] For Rowe, therefore, the really controversial premise is the first, and he admits that it might be false. Suppose we try to imagine an instance of pointless suffering. Though we may not be able to see that it serves a good which cannot be obtained without it, there might, Rowe agrees, be such a good. And yet, he continues, we have *good reason* to suppose that there *are* instances of pointless suffering even if we cannot definitively *prove* that there are such instances.

Take, for example, the case of a fawn dying in agony as the victim of a forest fire. 'Is it reasonable', asks Rowe, 'to believe that there is some greater good so intimately connected to that suffering that even an omnipotent, omniscient being could not have obtained that good without permitting that suffering or some evil at least as bad?' Rowe's answer is: 'It certainly does not appear reasonable to believe this. Nor does it seem reasonable to believe that there is some evil at least as bad as the fawn's suffering such that an omnipotent being simply could not have prevented it without permitting the fawn's suffering.'[27] For the sake of argument, Rowe concedes that perhaps he is wrong with respect to the example of the fawn. But what of the multitude of instances of 'seemingly pointless human and animal suffering that occur daily in our world'? Turning to this question, Rowe maintains that the only reasonable conclusion is one unfavourable to the theist:

> In the light of our experience and knowledge of the variety and scale of human and animal suffering in our world, the idea that none of this suffering could have been prevented by an omnipotent being without thereby losing a greater good or permitting an evil at least as bad seems an extraordinarily absurd idea, quite beyond our belief.[28]

With this point made, Rowe holds that his first premise is a reasonable one and that, given also the reasonableness of his second premise, 'it does seem that we have *rational support* for atheism, that it is reasonable to believe that the theistic God does not exist'.[29]

(b) Theistic responses

Mackie and Rowe are clearly arguing for non-theistic conclusions.[30] What, however, have theists said in the face of evil? How have they responded to the charge that evil is proof of, or good evidence for, the non-existence of God? At the risk of simplifying somewhat, we may say that they have mostly done so by embracing one or more of the following lines of argument, some of which Mackie mentions.

(i) The 'We Know that God Exists' Argument

If I know that it often rains in England, I should rightly assume that something is wrong with any attempt to show either that frequent rain in England is impossible or that there is good evidence against its occurring. In a similar way, so it has been argued, we have grounds for supposing that God's existence is not impossible or subject to doubt even though evil exists. For, it has been said, we can know, not only that evil exists, but *also* that God exists, from which it follows (a) that something is wrong with any attempt to show that God cannot exist, and (b) that something is wrong with any attempt to show that there is good evidence against God's existence. Defenders of this line of thought sometimes offer arguments for God's existence. Taking *p* to be equivalent to 'There is a good, omnipotent, omniscient God', their suggestion is that there are positive grounds for accepting *p*, grounds which entitle us to hold that the existence of God is logically compatible with the existence of evil, grounds which also entitle us to hold that there is no evidence based on evil which shows that God does not exist. [31]

(ii) The Unreality of Evil Argument

This argument takes two forms. According to the first, evil is an illusion of some kind. Such is the view of the Christian Science movement, according to which, in the words of its founder, Mary Baker Eddy (1821–1910), 'Sin, disease, whatever seems real to material sense, is unreal . . . All inharmony of mortal mind or body is illusion, possessing neither reality nor identity though seeming to be real and identical'. [32] According to the second form of the argument, evil is unreal since it is no positive thing or quality. Rather, it is an absence or privation of goodness.

What is this second form driving at? It can be found in the work of writers like Augustine of Hippo and Thomas Aquinas, and the first thing to say about it (since this is often not appreciated) is that it is not siding with Mary Baker Eddy and is not claiming that there really is no pain, or that there are no wicked people or bad actions. Augustine and Aquinas would never have denied the reality of suffering or sin. They acknowledge that people and other animals suffer, and that people can be horribly vicious as well as slightly bad. Much of their thinking depends on this recognition. On the other hand, however, they hold that what makes suffering or wickedness bad is the fact that it always amounts to a lack of some kind. On their account, 'evil' or 'badness' is not the name of some independently existing individual (like a particular human being, e.g. Mary) or of some positive quality or attribute (like being feline). Rather, it is a word we use to signify a gap between what is *actually* there and what *could be* there (and *should be* there) but *is not*. There can be people, but there cannot, so Augustine and Aquinas think, be 'baddities' (things whose nature is captured simply by saying that they are bad). There can be wooden boxes, just as there can be wooden chairs. But, so Augustine and Aquinas would say, while 'wooden' signifies a positive property, shareable by different things (like boxes and chairs), 'evil' and 'bad' do not. 'Evil', says Aquinas, 'cannot signify a certain existing being, or a real shaping or positive kind of thing. Consequently, we are left to infer that it signifies a certain absence of a good.'[33] Just as to say 'There is nothing here' is not to say of *something* that *it* is here, so, in Aquinas's view, to say that *there is* evil is not to say that there is *any real individual* or *any positive quality*.[34] With respect to the topic of God and evil, Aquinas regards this conclusion as significant since he thinks of it as implying that God cannot be thought of as causing evil, considered as some kind of thing or as some kind of positive quality. Aquinas holds that God, as Creator, causes the being of all that can properly be thought of as existing (i.e. actual individuals and all their actual, positive properties). On his account, therefore, evil cannot be thought of as something caused (creatively) by God. It is, he thinks, real enough (in the sense that it would be mad to say that nothing is bad or defective or sinful). But it is not, he concludes, something created. Its 'reality' is always a case of something missing.

(iii) The Free Will Defence

As we have seen, Mackie refers to the Free Will Defence. As we have also seen, his verdict on it is negative. But according to many philosophers it is a good response to the charge that evil somehow shows that God cannot, or probably does not, exist. One such philosopher (famous for advocating the Free Will Defence) is Alvin Plantinga.

In 'Evil and Omnipotence' Mackie rejects the Free Will Defence on the ground that an omnipotent God could have made a world in which free people always behave well. According to Plantinga, however, we cannot know that this is so. He agrees that there is no contradiction involved in the notion of someone always behaving well. But, he adds, whether someone freely behaves well in some actual situation cannot be determined by God. Created people must freely decide to act well, and they cannot do that if the fact that they act as they do is determined by God. 'Of course', says Plantinga, 'it is up to God whether to create free creatures at all; but if he aims to produce moral good, then he must create significantly free creatures upon whose co-operation he must depend. Thus is the power of an omnipotent God limited by the freedom he confers upon his creatures.'[35]

It might appear from this last quotation that Plantinga wishes to deny God's omnipotence. Yet that is not the way he sees it. Theists have regularly denied that divine omnipotence means that God can do what is logically impossible, and Plantinga's basic point is that it is logically impossible for God to create a creature whose actions are both free and determined by him. Plantinga wants to say this since he thinks that a free action cannot be caused by anything other than the agent whose action it is. 'If a person *S* is free with respect to a given action,' he writes, 'then he is free to perform that action and free to refrain; no causal laws and antecedent conditions determine either that he will perform the action, or that he will not. It is within his power, at the time in question, to perform the action, and within his power to refrain.'[36]

(iv) The Means and Ends Approach

You would probably think me bad if I cut off someone's leg just for the fun of it. But you would probably not think me bad if I were a doctor who amputated a leg as the only way known to me of saving someone with gangrene. Why not? You would probably say something like: 'Because it is not bad to aim for something regrettable, something we might truly deem to be bad, if we are working toward a good at which we should aim (or are justified to intend) which cannot be achieved in any other way.' And this thought constitutes the basic thrust of what I am now calling the 'Means and End Approach'. Here again we have a line of thought referred to and rejected by Mackie, though it is one which has found many theistic supporters. According to them, the evil we encounter is a necessary means to what is good. Considered as such, evil cannot, they think, be appealed to as part of a *proof of* God's non-existence. Nor is it *evidence for* God's non-existence.

A notable and impressive contemporary defence of the Means and End Approach can be found in Richard Swinburne's book *The*

Existence of God.[37] To begin with, Swinburne endorses a version of the Free Will Defence. It is good, he thinks, that people should be significantly free, but God can only allow them to be this by also allowing them to act badly should they choose to do so. For this reason Swinburne deems human wrongdoing to be explicable as a means to an end (the end being a world of free creatures, the means being God's standing back and allowing them freedom). What, however, of pain and suffering not brought about by people? To this question Swinburne replies by suggesting that this can also be seen as a necessary means to a good. For it is good, thinks Swinburne, that people have serious moral choice to harm or help each other, and, he argues, choice like this can only arise against the background of naturally occurring pain and suffering. He writes:

> If men are to have knowledge of the evil which will result from their actions or negligence, laws of nature must operate regularly . . . if humans are to have the opportunity to bring about serious evils for themselves or others by actions or negligence, or to prevent their occurrence, and if all knowledge of the future is obtained by normal induction, that is by rational response to evidence – then there must be serious natural evils occurring to man or animals.[38]

One might say that there is *too much* naturally occurring evil. Swinburne, however, thinks it reasonable to conclude that this is not so. The fewer natural evils God provides, he suggests, the less opportunity he offers for people to exercise responsibility. To say that there is 'too much' naturally occurring evil, says Swinburne, is effectively to suggest that God should make 'a toy-world; a world where things matter, but not very much; where we can choose and our choices can make a small difference, but the real choices remain God's'.[39] Swinburne considers the possibility of God making himself evident to us so that we always choose well. He thinks, however, that God needs to be somehow hidden if people are to be genuine choosers. If God were really evident to us, says Swinburne, we would desire to be liked by him and our freedom of action would be undermined. 'We will be in the situation of the child in the nursery who knows that mother is looking in at the door, and for whom, in view of the child's desire for mother's approval, the temptation to wrongdoing is simply overborne.

We need "epistemic distance" from God in order to have a free choice between good and evil.'[40]

A line of thinking similar to Swinburne's can be found in John Hick's *Evil and the God of Love* (justly a modern classic on the topic of God and evil).[41] Hick also employs the Free Will Defence: human freedom is a good which entails the risk of evil (the assumption being that a good God would be happy to take such a risk). Then he endorses a line of thought which he claims to derive from the writings of St Irenaeus of Lyon (*c.* 140–*c.* 202). According to Hick, God cannot create a world in which people can morally mature and eventually enjoy a proper relationship with him (this being thought of as a good) unless he also creates a world in which there are obstacles to overcome. Hick understands evil in the light of God's desire not to coerce people into accepting him. He suggests that people are sin-prone creatures, created as such by God, but able, in a world containing naturally occurring evil, to rise to great heights precisely because they are given the opportunity to become mature in the face of evil. He writes:

> Let us suppose that the infinite personal God creates finite persons to share in the life which He imparts to them. If He creates them in his immediate presence, so that they cannot fail to be conscious from the first of the infinite divine being and glory, goodness and love, wisdom, power and knowledge in whose presence they are, they will have no creaturely independence in relation to their Maker. They will not be able to *choose* to worship God, or to turn to Him freely as valuing spirits responding to infinite Value. In order, then, to give them the freedom to come to Him, God . . . causes them to come into a situation in which He is not immediately and overwhelmingly evident to them. Accordingly they come to self-consciousness as parts of a universe which has its own autonomous structures and 'laws' . . . A world without problems, difficulties, perils, and hardships would be morally static. For moral and spiritual growth comes through response to challenges; and in a paradise there would be no challenges.[42]

Athletes say 'No pain, no gain'. This is basically Hick's position when it comes to God and evil.

(v) The 'We Can't See All the Picture' Argument

Another theistic response to arguments such as those of Mackie and
Rowe takes the form of suggesting that we just cannot be sure that
the evil we know about disproves, or is good evidence against, God's
existence since our perspective is limited – since we lack a God's-eye
view of things, so to speak. Shakespeare's Hamlet told Horatio that
'There are more things in heaven and earth than are dreamt of in your
philosophy'. The 'We Can't See All the Picture' Argument suggests
that, though we might find it *hard* to see why there is evil in a world
made by God, there *might* be a reason for it. More precisely, so
defenders of the argument tend to hold, the evil we encounter might
be something God allows or brings about while aiming at a good end
which cannot be reached without it (an end which somehow justifies
the evil) – though we might not be able to show this by argument (i.e.
God has his reasons, even if we cannot understand them). Or as
Demea says in Hume's *Dialogues Concerning Natural Religion*:

> This world is but a point in comparison of the universe: This point
> but a moment in comparison of eternity. The present evil phenom-
> ena, therefore, are rectified in other regions, and in some future
> period of existence. And the eyes of men, being then opened to
> larger views of things, see the whole connection of general laws,
> and trace, with adoration, the benevolence and rectitude of the
> Deity, through all the mazes and intricacies of his providence.[43]

A prominent contemporary writer who defends the 'We Can't See
All the Picture' Argument is William P. Alston.[44] An opponent of
theism (such as William Rowe) might suggest that there exist
instances of intense suffering that God could have prevented without
thereby losing some greater good (let us call this 'Thesis *A*'). According to Alston, however, 'the magnitude or complexity of the question
is such that our powers, access to data, and so on are radically insuf-
ficient to provide sufficient warrant for accepting' *A*.[45] Hamlet's words
to Horatio, says Alston, hit the nail on the head: 'They point to the fact
that our cognitions of the world, obtained by filtering raw data
through such conceptual screens as we have available for the nonce,
acquaint us with only some indeterminable fraction of what there is
to be known.'[46] Alston's thesis is that God knows what he is doing (or
allowing, or whatever); and God might have reasons for doing what

he does (or for allowing what he allows); but we might not be able to understand what God is about as he lives his life.[47]

(vi) What kind of world can we expect from God?
Those who believe evil to be a problem for theists tend to rely on assumptions about the kind of world which God (if he exists) would make. We should therefore note that many theists have addressed the topic of evil and God by trying to call into question some of these assumptions.

Consider, for example, the notion that relief from (or absence of) pain and suffering is an intrinsically good thing, something which God would always lay on for things like human beings. Many anti-theistic writers seem to embrace this notion, but many theists do not. As we have seen, some hold that pain and suffering can perfect human beings. They argue (roughly) that austerity, sacrifice, poverty, and pain can lead to desirable results. And some suggest that what we may loosely call 'an absence of happiness' is not necessarily something which ought not to be brought about even though it could be prevented and even though we know nothing about desirable results. Some critics of theism have said that God (if he exists) would create 'the best possible world'. Others have said that God (if he exists) would maximize happiness for his creatures. But theists have challenged these assumptions as well. They have said, for example, that talk of a 'best possible world' is as incoherent as talk of a 'greatest prime number'. According to C. J. F. Williams, for example, 'It is a consequence of God's infinite power, wisdom and goodness that, for any world we can conceive him creating, it is possible to conceive him creating a better world. More than that – for this has nothing to do with what we can or cannot conceive – for any world which God can create, there is another, better world which he could also have created.'[48] And, though one might be tempted to suppose that 'Maximize happiness' is an imperative which any decent-minded God could be expected to act on, some theists have challenged the idea that such an imperative is intelligible. Suppose we have a happy human being. This person could, presumably, be happier. Is there, then, a limit to happiness – some stage at which further increased happiness is impossible, some stage which God should have brought about for all from the start? Arguing somewhat along the lines of the passage from Williams just cited, George N. Schlesinger has suggested that there is no such specifiable limit. We can, he suggests, always think of ways in which a person's happiness can be in some way increased, and it is no good objection to God's existence to say that God has made a world in which people are less happy than they could be.[49]

With an eye on the question 'What kind of world can God be expected to make?', we should also note that some theists have urged that we can have no reasonable expectations one way or the other. An example here is Aquinas. Taking his lead from the Bible and his own philosophical reflections, Aquinas thinks of God as the source of the being (*esse*) of creatures. For Aquinas, God alone exists by essence or nature, and anything other than God exists because it is made to be by God. It is not, thinks Aquinas, characteristic of God that he should make things like *this* as opposed to things like *that* (though Aquinas is clear that God has made a world of varied things). In so far as anything can be deemed a 'characteristic effect' of God, says Aquinas, it is being (*esse*) – the fact that there is something rather than nothing, the fact that there is any world at all – and this thought leads Aquinas away from suppositions as to what we can expect in a world created by God. We can, he thinks, expect that poison will have certain effects when swallowed by human beings. In general, so he thinks, we can have lots of expectations about what will be produced by what (such expectations are part of what Aquinas would have called a scientific understanding of the world). For Aquinas, however, God is not an object of scientific enquiry, not a part of the world in which science can be developed. For him, God 'is to be thought of as existing outside the realm of existents, as a cause from which pours forth everything that exists in all its variant forms'.[50] If it is logically possible for something to be, then, thinks Aquinas, God can make it to be. But, Aquinas also thinks, we have no means of determining what logically possible things God will make to be. For Aquinas, we have to start by noting what God has, in fact, made to be. Reflections on the topic of God and evil must, so he thinks, start from that, and not from assumptions we might have dreamed up (on what basis?) concerning what God is or is not likely to create.

While defending Aquinas's account of what we can and cannot know of God by rational reflection, Herbert McCabe writes: 'We do not appeal specifically to God to explain why the universe is this way rather than that, for this we need only appeal to explanations within the universe. For this reason there can, it seems to me, be no feature of the universe which indicates that it is God-made.'[51] Like Aquinas, McCabe is suggesting that, since God accounts for there being something rather than nothing, we have no basis as philosophers (i.e. apart from recourse to divine revelation) for expectations concerning the kind of world which God (if he chooses to create) will make.

(vii) God suffers also

A survey of recent theistic responses to those who deny or call into question the existence of God because of the reality of evil would not be complete without a mention of a very contemporary angle on the topic of God and evil. According to this, evil is no more a ground for denying God's existence than it is for denying mine or yours. That is because, so it has been argued, God (like all human beings) is also a victim of evil and also suffers. Authors who might be cited as defending this line of thought include the German theologian Jürgen Moltmann and the Latin American liberation theologian Jon Sobrino.

Classical Christian theists take it for granted that God is utterly changeless (immutable).[52] From this belief it follows that God cannot be acted on (i.e. modified) by anything. It also follows that God cannot undergo suffering (since to suffer is to be passive to the action of something which acts on one to bring about a change of a certain kind). Moltmann and Sobrino, however, deny that God is utterly changeless. According to them, if God is to be really acceptable to human beings he must be capable of suffering and, in this sense, must be affected by evil. In Moltmann's view, the great thing about Christianity is that it offers us a suffering God revealed as such in the person of Christ. Traditional Christian teaching holds that Christ is God, but it also denies that this implies that we can say, without qualification, 'God suffers'. A distinction is made between what is true of Christ *as man*, and what is true of him *as God*. The conclusion then proposed is that, though Christ could suffer as man, he could not suffer as God. Moltmann rejects this traditional way of speaking, however. For him, the divinity of Christ means that divinity *as such* is capable of suffering, and, he says, in the light of this point we can offer comfort to suffering human beings (considered as victims of evil). People in distress can be driven to say that because of their suffering they cannot believe in God. According to Moltmann, however, God and suffering are not to be thought of as irreconcilable with each other. For God suffers too. And that is what Sobrino also wants to say. As he puts it:

> For Saint John, God is love . . . Is that statement real? . . . We must insist that love has to be credible to human beings in an unredeemed world. That forces us to ask ourselves whether God can really describe himself as love if historical suffering does not affect him . . . We must say what Moltmann says: 'We find suffering that is not wished, suffering that is accepted, and the suffering of love. If God were incapable of suffering in all those ways, and hence in an absolute sense, then God would be incapable of loving'.[53]

As we have seen, in his discussion of the problem of evil J. L. Mackie accepts that (what he identifies as) the problem disappears if one gives up on the claim that God is omnipotent. Since Moltmann and Sobrino want to conceive of God as passive to the action of creatures and as himself suffering (a notion which seems at odds with traditional theistic accounts of omnipotence), they can fairly be taken as rejecting belief in God's omnipotence and as representing a response to the problem of evil which writers like Mackie would presumably deem to dissolve the problem as conceived by them.

God and the problem of evil

As you can see, therefore, there are many different approaches on offer when it comes to the topic of God and evil. Can we adjudicate between them? If we are concerned with truth, we presumably ought to try to do so. But how should we proceed? My view is that we cannot proceed to any good effect if we do not start by returning to what, in the Introduction to this book, I referred to as certain 'basics'. When it comes to the problem of evil we cannot, I think, bypass the question 'Is there any reason to believe in God before we start talking about God and evil?' We cannot, I think, make good progress when trying to think about God and evil if we do not (and apart from the issue of evil) ask if there are positive grounds for believing in God to start with. If there are such grounds, the next obvious question to ask is 'What should we suppose God to be?' God is often (though certainly not always) said to be omnipotent, omniscient, and good. But how, when it comes to God, should we construe 'omnipotent', 'omniscient', and 'good'? You might reply: 'It is obvious, is it not?' My view, however, is that it is not obvious. If we are right to think (as I believe we are) that cats are animals which fear water, that is because of what we know of actually existing cats. No sensible scientist would dream of telling us what *X*, *Y*, and *Z* are without copious study of them. By the same token, so it seems to me, talk of God's omnipotence, omniscience and goodness needs to be grounded (should this be at all possible) in a study of God – something, in turn, that needs to come before a discussion of God and evil (or the problem of evil). When turning to such a discussion one needs some serious context. In the next chapter, therefore, I begin to spell out what I think we should take this to be.

Notes

1. Hume's *Dialogues Concerning Natural Religion* was first published in 1779. A second edition appeared in the same year.
2. See, for example, ibid., part 4.
3. I quote from David Hume, *Dialogues Concerning Natural Religion*, ed. Stanley Tweyman (Routledge: London and New York, 1991), p. 152. All my subsequent quotations from the *Dialogues* are from this edition.
4. Ibid., p. 153.
5. Ibid.
6. Ibid., p. 154.
7. Ibid., p. 155.
8. Ibid., p. 157. Epicurus lived from 342/1 to 270 BC. He is quoted by Lactantius (*c.* 260–*c.* 340) thus: 'God either wishes to take away evils, and is unable; or he is able, and is unwilling; or he is neither willing nor able; or he is both willing and able. If he is willing and able, he is feeble, which is not in accordance with the character of God; if he is able and unwilling, he is malicious, which is equally at variance with God; if he is neither willing nor able, he is both malicious and feeble and therefore not God; if he is both willing and able, which is alone suitable to God, from what source then are evils? Or why does he not remove them?' *Patrologia Latina*, 7, 121; I quote from the translation offered in M. B. Ahern, *The Problem of Evil* (Routledge & Kegan Paul: London, 1971), p. 2.
9. I take a theist to be someone who believes in God (and theism to be the belief that there is a God). For the moment, however, I pass over the question 'What is God?' As we shall see, one's approach to the topic of God and evil will be much affected by how one construes the term 'God'.
10. I find it hard to believe that planes can get off the ground and stay in the air. Jilted lovers often find it hard to believe that their former 'others' can have treated them as they did.

11. Hume, *Dialogues Concerning Natural Religion*, p. 158.
12. Ibid.
13. I am not here assuming, of course, that acting well on some occasion makes one a morally good person. One might do a good deed one day and a bad one the next. And so on.
14. Hume, *Dialogues*, p. 160.
15. As readers of the *Dialogues* will quickly discover, Hume certainly seems to think that there is no good proof of the existence of a morally good and all-powerful God.
16. Books by Mackie in which much reference is made to Hume include: *The Cement of the Universe* (Clarendon Press: Oxford, 1974), *Ethics: Inventing Right and Wrong* (Penguin Books: Harmondsworth, 1977), and *Hume's Moral Theory* (Routledge & Kegan Paul: London and Boston, 1980). Mackie's 'Evil and Omnipotence' originally appeared in *Mind* 64 (1955). It has been reprinted a number of times. My page references to this text are linked to the conveniently available reprint of it in Marilyn McCord Adams and Robert Merrihew Adams (eds), *The Problem of Evil* (Oxford University Press: Oxford, 1990).
17. Mackie, 'Evil and Omnipotence', p. 25.
18. Ibid., p. 26.
19. Ibid.
20. Ibid.
21. Ibid., p. 30.
22 Ibid., p. 33.
23. In ch. 9 of *The Miracle of Theism* (Clarendon Press: Oxford, 1982), Mackie softens his charge of contradiction and argues, instead, that evil renders God's existence unlikely.
24. Rowe's paper was first published in *American Philosophical Quarterly* 16 (1979). It is reprinted in Adams and Adams (eds), *The Problem of Evil*. My page references are linked to this text. Although, as I say, Rowe's position is comparable to that of Hume, it is developed somewhat differently and is worth drawing attention to since it has been taken very seriously by a large number of thinkers.
25. Rowe, 'The Problem of Evil and Some Varieties of Atheism', pp. 127f.
26. Ibid., p. 129.
27. Ibid., p. 131.
28. Ibid.
29. Ibid., p. 132.
30. The reader should recognize that I focus on Mackie and Rowe because they present in a clear form arguments offered by a variety of contemporary non-theistic critics of theism writing with respect to the topic of God and evil.
31. What I am calling the 'We Know that God Exists' Argument is implicit in a great deal of Christian philosophical thinking. I take it to be evident, for instance, in the writings of Augustine of Hippo (354–430) and Thomas Aquinas. In recent years, it has been (briefly) defended by Nelson Pike

and (at greater length) by Alvin Plantinga (though by others also). See Nelson Pike (ed.), *God and Evil* (Prentice-Hall: Englewood Cliffs, NJ, 1964), pp. 97f. For Plantinga, see, for example, 'Epistemic Probability and Evil', rep. in Daniel Howard-Snyder (ed.), *The Evidential Argument from Evil* (Indiana University Press: Bloomington, Ind. and Indianapolis, 1996). I shall be defending the 'We Know that God Exists' Argument in this book, but not in the terms in which Pike and Plantinga seem to do so.

32. Mary Baker Eddy, *Science and Health with Key to the Scriptures* (Christian Science Board of Directors: Boston, 1971), p. 257.
33. Thomas Aquinas, *Summa Theologiae*, Ia. 48.1. I quote from vol. 8 of the Blackfriars edition of the *Summa Theologiae* (Eyre and Spottiswoode: London and McGraw-Hill: New York, 1967).
34. Augustine expresses the same line of thought; see *Enchiridion*, 11 and *Confessions*, III.vii.12. For contemporary defences of the view that evil is an absence of a due good (*privatio boni*) see Paul Helm, *The Providence of God* (Inter-Varsity Press: Leicester, 1993), pp. 168ff. and Herbert McCabe, *God Matters* (Geoffrey Chapman: London, 1987), pp. 27ff.
35. Alvin Plantinga, 'God, Evil, and the Metaphysics of Freedom', ch. 9 of *The Nature of Necessity* (Clarendon Press: Oxford, 1974), reprinted Adams and Adams, *The Problem of Evil*, p. 106. Plantinga's position is echoed by many contemporary philosophers of religion. Cf., for example, William Alston, according to whom 'It is logically impossible for God to create free beings with genuine freedom of choice and also guarantee that they will always choose the right' ('The Inductive Argument from Evil', in Howard-Snyder (ed.), *The Evidential Argument from Evil*, p. 112).
36. Plantinga, 'God, Evil and the Metaphysics of Freedom', in Adams and Adams (eds), *The Problem of Evil*, pp. 84f.
37. Richard Swinburne, *The Existence of God*, 2nd edn (Clarendon Press: Oxford, 2004). Swinburne has developed a position on God and evil in *Providence and the Problem of Evil* (Clarendon Press: Oxford, 1998).
38. Swinburne, *The Existence of God*, p. 252.
39. Ibid., p. 264.
40. Ibid., p. 269.
41. *Evil and the God of Love* was first published in 1966. A second edition appeared in 1977. I quote from the 1985 reissue of the second edition (Macmillan Press: Basingstoke and London, 1985).
42. Ibid., pp. 372ff.
43. Hume, *Dialogues Concerning Natural Religion*, p. 158.
44. This argument has defenders earlier than Alston. It can be found, for example, in *An Essay on Man* by Alexander Pope (1688–1744).
45. William P. Alston, 'The Inductive Argument from Evil and the Human Cognitive Condition', in Howard-Snyder (ed.), *The Evidential Argument from Evil*, p. 98.
46. Ibid., p. 109.
47. Alston's line of reasoning may be compared with that found in Peter van

Inwagen's 'The Problem of Evil, the Problem of Air, and the Problem of Silence', ibid., pp. 151ff. For thinking similar to Alston's see also Stephen Griffith, 'The Problem of Pomegranates' in Peter van Inwagen (ed.), *Christian Faith and the Problem of Evil* (Eerdmans: Grand Rapids, Mich., and Cambridge, 2004). Griffith writes: 'Not even the wisest among us is capable of understanding things in the manner that our Creator understands them . . . We are thus free to believe that there is some reason for all the evils in the world, even if we do not always know what that reason might be. To claim that there is not, much less that there cannot be, such a reason, is to claim to know more than any human being could possibly know' (p. 94).

48. C. J. F. Williams, 'Knowing Good and Evil', *Philosophy* 66 (1991), p. 238.
49 George N. Schlesinger, *New Perspectives on Old-Time Religion* (Clarendon Press: Oxford, 1988), ch. 2.
50. Thomas Aquinas, *De Interpretatione*, I.14.
51. Herbert McCabe, 'God:1 – Creation', *New Blackfriars* 61 (1980), p. 412. This article is reprinted in Herbert McCabe, *God Matters* (Geoffrey Chapman: London, 1987).
52. Examples of such theists would be Augustine, Boethius (*c.* 480–*c.* 524), Anselm of Canterbury (1033–1109), and Aquinas. The teaching that God is immutable is a matter of faith (*de fide*) for Roman Catholics. On this see Vatican I's *Dogmatic Constitution Concerning the Catholic Faith* (*Constitutio dogmatica de fide catholica*), ch. 1. The text is conveniently available in Norman P. Tanner (ed.), *Decrees of the Ecumenical Councils*, vol. 2 (Sheed & Ward and Georgetown University Press: London and Washington, DC, 1990).
53. Jon Sobrino, *Christology at the Crossroads* (SCM Press: London, 1978), p. 197. For Moltmann, see his *The Crucified God* (SCM Press: London, 1974).

Two

God the Creator

Why did people ever start saying that God exists? The question is probably impossible to answer with any degree of confidence, but much theistic belief is surely grounded in (even if it does not always directly spring from) a belief that the world or universe is somehow derived from and governed by what is distinct from it. According to the book of Genesis God created the heavens and the earth 'in the beginning'.[1] According to the Qur'an, God, 'the Compassionate, the Merciful', 'created the heavens and the earth to manifest the Truth'.[2] Then again, consider the start of the Apostles' Creed ('I believe in God, the Father Almighty, Maker of heaven and earth') or the beginning of the Nicene Creed ('I believe in one God, the Father Almighty, maker of heaven and earth, and of all things visible and invisible').[3] A traditional development of all these statements insists that God is the Creator in that he makes the world or universe continually to exist from nothing (*ex nihilo*). The basic idea here is that the world depends for its being on God all the time that it exists (and whether or not it *began* to exist), and this idea is certainly central to anything that we might now take to be an orthodox account of what belief in God amounts to.

Many theistic authors have tried to argue that belief in God as Creator is philosophically defensible. Need they bother to do so? More precisely, is it irrational to believe in God as Creator without reference to argument or without the presentation of evidence of some sort? Some philosophers have said that it most certainly is. A notable example is Antony Flew, who urges us to proceed on a 'presumption of atheism'. People on trial in civilized law courts are presumed to be innocent until they are proved guilty. In a similar way, says Flew, the proposition 'God exists' should be deemed to be false until it is shown to be true by reasonable arguments. 'If it is to be established that there is a God,' Flew argues, 'then we have to have good grounds for believing that this is indeed so. Until and unless some such grounds are produced, we have literally no reason at all for believing; and in that situation the only reasonable posture must be that of either the negative atheist or the agnostic.'[4] By 'good grounds' here Flew is clearly not demanding irrefutable demonstrations. Rather, he is looking for a reasonable case, something which suggests that it is more likely than not that God exists. Effectively he is asking that belief in God be supported by some good natural theology – taking 'natural theology' to be an argument, or a set of arguments, designed to show that, without presupposing God's existence at the outset, it is reasonable to conclude that there is, in fact, a God.

Yet Flew's position is too extreme. For it is often perfectly in order (i.e. reasonable) to believe statements that one cannot, in fact, defend by appeal to arguments or evidence. Suppose that you and I meet at a party. I tell you that my name is Brian Davies, and you believe me. Are you being unreasonable here? Surely not, even though you have no arguments or evidence to support what I say at the time that I say it (and even though I might, of course, be lying). Or again, suppose that you get on a plane and arrive at an airport where all the signs tell you that you are, say, in Munich, and where all the airport staff have the same story to offer. You are in no position to offer a reasoned case for believing the signs or the staff, but would you be unreasonable in acting on the supposition that you are, indeed, in Munich (even though it might subsequently turn out that you are the victim of a fantastically elaborate hoax)? Surely not. Believing that such and such is the case on someone's saying so (or believing that such and such is the case because of what is asserted by signs, or books, or the like) is, in general, a perfectly rational thing to do. Indeed, we could hardly get along without believing in this way.[5]

To concede this, however, is not to say that there is no reasonable case to be made for concluding that there is a Creator God, and I now want to suggest that there is such a case to be made (even if we do not need recourse to it, or to comparable cases, in order to be reasonable in believing that there is, in fact, a Creator God).[6] Arguments for God's existence (considered as Creator, but also under other descriptions) are legion and take many different forms. In my view (and as I have argued elsewhere), a number of them deserve respect, but I shall here concentrate on what I take to be the most fundamental and best of them, one for which I am basically indebted to Thomas Aquinas, and one which takes us right to the heart of what the notion of God as Creator seems classically to involve.[7]

The asking of questions

Is there anything that distinguishes people from the other animals among whom they live? Obviously there is. People are *linguistic* animals. They talk to each other using symbols which allow them to communicate on a world-wide basis. Dogs and cats can smell each other (and thereby be familiar with each other at a bodily level), but we can *talk* about the sense of smell. We can also talk about dogs and cats, and we can share an understanding of all these things in a way that non-linguistic animals cannot. When Fido smells Rover, the smell of Rover is in Fido as a sensation he has (so it is Fido's private property, something that belongs to him, and to him alone, just like his nose). But when you tell me that you have just acquired a dog, I have in me exactly what you have in you (the understanding that you have just acquired a dog). Mutual understanding among linguistic animals is not private property. When it occurs, we share thoughts.[8]

We often express our thoughts in positive terms. 'Some dogs have fleas' expresses a thought. So does 'It is often cold in Chicago in January'. We can, however, negate statements like these so as to say 'It is not the case that: some dogs have fleas' or 'It is not the case that: it is often cold in Chicago in January'. And, though our ability to understand signs of negation may seem boringly familiar (second nature, as it were), it has at least one major non-boring function. For it allows us to recognize the possibility of alternatives, the fact that things might be other than they are. And with this recognition comes the tendency to ask questions. For questions, after all, are basically designed to prompt us to work out why things are as they are and not otherwise. This, at any rate, is always the case with sensible questions. One can make up silly questions like 'Why is the number 2 taller than the Eiffel Tower?' or 'Why is green heavier than yellow?' Even if each of the words in these questions has a meaning taken in isolation (which I doubt), the questions themselves are meaningless. With sensible questions, however, such is not the case. With these we pose genuine queries because they latch onto genuine puzzles presented by the fact that things are thus and so rather than some other possible way in which they might have been. At least part of the reason that 'Why is John sneezing?' makes sense is because John might not be sneezing. At least part of the reason that 'Why is it snowing in New York today?' makes sense is because it is not always snowing in New York.[9]

So there are thoughts expressible in statements which can be negated and which therefore naturally lead us to ask 'Why are these statements true?' Of course, there are statements that cannot *but* be true. '9 is greater than 6' is a case in point. There are also statements which cannot *but* be false – e.g. 'What happened last year did not happen'. Statements like these, however, do not give rise to the questions 'Why are they true?' or 'Why are they false?' When something cannot be other than it is, questions as to why it is as it is simply do not arise. Such questions do, however, arise when alternatives are possible. Once we understand what the numbers 9 and 6 are, there is no question as to how 9 comes to be greater than 6. Once we grasp that 'it was the case that such and such happened' and 'it was not the case that such and such happened' are simply contradictory, no question arises as to why it is not true that what happened last year did not happen. Things, though, are different when we come to statements like 'John is sneezing' or 'It is snowing today in New York'. Neither of these statements is true of necessity. If they are true, therefore, it makes sense to ask what accounts for the fact that they are true.

Or does it? It should be clear that I am suggesting that true statements which do not *have* to be true (*contingently* true statements, as we might call them) raise causal questions. They invite us to ask what brings it about that what they report is true. To be sure, some of them might reasonably lead us to ask questions of a different kind – questions concerning what something is by nature, for example. If I simultaneously throw a plastic cup and a crystal wine glass onto a hard surface, the cup may be unharmed while the glass will probably shatter. Someone might ask, 'Why did the cup survive while the glass was destroyed?' This question is not asking what agent or agents brought about a certain outcome. It is asking what it is about something that explains its fate; it is raising a question to be solved by an account of the natures of certain things. But even questions like these readily lead to questions about what we might call 'agent-causation' (the coming about of an effect by virtue of an individual agent – as, for example, when a stick moves a stone). Plastic cups and crystal glasses, whether shattered or not, do not have to be in any particular place. So one might wonder how some particular cup or glass came to be where someone (truly) says that it was (to fall and remain intact, or to fall and be shattered). Or, rather, one might do so if one thinks that it is reasonable to do so, which not everyone has thought. For it has been suggested that, even where we are dealing with a true statement that does not (absolutely speaking) have to be true, it could be that no agent-cause accounts for what the statement reports.

What does this suggestion amount to? It seems to boil down to the conclusion that, *possibly*, not everything that comes to pass in the world, or not everything that exists in it, needs to be accounted for in terms of agent-causation, or the concurrent activity of more than one agent-cause. Someone who defends this conclusion is David Hume. According to him, the ideas of cause and effect are distinct, and it is possible for something to arise (begin to exist), or for something to undergo change, without a cause (an agent-cause). As Hume himself expresses the point:

> We can never demonstrate the necessity of a cause to every new existence, or new modification of existence, without shewing at the same time the impossibility there is, that any thing can ever begin to exist without some productive principle; and where the latter proposition cannot be prov'd, we must despair of ever being able to prove the former. Now that the latter proposition is utterly incapable of a demonstrative proof, we may satisfy ourselves by considering, that as all distinct ideas are separable from each other, and as the ideas of cause and effect are evidently distinct, 'twill be easy for us to conceive any object to be non-existent this moment, and existent the next, without conjoining to it the distinct idea of a cause or productive principle. The separation, therefore, of the idea of a cause from that of a beginning of existence is plainly possible for the imagination, and consequently the actual separation of these objects is so far possible that it implies no contradiction or absurdity.[10]

Hume's argument here, however, is a weak one, based only on imagination. The fact that I can 'imagine' something arising without agent-causation settles nothing when it comes to how things start to be. I can imagine all sorts of things which do not, and maybe cannot, exist, and, if I am a movie producer, perhaps I can put my imaginings onto a very big screen. Yet nothing follows from this when it comes to reality. Or, as Elizabeth Anscombe observes:

> If I say I can imagine a rabbit coming into being without a parent rabbit, well and good: I imagine a rabbit coming into being, and our observing that there is no parent rabbit about. But what am I to imagine if I imagine a rabbit coming into being without a cause? Well, I just imagine a rabbit coming into being. That this *is* the imagination of a rabbit coming into being without a cause is nothing but, as it were, the *title* of the picture. Indeed I can form an image and give my picture that title. But from my being able to do *that*, nothing whatever follows about what it is possible to suppose 'without contradiction or absurdity' as holding in reality.[11]

In reply to Anscombe you might say that you can imagine something coming into existence at some time and place and there being no cause of this. But how do you know that the thing in question has come into existence at the time and place you picture it as beginning to exist? You have to exclude the possibility of it having previously existed elsewhere and, by some means or other, come to be where you picture it as beginning to exist. Yet how are you to do that without supposing a cause which justifies you in judging that the thing really came into existence, rather than just reappeared, at one particular place and time? The truth surely is that recognizing that we are dealing with a genuine beginning of existence is something we are capable of because we can identify agent-causes. As Anscombe writes: 'We can observe beginnings of new items because we know how they were produced and out of what . . . We know the times and places of their beginnings without cavil because we understand their origins.'[12] In other words, to know that something began to exist seems already to know that it has been caused, and to know something about its cause or causes. So it appears odd to suppose that there really could be a beginning of existence without a cause (i.e. an agent-cause).[13]

It seems equally odd to suppose that change in a subject could occur without such a cause. Suppose that my ankle starts to swell. Hume might say 'This could be happening without any agent-cause'.

But what is the force of the 'could' here? When we say that such and such could happen we normally mean that its coming to be is genuinely possible given the way the world is now. Suppose someone says that there could be a change of government in Brazil soon. We would take this to mean something along the lines of 'Many people in Brazil are dissatisfied with its present government, and their votes will bring the government down' or 'Anti-government rebels in Brazil are now sufficiently armed so as to effect a successful revolution'. 'Could', in 'could happen', normally means 'is able to come about given the existence of what is able to bring about certain effects'. In that case, however, why should we pay any attention to the suggestion that my ankle could swell up without an agent-cause? There is a sense of 'could' where it only means 'is not logically impossible', and with this sense in mind someone might say 'Your ankle could swell up without an agent-cause'. But how does such a person know that it *is* logically possible for ankles to swell without anything causing them to do so? If ankles are things which *by nature* only swell because acted on in some way, then it is *not* logically possible for them to swell without anything causing them to do so.

In any case, we do, in fact, look for agent-causes when things begin to exist or get modified. Some people (e.g. Hume) have suggested that we do so only on the basis of 'custom'. Being used to things happening in certain ways, they argue, we naturally expect them always to happen in these ways. This line of thinking, however, is surely wrong. We do not always form causal expectations on the basis of experience. Sometimes we interpret our experience in the light of causal expectations we have. People who have never experienced a tidal wave will normally take very precise (and self-saving) action when told that such a thing is coming their way. Why so? Not because they have personally become accustomed to tidal waves and what they tend to effect. Unless they have studied the nature and effects of tidal waves (this not being something that they are likely to have done by personal contact with tidal waves and their effects), they are probably going to act as they do because of their beliefs about tidal waves, which might well not be based on personal experience of them. They interpret their experience in the light of causal expectations that they have.

And why should they not? We might think that they should not if we suppose that they are disoriented, confused, or even insane. As we all know very well, however, people can form causal expectations which by any interpretation of the word 'rational' are surely rational. I have no serious understanding of (and, given the history of the universe, only a limited experience of) eggs, water, and heat. But I think that I know what to do in order to enjoy a boiled egg for breakfast. My expectations here are based on what I have been taught about the natures of eggs, water, and heat, teaching that I have taken on faith. Are my expectations irrational? If they are, then I have to wonder what the word 'rational' is supposed to mean. 'It is irrational to suppose that putting eggs into boiling water will result in boiled eggs.' 'It is irrational to suppose that hot, solid eggs got to be that way because of immersion in boiling water or the like.' Are we to subscribe to those two statements? Well, people can believe all sorts of things, but I see no reason to suppose that these statements are remotely credible. If they are not, however, then there is something to be said for the view that human causal expectations are not automatically to be dismissed as unreasonable just because they are *expectations*. And we certainly do have causal expectations, which is why we seek causally to account for what lies before us but does not, absolutely speaking, *have* to be there.[14]

If I find gallons of water pouring through the roof of my apartment, I might side with Hume and say that the coming to be of this might have had no agent-cause (this being great news to my landlord, who will not, therefore, worry about me and my lawyers, assuming that he can get a jury or a judge to think as Hume does). But why *should* I agree with Hume here? You might say, 'You should do so unless you can prove that whatever has a beginning of existence always has an agent-cause (or agent-causes) or that every change that takes place always has an agent-cause (or agent-causes).' But that response seems to imply that we should never believe (or are never reasonable in believing) what we cannot prove, which seems positively unreasonable – if 'to prove' means 'formally to demonstrate a conclusion from premises that cannot consistently be denied'. If we are unreasonable in believing what cannot, in this sense, be proved, then we are unreasonable when it comes to most of what we believe. One might, of course, take 'to prove' to mean 'to supply reasonable grounds for believing something or other'. In that case, however, we *can* prove that whatever has a beginning of existence always has an agent-cause (or agent-causes) or that every change that takes place always has an agent-cause (or agent-causes). We can say, for example, that something beginning to exist does so at some particular time and place and that something other than itself must therefore be responsible for it coming to be when and where it does (surely a reasonable assumption?). Or we can say that something which undergoes change cannot itself totally account for the state in which it comes to be, since that state is a way of being which is not present in the thing before the change it undergoes, and since something cannot give itself what it does not have to start with (surely another reasonable assumption?).

A question we might ask

I am suggesting, therefore, that we can reasonably continue with our common practice of asking what it is that accounts for what does not, absolutely speaking, have to be there in our world, and there in the way that it is. So let us now consider just how far this practice can take us – starting with Smokey, my cat, whom I first encountered in a shelter for stray animals.

I wondered where he came from. The people who ran the shelter had no answer. Yet they did not, of course, assume that there was no answer. They did not suppose that Smokey popped into existence uncaused where the person who brought him to the shelter found him. They assumed (and rightly so, surely) that Smokey had parent cats. We can reasonably wonder about the feline sources of cats of our acquaintance (while presuming that there are, indeed, such sources). In a similar way we can ask (while assuming that there are true answers) who people's parents are, or who (or what) produced the buildings we see through our windows.

But we might now push our questions onwards a stage – to move beyond particular individuals belonging to a single kind or class. Suppose that I were to discover that Smokey is the offspring of Caesar and Cleo – two real (or once real) cats. Knowing this fact would explain, to some extent, how Smokey is there for us to talk about. But it would not explain how cats, as such, are there. So we might now ask 'How come cats?' How did cats get going in the first place? And what keeps them going? These are surely reasonable questions. Indeed, so one might say, they are questions which *ought* to be raised. And, perhaps (and as I think many people suppose), there are answers to them which make good scientific sense (answers in terms of evolution, genetics, and whatever in the universe helps to support or promote the lives of cats). We naturally seek to account for the existence of kinds of things, and we presume (or, at least, many of us presume) that we can, in principle, account for this scientifically – in terms of what exists in the universe.

Yet what about the universe itself? If it had a beginning, should we not also seek to account for this causally? And, even if we suppose that it had no beginning, should we not seek causally to account for its existence at any time? If we suppose that the universe did have a beginning, and if, against Hume, we conclude that whatever begins to exist has a cause, then we should presumably posit a cause, or a collection of causes, for the beginning of the existence of the universe (a cause, or a collection of causes, which would have to be distinct from the universe).

Yet why should we suppose that there is a need causally to account for the existence of the universe at any time? It seems (at least to many people) natural and proper to ask what *within* the universe accounts for what it contains at particular times. So it does not seem especially strange or unreasonable to ask 'How come Smokey?' or 'How come cats?' (or 'How come mountains, oceans, deserts, people, the planet Earth, the conditions that exist on Earth, or on the Moon, or on Mars?' – and so on). But what are we to make of 'How come the existence of the universe as such?' I use the phrase 'as such' here in order to highlight the fact that 'How come the universe?' is not asking 'What accounts (or accounted) for the fact that the universe *began* to exist?' but 'What accounts for the existence of the universe *at any time?*' The question seems to amount to 'How come any universe at all (regardless of whether or not the universe is something that had a beginning)?'[15]

This is a puzzling query, to say the least. Be that as it may, however, I now want to suggest that we absolutely do need to ask 'How come the universe, whether or not it had a beginning?' My argument for doing so is a fairly simple one and goes as follows:

(1) Take any object in the universe you care to mention or of which you can conceive (while supposing that it is real).
(2) Any such object has intrinsic properties or qualities – i.e. proper-

ties or qualities which it has in and of itself. (Of *X* we might say that 'John finds it frightening', but being frightening is not a property that is intrinsic to anything. Being mammalian, however, is such a property, as is being human, being made of wood, being a whale, and so on.)

(3) The intrinsic properties of any object are, in principle, ones that can be had by other objects. There are more mammals than one. Many individuals count as human beings. Lots of things are made of wood. There are many whales. And so on.

(4) Therefore, knowing that real objects in the universe have whatever properties they have is not to know that they, as the individual things that they are, actually exist. In this sense, we can distinguish between what real objects in the universe are and whether or not they exist (we can distinguish, if you like, between their existence and their nature).

(5) But if the existence of something is not part of its nature (if it is not something's nature to exist), the thing's existence cannot be accounted for in terms of its nature and requires an external cause. And if the existence of nothing in the universe is accountable for in terms of its nature, the existence of the universe as a whole (and at any time) requires an external (agent-) cause.

In short, we can know what something in the universe (e.g. Smokey) is without knowing that it has to exist, which means that its existence has to be derived, which, in turn, means that the existence of the universe as a whole is derived.

Objections and replies

Can we fault this argument?

(1) is not a premise; it is simply an invitation to think about something. So I cannot see that there is anything to quarrel with here.

(2) might be thought to raise questions about what counts as an intrinsic property. But the examples I give surely indicate what (2) is saying and that (2) is true. It is focusing on what one might say while trying truly to describe what something that exists is actually like. It is not drawing attention to any old predicate that we might use when seeking to say something about something. '____ is identical with itself', '____ is either bigger or smaller than something or other',

'___ is loved by James', and '___ is to the right of the tree' are all examples of predicates that we might use when trying to talk about something. But none of them tells us what anything might be in itself. They do not describe – in the perfectly ordinary sense of 'describe' that we have in mind when we say, for example, 'Tell me what your pet is'. If someone were to say this to me then I would briefly reply somewhat along these lines: 'My pet is a cat. He is male. He has grey fur. His dimensions are thus and so. He is energetic and healthy.' This answer first places my pet into a species (of which there are detailed scientific descriptions available). It then goes on to note positive features that he has which some members of his species lack. In this sense, my answer describes what he is actually like in and of himself. So it seems perfectly proper to say that objects in the universe can be thought of as having intrinsic properties or qualities.

We might, of course, ask 'What should we count as an object?', and that is a difficult question, largely because 'object' (one can say the same of 'thing') is what Ludwig Wittgenstein (1889–1951) once called a 'formal concept'.[16] If you are only told that such and such is an object, you learn nothing when it comes to what it actually is. And even if you think that you know an object when you see one, and if you give an example of what you take to be an object, you might be argued into agreeing that it is really many objects. You might, for example, say that a telephone is an object. Yet even the simplest telephone has many parts. So might not each of these be thought of as objects? And might not their microscopic constituents also be thought of as objects? Given that 'object' is, indeed, a formal concept in Wittgenstein's sense (and I do not deny this), one might well wish to conclude that we have no idea as to what objects there are.

To do so, however, would surely be to end up with a pretty odd belief. Think, once again, of Smokey. He is a single living being. He has parts, of course, and these might be thought of as objects.[17] But, considered as a living and breathing cat, he is obviously an entity in his own right. He is a natural unit. Or again, think of a carrot, or a cabbage, or a stone, or a shell, or a planet, or a star. These are things which are also naturally referred to as entities in their own right. The same can even be said of distinguishable individuals which are not naturally occurring ones – like houses, books, or cars.[18] The same can also be said of everything that makes up our world. We live in a universe in which things can intelligibly be singled out as subjects to be studied, categorized, analysed and described. We live in a universe made up of distinguishable, concrete things (some made up of distinguishable parts, some not), things we can refer to and to which we can apply predicates. There have been philosophers who have denied this, but most (with differing levels of interpretation and elaboration) have affirmed it.[19] So, for present purposes, I am going to suggest that (2) is not a particularly dubious premise on which to draw and that it is, therefore, acceptable even in spite of the formal character of 'object' (for which, also, read 'thing').

(3) seems to be an equally tenable premise to employ. Anything we can predicate of something can also, in principle, normally be predicated of something else. It is, of course, easy to think of possible predicates which could only apply to one thing. Examples would be '____ is the one and only human being who knows about the imminent alien invasion', or '____ is the only daughter of James and Maria Smith'. When we describe things, however, we are rarely picking out features, or descriptions, which are not shareable, and we are not completely doing that even as we use predicates like the two just mentioned. There may be only one human being who knows about the imminent alien invasion, but (a) being a human being, and (b) knowing about an imminent invasion, is what could in principle be truly affirmable of more than one individual. And though James and Maria Smith might have only one daughter, she shares what she is in herself with millions of others (e.g. she is human and female). In so far as we are concerned with what I am calling intrinsic properties (what we can predicate of something as we analyse it and attempt to describe it scientifically), we are concerned with things that are not, in principle, unique.

If this is so, however, we can, following (4), surely draw a serious distinction between what something is and the fact that it exists. One true answer (I am sure that there are more) to the question 'What is Smokey?' is 'A cat'. And we know what cats are (though, while some of us know a lot about them, most of us know only relatively little). Knowing what cats are, however, does not help us in the slightest when it comes to knowing whether there is any such cat as Smokey. The same is true when it comes to other things.

Notice that I am not here suggesting that it is impossible to deduce the existence of cats from something like a nominal definition of 'cat' (i.e. a definition which tells us what the word 'cat' means). That suggestion is different from what I am now proposing. Let us suppose that, along with standard English dictionaries, we take it for granted that 'unicorn' means 'a horse-like creature with a horn on its forehead' (or something along those lines). In that case, there is obviously a sense in which it would be false to say 'It is not the case that: a unicorn is a horse-like creature with a horn on its forehead'. If I talk about unicorns as though they were exactly like dogs, then I am clearly labouring under a delusion and you would be justified in correcting me and insisting that I am somehow in error. But none of this implies that there actually are any unicorns. The fact that the meaning of a word seems to name or designate an existent object does not imply the existence of such an object (as critics of a famous theistic argument commonly called 'the Ontological Argument' have often observed).[20] Yet I am not denying this. I am suggesting that with respect to *actually existing* things in the world we can distinguish between what they are intrinsically and the fact that they exist. Understanding their natures, I am saying, does not involve understanding that any particular one of them exists. You can, for example, know what cats are (you can be scientifically expert when it comes to cats) without knowing that Smokey exists.

Does it therefore follow, however, that things in the world cannot account for their own existence and that the same is true of the universe as a whole at any given time? In other words, is (5) true? I can think of at least five reasons why someone might argue that it is not. These can be expressed as follows:

(a) Even if the existence of particular things in the universe needs to be accounted for with respect to something other than what they are, it does not follow that the existence of all particular things, or the existence of the universe as a whole, needs to be so accounted for.

(b) Even if we grant that the existence of some object does not follow from its nature (and even if we grant that something other than the object accounts for its existence), we need not suppose that there is something distinct from the universe accounting for its existence at any time. We need only suppose that for anything in the universe there is something else within the universe accounting for its existence.

(c) It is wrong to ask what accounts for the sheer existence of anything. We can sensibly ask what accounts for something having a particular nature or a particular property, but we cannot sensibly ask what accounts for something simply existing. For existence is not a property of objects or individuals.

(d) Even supposing that an object's existence cannot be deduced from a knowledge of what it is, there is no reason to suppose that the object's existence is brought about by anything. Why not say that objects in the world can exist uncaused? Why not say that the universe as a whole exists uncaused?

(e) There is no serious alternative to the universe not existing. If we ask 'How come the universe as a whole and at any time?', we must be supposing that there not being a universe is some kind of possibility that might have been realized. Yet the alternative to there being a universe is there being absolutely nothing, which is not an alternative at all.

Yet these lines of thinking are unacceptable, as I shall try to explain by discussing them in order.

In defence of (a) one might argue that (5) commits the fallacy of composition. If every brick in a wall weighs two pounds, it does not follow (and is, in fact, false) that the wall as a whole weighs two pounds. What is true of X, Y, and Z, taken individually, might not be true of X, Y, and Z considered as a collection. Sometimes, however, what is true of members of a collection taken individually *is* true of the collection as a whole. If every brick in a wall is yellow, the wall as a whole is yellow. If every fibre of a rug is made of wool, then the rug as a whole is made of wool. And, so it seems obvious to me, if every object in the universe needs something other than itself to account for its existence, the universe as a whole does so as well. If the universe is nothing but the sum of the objects that make it up, and if each of them in turn needs something other than itself to account for its existence, then the same must be true of the universe itself. You might say that a brick wall is nothing but the sum of its parts and that, just as we should not conclude that if every brick in a wall weighs two pounds, the wall as a whole weighs two pounds, we should not conclude that if every object in the universe needs something other than itself to account for its existence, the universe does so as well.

Weighing two pounds, however, is only attributable to particular bricks in a wall of which each brick weighs two pounds. Depending for its existence on something else is, by contrast, attributable to the universe as a whole if everything in it depends for its existence on something else.[21] One two-pound brick plus another two-pound brick leaves us with what weighs four pounds. One thing which depends for its existence on something else plus another thing which depends for its existence on something else merely leaves us with what depends for its existence on something else.

(b) might be thought plausible on the basis of one or both of two assumptions: (i) the universe never had a beginning, and everything now existing has a series of (agent-) causes within the universe going back infinitely into the past, and (ii) anything having a cause of its existence owes that existence to an infinite series of agent-causes within the universe. Now (i) and (ii) here clearly depend on assumptions about infinite collections of things. In the case of (i), the assumption is that there could be an infinite series of completed past events, states, or times, or something along those lines. In the case of (ii) the assumption is that there could be an infinite series of causes acting simultaneously. Neither assumption seems plausible to me, but I shall quarrel with neither of them here. For, even if true, they do nothing to refute what I am arguing at present. Whether backwardly or contemporaneously infinite, the universe is still a collection of objects the natures of which do not entail the existence of the objects having those natures. This, I am suggesting, ought to leave us asking what accounts for the existence of the universe as a whole and at any time.

(c) brings us to a very tricky topic, one much discussed by philosophers especially since the time of Immanuel Kant (1724–1804). According to him, '*Being* is obviously not a real predicate, i.e., a concept of something that could add to the concept of a thing'.[22] Kant's statement here, and the subsequent justification he provides for it, might seem somewhat opaque, but he appears at least to be claiming that we do not *describe* something in any way when we say that it exists – a claim which has received its most sophisticated elaboration and defence in the late C. J. F. Williams's book *What is Existence?*[23] And the claim clearly has merit. Obviously I do not tell you what something is when I say that it exists ('There are rats in the New York Subway' does not tell you what a rat is). Also, statements of existence are very commonly nothing but assertions to the effect that certain predicates (none of them being '____ exists') are truly affirmable of something. If, for example, I say that 'Horses exist', I am not saying anything about any particular horse. I am saying that '____ is a horse' is truly affirmable of something or other.

But this does not mean that we are not making true affirmations about things when saying that they exist. It does not mean that '____ exists' cannot be a genuine predicate of individuals. The reason most commonly given for supposing that it cannot is that thinking so allows us to make sense of negative existential propositions such as 'Blue daffodils do not exist'. In such propositions, the predicate '____ do(es) not exist' cannot tell us something about anything (cannot be a predicate of individuals) since the propositions themselves are telling us that there is nothing to which any predicate can be truly assigned. And, with this thought in mind, it has often been suggested that '____ exists' is not a predicate of individuals either. But that suggestion assumes that negative predications carry existential import, that they imply or state that something exists, which is open to question. In other words, we do not have to suppose that 'Blue daffodils do not exist' implies the existence of blue daffodils and amounts to a contradiction on the supposition that '____ do(es) not exist' (like '____ exist(s)') is a first-level predicate (a predicate of individuals). All we have to suppose is that 'Blue daffodils do not exist' is true if nothing is a blue daffodil, and false if some daffodil is blue.

In any case, it clearly does sometimes make sense to say of something that it exists. It makes sense, for example, to say 'The Great Pyramid still exists, but the Library of Alexandria does not'. It makes equal sense to say 'The Statue of Liberty exists, but the World Trade Towers do not'. And it makes perfect to sense to say that, for example, Smokey exists – meaning that he is actually there to be examined, petted, fed, cleaned up after, and so on. This is the sense of 'exists' that Aquinas has in mind as he employs the Latin term *esse*. For Aquinas, something can be said to have *esse* in so far as it is actually there to be analysed or described.[24] He does not think of *esse* as a distinguishing quality or property of things (so he denies that to know that something has *esse* is to know *what* it is). At the same time, however, he thinks that we can distinguish between, say, Smokey and the last living (but now dead) dinosaur. Smokey, for Aquinas, would be something actual, a genuinely existing individual, and, so far as I can see, such a view is hardly unreasonable. In that case, however, one can fairly claim that existence is something we can reflect on causally. It makes sense, for example, to ask what accounts for Smokey's existence at any time, and the existence of any other object, for that matter.

Yet, do we *need* to do this? (d) suggests that we do not, that we might take the existence of things in the universe, and the existence of the universe as a whole, not to raise questions about agent-causality. The fact of the matter, though, is that we just do seek causally to account for what exists but does not intrinsically have to, and we take seeking of this kind to be the mark of a reasonable person. When asked if he would speak of the universe as 'gratuitous', Bertrand Russell (1872–1970) once famously replied, 'I should say that the universe is just there, and that's all.'[25] His position on that occasion was based on three stated assumptions: (a) that the word 'universe' does not stand for anything that has meaning, (b) that something in the world might arise without an agent-cause (or agent-causes), and (c) that, while it might be legitimate to ask what in the world caused some object or event in the world, there is no warrant for asking what causally accounts for the world as a whole. Yet (a) here is plainly false, if only because 'universe' is a word that people use in conversation. I have already commented on (b). With respect to (c), all I can say is that it seems arbitrary to stop asking causal questions unless we arrive at a cause (or causes) the existence of which is somehow necessary or self-explanatory. I have argued that the existence of the universe is not necessary or self-explanatory since we cannot account for the existence of any object in the universe in terms of what it is. So I now suggest that we ought to presume that the existence of the universe has a cause (or causes).

What kind of difference, however, would such a cause (or causes) be making? If it (they) account(s) for the existence of the universe as a whole, it (they) cannot be making the kind of difference which agent-causes within the universe typically make. Without exception, these achieve their effects only by bringing about a change of some kind. Artists produce paintings by moving bits of paint around. People write books by fiddling with computers, pens, or typewriters. Tropical storms wreak havoc by modifying the environments they hit. And so on. Yet for something causally to account for there being any universe at all cannot be for it to change the universe (or anything in it) in any way – since nothing can undergo change unless it exists to start with. So if anything accounts for the existence of the universe, then it must simply make the universe to be. It cannot be altering the universe in any way. Rather, it must account for there being a universe as opposed to there being nothing at all.

Yet how can we sensibly think of there being nothing at all as a genuine alternative that we might have in mind when wondering why the universe exists at all? Here we come to (e). The position I am defending could well be expressed as 'We are entitled to ask and, therefore, entitled to suppose that there is an answer to the question "How come something rather than nothing?"' (e) represents a challenge to this position since it denies that there being nothing is a genuine alternative to there being something. And it is easy to see the force of (e). For is there really an intelligible distinction to be drawn here? Can we take *nothing* to be a genuine possibility to be set beside *something*? We may speak of there being nothing in the room, or of there being nothing between Australia and New Zealand. But here we mean something like 'There is no furniture in the room' or 'There is no land between Australia and New Zealand'. In other words, the notion of there being *absolutely nothing* is not one with positive content. So why suppose that there being *something* rather than *nothing* is something to get worked up about?

Yet is the notion of nothing really so problematic in this context? Suppose that we are searching through the drawers in my kitchen. I open one of them and I say 'Well, there is nothing in here'. You will understand what I am saying. You will know that I am saying that there are no knives, forks, spoons, and so on in the drawer. In that case, however, can you not equally well understand me if I were to claim that there is nothing at all? I would obviously be speaking falsely. But would you not be able to understand why that is so? Would you not take me falsely to be insisting that there are no nameable and describable individuals? Surely you would, and rightly so. We do not have a concept of nothing as we have a concept of longevity or tallness or liquidation. But might it not be thought that we *do* have a concept of nothing in so far as we have a knowledge of things that there are in the world, and in so far as we might think of them *just not being there*? And might it not also be thought that there being nothing at all is a genuine possibility in so far as the 'all' we are concerned with is what we take to make up the world or universe? It has been said that 'There might have been nothing' is not a believable proposition since there is no alternative to being. According to Bede Rundle for example,

> When we say 'Nothing is . . .', far from talking about nothing, we are talking about everything. Nothing is immortal; that is, everything is mortal. Nothing might have been here – neither you nor I, the cat, the dog, and so on indefinitely . . . We cannot conceive of there being nothing, but only of nothing being this or that, and that is a use of 'nothing' that presupposes there being something. Intelligible contrasts are within *ways of being* – near or far, long or short, young or old. Existing and not existing fit into the scheme – existing now, not existing then, and, more radically, there being a so and so and there being no so and so – but the contrast is still within how things are: at least one thing's being a dragon, say, and the failure of every single thing to be a dragon. This is as far as it goes, there being something and there being nothing not being contrasting poles with respect to the way things might be.[26]

Yet saying that there might have been nothing need not amount to claiming that there being nothing is a way things might be, or that there is something called 'nothing' which might be thought to be in some way. To say that there might have been nothing could, and as far as I am concerned *does*, amount to the suggestion that nothing in the universe is such that its nature guarantees its existence – this also being true of the universe as a whole.

Of course, 'Why is there something rather than nothing?' is an unusual and radical question. But that is not a reason for dismissing it. The asking of unusual and radical questions often leads people to expand their intellectual horizons and to make serious intellectual progress. One might suggest that the question is intrinsically silly or ill-formed. But is it? Questions like 'How thick is the Equator?' or 'How much money does algebra earn?' certainly make no sense. Another example of an intrinsically absurd question occurs in an amusing dialogue reported by Peter Geach:

> Two Rabbinical scholars were reading the Law. They had not got very far – in fact not beyond Genesis 1,1, which contains the word

'eretz' ('earth'). The initial question of the dialogue which follows is like asking in English: Why should there be a letter G in the word 'earth'? – *gimel* being the corresponding letter in Hebrew.

Why should there be a *gimel* in 'eretz'?
But there isn't a *gimel* in 'eretz'.
Then why isn't there a *gimel* in 'eretz'?
Why should there be a *gimel* in 'eretz'?
Well, that's what I just asked you![27]

Is the question 'Why is there anything at all?' intrinsically absurd, however? I do not see that it is. One might side with Bertrand Russell and assert that things are just there and that there is nothing more to be said. Yet (going by his writings in general) Russell would never have suggested that, for example, cats are *just there*. He would have asked how cats came to be and continue to be. So why should we not ask why there is anything at all? Why should we not ask 'Why is there something rather than nothing?' It might be said that we have not familiarized ourselves with the answer to this question and that this is a reason for fighting shy of it. But not understanding what the answer to a question might be does not justify refusing to ask it and refusing to suppose that there must be an answer to it. The earliest scientists who puzzled over the world had not acquainted themselves with realities that we now casually refer to in giving what we take to be accurate scientific answers. They were venturing into the unknown. Yet we commend them for their efforts and are seriously indebted to them. They might have said that X, Y, or Z was 'just there'. Fortunately, however, they did not.

God and creation

If I am right in what I have just been saying, then we ought to suppose that the universe is caused to exist for as long as it exists, which is what those who believe in God have traditionally believed.[28] Or, to put it another way, people have traditionally used the word 'God' in order to talk about what produces the sheer existence of the universe, that which makes the world to be (at any time). And, of course, in doing so they have used the word 'Creator'. God, they have said, is the Creator of all things. Hence, for example, we find Aquinas writing: 'It is not enough to consider how some particular being issues from some particular cause, for we should also attend to the issuing of the whole of being from the universal cause, which is God; it is this springing forth that we designate by the term "creation".[29] Similarly, the recently promulgated *Catechism of the Catholic Church* says: 'God does not abandon his creatures to themselves. He not only gives them being and existence, but also, and at every moment, upholds and sustains them in being.'[30] So I shall henceforth use the word 'God' to mean 'whatever it is that makes things to be for as long as they are'.

Yet what understanding of God should we take ourselves to have on that basis? Some have suggested that we pretty much know what God the Creator is. Indeed, so it is often said, he is somewhat like us. Hence, for example, Richard Swinburne (who believes that there is a God) tells us that God is something like a 'person without a body (i.e., a spirit) who is eternal, free, able to do anything, knows everything, is perfectly good, is the proper object of human worship and obedience, the creator and sustainer of the universe'.[31] Like many philosophers, especially since the time of René Descartes (1596–1650), Swinburne thinks that people (persons) are composed of two kinds of stuff – mental, incorporeal, indivisible stuff (mind) and physical, extended, divisible stuff (body). On this account, the real me is my mind (or soul), and so I, like all persons, am essentially incorporeal. I am causally connected to what is material, but I am not myself a material thing. I am a spirit. And, so Swinburne thinks, this is what God is – a 'person without a body'. Of course, Swinburne (and those who agree with him) do not think that God is just like any human person you care to mention. They take him to be, for example, more long-lived than we are. They also take him to be uncaused, and more powerful and knowledgeable than we are. So they think of God as an extra-ordinary person. Yet they still presume that God belongs to the same class as people (or persons). He is, for them, one among many, and with this thought in mind they have said that we have a fairly good idea of what he actually is. We know what people are, they reason; so we have a fair understanding of what God is. Swinburne, indeed, suggests that we can actually *imagine* what it is like to be God. God, says Swinburne, is not just a spirit; he is an omnipresent one, and we can understand what it is to be such a thing. Says Swinburne:

Imagine yourself, for example, gradually ceasing to be affected by alcohol or drugs, your thinking being equally coherent however men mess about with your brain. Imagine too that you cease to feel any pains, aches, thrills, although you remain aware of what is going on in what has been called your body. You gradually find yourself aware of what is going on in bodies other than your own and other material objects at any place in space . . . You also come to see things from any point of view which you choose, possibly simultaneously, possibly not. You remain able to talk and wave your hands about, but find yourself able to move directly anything which you choose, including the hands of other people . . . You also find yourself able to utter words which can be heard anywhere, without moving material objects. However, although you find yourself gaining these strange powers, you remain otherwise the same – capable of thinking, reasoning, and wanting, hoping and fearing . . . Surely anyone can thus conceive of himself becoming an omnipresent spirit.[32]

Speaking for myself, I have to say that I cannot imagine what Swinburne is here telling me that I can.[33] But that is neither here nor there for the moment. The point to grasp is that Swinburne thinks that an understanding of people takes us a long way towards an understanding of God, and the same can be said of many other writers.

Yet why should we suppose that anything with which we are acquainted gives us an understanding of what God is? Biblical authors often speak as though God is very much like a human being. In the Old Testament, for example, he is depicted as having hands, eyes, ears, and a face.[34] He laughs, smells, and whistles.[35] And he has emotions such as hatred, anger, joy, and regret.[36] Yet we also find biblical passages stressing the difference between God and anything created. A classic one is in Isaiah:

> To whom then will you liken God,
>> or what likeness compare with him?
>
> . . .
>
> To whom then will you compare me,
>> or who is my equal? Says the Holy One.
> Lift up your eyes on high and see:
>> Who created these? (Isaiah 40:18, 25–26)

Here we have a text which seems strongly to say that God's creatures provide no serious model at all for what God is. It seems to imply a sharp distinction between God and creatures. My view is that this is a distinction we need to respect, given that we take God to be the source of the being of everything other than himself, the Maker of all things visible and invisible (as the Nicene Creed puts it). For if that is what God is, then must he not be *radically* different from anything with which we are acquainted – so different that seriously using any creature as a model for God is simply absurd? In the next chapter I shall argue that the correct answer to this question is 'Yes', though I shall also suggest (not only in the next chapter but in subsequent ones) that we may truly speak of God while using terms (words) that we employ when talking of creatures.

Notes

1. Genesis 1:1.
2. Qur'an, 16:3. I quote from *The Koran*, tr. N.J. Dawood (Penguin Books: London, 1999), p. 187.
3. The Apostles' Creed in its present form dates from around the fourth century AD. The Nicene Creed (which comes to us in two versions) derives from the Council of Nicaea (325 AD). I am citing these texts in their traditional English versions, which are multiply reprinted.
4. Antony Flew, *The Presumption of Atheism and Other Essays* (Elek/Pemberton: London, 1976), p. 22.
5. For a more detailed defence of this conclusion see G. E. M. Anscombe, 'What Is It to Believe Someone?', in C. F. Delaney (ed.), *Rationality and Religious Belief* (University of Notre Dame Press: Notre Dame, Ind. and London, 1979). See also Norman Malcolm, 'The Groundlessness of Belief', in Stuart C. Brown (ed.), *Reason and Religion* (Cornell University Press: Ithaca, NY and London, 1977). See also Michael Welbourne, *The Community of Knowledge* (Aberdeen University Press: Aberdeen, 1986) and *Knowledge* (McGill-Queen's University Press: Montreal and London, 2001). Finally, see also C. A. J. Coady, *Testimony: A Philosophical Study* (Clarendon Press: Oxford, 1992).
6. By 'we' here I simply mean 'any particular person you know that you care to name'. I do not mean that it is reasonable to claim that there is a Creator God if *nobody* can give us grounds for supposing that there is such a God, grounds which leave us (or at least some people) with knowledge rather than mere belief. 'Mere belief' is not necessarily a bad thing. But we can distinguish it from knowledge, which, in my view, does rest on grounds. It always makes sense to ask 'How do you know?' You might say that we frequently use the word 'know' when thinking of assent based

on something like someone's say-so (as in 'Because he told me', given as an answer to 'How do you know that he lives in London?'). And that is obviously the case. So one might argue that knowledge is something that can be passed on simply by word of mouth. I have no special quarrel with that suggestion but would also draw attention to the fact that we can distinguish between taking something on say-so and coming to see for oneself that what one is told is true, and why it is true (this, surely, being more worthy of being called 'knowledge' than a belief based on someone's say-so). Therefore, if the claim is that there is such a thing as knowledge that there is a Creator God, it seems reasonable to look for more than mere say-so when inspecting that claim's intellectual credentials.

7. One line of thinking on which I do not touch in this book, but have previously defended, is often called 'the Argument from Design'. I discuss this in ch. 4 of my *An Introduction to the Philosophy of Religion* (3rd edn, Oxford University Press: Oxford, 2004). Texts of Aquinas lying behind what I go on to say in the present chapter include: *De Ente et Essentia*, 4; *Summa Contra Gentiles*, I.12, 22; *Summa Contra Gentiles*, II.15–21; *Summa Theologiae*, Ia.2.3.44–45; and *In Aristotelis Librum Peri Hermeneias*, 1.14.

8 The *occurrence* in John of the thought that-*p* is, of course, not identical with the *occurrence* in Jane of the thought that-*p*. But the content of the thought is the same. When John and Jane think that-*p*, they both think the same thought. One might object to this suggestion on the ground that *p* here might be something like 'I'm tired', which can hardly express the same thought as uttered by both John and Jane. Here, however, I am not concerned with sentences including indexical terms (like 'I') – sentences which, arguably, do not express genuine propositions. I am taking a thought to be what can be expressed without reference to particular thinkers. Paradigm examples of thoughts in my sense would be 'Green is a colour', 'Cats are mammals', 'Paris is a city containing many buildings', 'Leibniz was a philosopher', and so on.

9. I take it that 'Why is it snowing in New York?' would be a sensible question to raise even if it is *always* snowing there.

10. David Hume, *A Treatise of Human Nature*, ed. L. A. Selby-Bigge (Clarendon Press: Oxford, 1978), pp. 79f.

11. G. E. M. Anscombe, '"Whatever Has a Beginning of Existence Must Have a Cause": Hume's Argument Exposed', *Analysis* 34 (1974), p. 150, repr. in G. E. M. Anscombe, *Collected Philosophical Papers* (Basil Blackwell: Oxford, 1981), vol. 1.

12. G. E. M. Anscombe, 'Times, Beginnings and Causes', *Proceedings of the British Academy* 60 (1974); quotation from reprint G. E. M. Anscombe, *Collected Philosophical Papers* (Basil Blackwell: Oxford, 1981), vol. 2, p. 162.

13. For what I take to be another defence of this conclusion, see Peter van Inwagen, *Metaphysics* (Westview Press: Boulder, Col., 1993), pp. 108ff.

14. Perhaps I should modify that last sentence. Maybe there are people who do not seek causally to account for contingent events. It is hard to imagine them living a successful human life; it is also impossible to conceive of them being even slightly sympathetic to what we commonly call 'scientific reasoning'; but perhaps they exist. We could not, however, regard them as reasonable. We might hesitate to call them unreasonable, since we might find them to be so alien from us as not to be rationally assessable in our terms; but we could not view them as reasonable.

15. There are philosophers who have taken God to be a part of the universe. It should, I hope, be obvious that I am not doing so. For what I take to be a good defence by a recent philosopher of the position I am adopting in this chapter see H. D. Lewis, *Philosophy of Religion* (English Universities Press: London, 1965), ch. 14.

16 See Ludwig Wittgenstein, *Tractatus Logico-Philosophicus*, tr. C. K. Ogden (Routledge & Kegan Paul: London, 1922), 4.126ff.

17. Notice, however, that Smokey's parts are not independently existing objects. They are parts of him. What they are depends on what they are as parts of him.

18. Medieval authors sometimes distinguish between *entia per se* and *entia per accidens*. For them, an *ens per se* is a naturally occurring unit (a substance) while an *ens per accidens* is an artefact the parts of which pre-exist the whole of which they are parts. The distinction seems to me a fair one to make, but it does not affect what I am currently arguing.

19. Philosophers who have denied this include those (sometimes called Idealists) who have said that there really is no universe distinct from our (individual?) minds. You will have to pardon me for not here engaging with Idealism, something which seems to me to be discredited by the fact that we cannot make sense of it using the language in which we talk about what there is. It is, for example, part and parcel of the concept of dog that dogs are distinct from people (meaning that dogs are not just parts of people's minds). Or again, the concept of conversation presupposes the existence of distinct speakers. And so on.

20. The invention of the Ontological Argument is usually credited to Anselm of Canterbury (*c.* 1033–1109). See his *Proslogion*, ch. 2 and 3. An English translation of these texts can be found in Brian Davies and G. R. Evans (ed.), *Anselm of Canterbury: The Major Works* (Oxford University Press: Oxford and New York, 1998).

21. For more on God's existence and the fallacy of composition see Patterson Brown, 'Infinite Causal Regression', *Philosophical Review* 75 (1966), repr. in Anthony Kenny (ed.), *Aquinas: A Collection of Critical Essays* (University of Notre Dame Press: Notre Dame, Ind., 1976).

22. Immanuel Kant, *Critique of Pure Reason*, A599/B627. I quote from the translation by Paul Guyer and Allen W. Wood (Cambridge University Press: Cambridge, 1997), p. 567. (Macmillan: London, 1964), pp. 502f.

23. C. J. F. Williams, *What is Existence?* (Clarendon Press: Oxford, 1981).

See also C. J. F. Williams, *Being, Identity, and Truth* (Clarendon Press: Oxford, 1992), ch. 1.

24 For an excellent account of Aquinas on *esse* see Herbert McCabe, *God Still Matters* (Continuum: London and New York, 2002), ch. 2.

25. Russell's reply comes in a radio debate he engaged in with Frederick Copleston in 1948. The debate is reprinted in John Hick (ed.), *The Existence of God* (Macmillan: New York, 1964); quotation from p. 175.

26. Bede Rundle, *Why there is Something Rather than Nothing* (Clarendon Press: Oxford, 2004), p. 112.

27 P. T. Geach, *Reason and Argument* (Basil Blackwell: Oxford, 1976), p. 85.

28. It has been argued that any attempt to reason to God's existence is thoroughly un-Christian and something to be condemned on biblical grounds. I cannot directly engage with this view here; for what seems to me a definitive refutation of it, see James Barr, *Biblical Faith and Natural Theology* (Clarendon Press: Oxford, 1993), esp. ch. 1–5.

29. Aquinas, *Summa Theologiae*, Ia.45.1; quotation from vol. 8 of the Blackfriars edition of the *Summa Theologiae* (Eyre & Spottiswoode: London and McGraw-Hill: New York, 1967).

30. *Catechism of the Catholic Church* (Geoffrey Chapman: London, 1994), p. 71.

31. Richard Swinburne, *The Coherence of Theism*; revd edn (Clarendon Press: Oxford, 1993), p. 1.

32. Ibid., p. 107.

33. For someone who seems to be of the same mind as me on this, see Peter van Inwagen, *God, Knowledge, and Mystery* (Cornell University Press: Ithaca, NY and London, 1995), p. 20. I might add that what Swinburne describes as what it would be like to imagine oneself to be an omnipresent spirit might well be taken to be what it is like to be severely affected by alcohol or other drugs.

34. See I Samuel 5:11; Psalm 8:4; Isaiah 52:10; II Kings 19:16; Numbers 11:1; Genesis 3:8; 32:31.

35. See Psalm 2:4; 37:13; Genesis 8:21; Isaiah 7:18.

36 See Deuteronomy 16:22; Isaiah 61:8; Exodus 22:24; Genesis 9:5; Deuteronomy 30:9; 32:35; Isaiah 62:5; Genesis 6:6.

Three

Identifying God

If you think that evil renders God's existence impossible or unlikely, you must presumably take yourself to have a fairly good understanding of what God is. At any rate, those who have claimed that evil shows that God's existence is impossible or unlikely normally *do* take themselves to have such an understanding. They sometimes tell us, for example, that God is an omnipotent, omniscient, good person whose existence is impossible or unlikely given the evil that exists. They do not, of course, mean that there *is* an omnipotent, omniscient, good person. They are indulging in what we might call 'parasitic reference'. They are talking about God while, so to speak, sceptically riding on the backs of those who speak of God as believers. They are picking up on what believers say without actually agreeing with them (just as I might tell you lots about Santa Claus without actually supposing that there is any such individual). Yet can we (whether as believers in him or not) have a fair understanding of what God is? The question may seem odd, since those who believe in God have plenty to say about him. They commonly tell us that he is, for example, omnipotent, omniscient and good. Even if God does exist, however, we should not presume that any of us understand what he is. Indeed, so I now want to argue, there is a serious sense in which none of us can do any such thing – a sense which has a considerable bearing when it comes to the topic of God and evil.

What is God?

It is sometimes said that we should think of God as an explanation. Of what? Answers differ. Some hold that God explains the universe as accounting for its existence. Others say that, for example, God explains why the world has the character it has, or why there are moral truths, or why what the Bible says is true. Yet it is surely hard to see why we should speak of God as being an explanation of anything. An explanation is always something which we understand better than what we invoke it to explain, and why should we think that we understand God better than anything with respect to which we invoke him as an explanation?[1] Let us, for example, suppose that there is indeed something (let us call it 'God') which accounts for the existence of the universe at any time. Is this thing something we understand better than the universe, or better than anything in it? Or again, suppose that something (call it 'God') imposes on things the natures they have, accounts for there being moral truths, or is somehow the ground of what we read in the Bible. Why should we suppose that such a thing is something we understand better than the natures of things around us, the moral truths we subscribe to (supposing we take ourselves to subscribe to moral truths), or whatever we find ourselves reading in the Bible?

Following authors like Richard Swinburne, we might reply to these questions by saying that we have an understanding of God which is at least comparable to that which we have of ourselves. We might say that we know what we are, that God, like each of us, is a person, and that we therefore have an understanding of God, one which allows us to think of him as an explanation of something or other. But why (whether as a theist or a non-theist) should one suppose that God is a person?

The formula 'God is a person' is (given the history of theistic thinking and writing) a relatively recent one. I believe that its first occurrence in English comes in the report of a trial of someone called John Biddle (b. 1615), who in 1644 was brought before the magistrates of Gloucester, England, on a charge of heresy. His 'heresy' was claiming that God is a person. Biddle was explicitly defending Unitarian beliefs about God, already in evidence among Socinians outside England.[2]

In other words, Biddle's 'God is a person' was intended as a rejection of the orthodox Christian claim that God is three persons in one substance (the doctrine of the Trinity). One can hardly take it to be a traditional Christian answer to the question 'What is God?' According to the doctrine of the Trinity, God is certainly not three persons in *one* person. And when orthodox exponents of the doctrine speak of

Father, Son, and Spirit as 'persons', they certainly do not take 'person' to mean what it seems to mean for Swinburne and those who agree with him. They do not, for example, think of the persons of the Trinity as distinct centres of consciousness, or as three members of a kind. The teaching as given in English that God is three persons derives from Latin authors who, employing the term *persona*, said that God is three *personae*. The use of *persona* in Trinitarian discussions has a complicated history, but it seems clear that the Latin *persona* as employed in such discussions was intended to be equivalent in meaning to some (and I stress *some*) Greek usages of the terms *prosopon* (πρόσωπον) and *hypostasis* (ὑποστασις) – neither of which terms, as understood in the context of Trinitarian thinking, can be taken to suggest that God is three persons in the sense, say, that three people are persons. Drawing on biblical passages, they were employed to preserve the thought that, though God is one and undivided, there has to be distinction within him (even if we cannot understand how), since the Father is not the Son and since the Holy Spirit is neither the Father nor the Son.[3]

Suppose, however, that someone should insist that God must be a person and, therefore, something whose nature we can pretty well grasp even if we do not fathom its depths. What are we supposed to mean by 'person' here? As I noted in the previous chapter, Richard Swinburne takes 'God is a person' to mean that God is something like what Descartes thought himself essentially to be – an incorporeal thinking thing. 'What then am I?', asks Descartes. He replies: 'A thing that thinks. What is that? A thing that doubts, understands, affirms, denies, is willing, is unwilling, and also imagines and has sensory perceptions.'[4] Now I do not claim that Swinburne really takes God to doubt, to imagine, or to have sensory perceptions (though his language seems to me often to pull in this direction), but he certainly appears to think that God is somewhat as Descartes takes himself to be in so far as he thinks of himself as essentially incorporeal. For Swinburne, God is a non-material conscious mind, existing over time, having beliefs, and willing some things but not others. Swinburne's God acquires beliefs and has a life history. So we may take Swinburne to have an answer to the question 'What does it mean to call God a person?', an answer which we also find in the work of other writers. Yet why should we suppose that God really is a person in this sense?

Some philosophers would say that we should not since, so they would argue, there are no such persons. Those who construe 'God is a person' along Swinburne's lines begin with (or have arrived at) a view about people which takes them to be incorporeal individuals (albeit ones somehow attached to what is bodily). Or they assume that it at least makes sense to think of people along the lines presented by Descartes.[5] As students of philosophy know well, however, many philosophers have rejected the view of people which sees them as essentially incorporeal. Cartesian accounts of human beings have met with strong philosophical resistance from writers like Gilbert Ryle (1900–1976), Ludwig Wittgenstein (1889–1951), and mind–brain identity theorists such as J. J. C. Smart and David Armstrong.[6] None of these authors would take you or me to be essentially incorporeal objects, and some of them would say that it is conceptually confused to do so. Are they right? I would say that they are, since I take people to be essentially bodily. In my view, we cannot think of what it is for there to be people (individuals like you and me) without supposing that they, even if not *reducible* to what is wholly physical, are never less than bodily individuals whose life stories cannot be made sense of if conceived as taking place in a wholly immaterial realm. Yet suppose that I am completely wrong about this. Suppose that all the truth as to what people are lies with authors like Descartes, Swinburne, and others who get to 'God is a person' in the light of the thought that human persons are essentially incorporeal. It still does not follow that we (whether theists or atheists) should be happy with the formula 'God is a person'.

For let us, for the sake of argument, take 'God is a person' to mean something like this: 'God is an immaterial, conscious individual, with thoughts, beliefs, memories, and, perhaps, hopes. He undergoes various mental changes. He can will and act, and, indeed, he does so.' Why should we take such an individual to be God? Why should we think of God as an individual like this? If we do so, then, so it seems to me, we are supposing that God is nothing but an inhabitant of the universe (albeit an invisible inhabitant), one of a kind of which there are many members, something the existence of which we might ask 'How come?' just as much as we might ask how it comes to be that there are dogs or cats. In my view, whatever you take people (the 'persons' we know best) to be, it still remains that they are parts of what, if the argument of the previous chapter has any merit, is a created world. And, considered as such, they should certainly not be thought of as providing an answer to the question 'What is God?' One might, of course, say that the person God is differs significantly from the persons that people are. One might say, for example, that he is more powerful or more knowledgeable than other persons. Yet it would still remain the case that this extraordinary person would be nothing more than that – an extraordinary person, one of a kind, hardly the Creator of the Universe, hardly that which accounts for there being any world at all, for there being something rather than nothing.[7]

What God is not

So suppose we start our reflection on what God's nature is by asking not 'What is God?' but 'What is God *not*?' Might turning to that question help when it comes to understanding what God is? You might reply, 'No, since one can hardly come to understand what something is by noting what it is not'. And that would be a response with some merit. After all, knowing that what I have in my bedroom is not a giraffe or a mouse or a replica of the Eiffel Tower is not to know what I have in my bedroom. Yet knowing what something is not may well help us towards some understanding of it (if only the kind of understanding which consists in not making mistakes about it). And, so I now suggest, we would do well to consider what God is not, or, indeed, *cannot* be, given that he is, indeed, the Creator of all things.[8]

(a) Is God a body?

We can agree at the outset, and perhaps uncontroversially, that God cannot be something bodily. For if God were that, he would be part of the physical universe, not its Creator. You might, of course, say that like can produce like. Thus, cats produce cats, and dogs produce dogs. So why cannot a material God be that which accounts for a material universe? This question, however, misses the force of what, in the previous chapter, I took to be a reason to believe that there is a God at all. On my account, anything material is part of what I call 'the universe' or 'the world'. And of any such thing we can, I think, ask 'What accounts for its existence (at any time)?' Any particular material object is always something of which there could, in

principle, be more than one. We might be able to imagine circumstances which would result in there being, say, only one living cat.[9]
But this last surviving cat would still be something the nature of
which can be distinguished from its existence, as would any material
thing of which there could in principle be more than one. It would be
something with respect to which we could ask 'How come this thing,
rather than nothing?' It would be part of a created world. It would
also, of course, be something changeable and potentially divisible,
which could hardly be the case with whatever accounts for there
being any universe at all (though more on that below).

(b) Nature and individuality

More controversially, we should, I think, go on to agree that God
cannot be something the individuality of which we can distinguish
from its nature. This, indeed, is a tricky thesis, but let me try to tease
it out a little.

You and I are human beings, and, considered as such, we can be
thought of as having natures (i.e. as being things of a certain kind).
This, of course, is not to say that anyone at present knows what a
human being is exactly. People are objects of ongoing scientific investigation, not to mention philosophical study. Yet we can single out
human beings as distinguishable objects to investigate, as, for
example, biologists and medical experts in general do. And (ignorant
though we might be about human beings) we can specify ways in
which they resemble each other and ways in which they differ from
other things. In this sense, we can speak of them as having a distinct
nature. This nature, however (and regardless of how our knowledge
of it might increase over time), is hardly something to be identified
with any human being who has it. 'Mary is human' can hardly be
thought to mean that Mary is human nature. Mary, of course, cannot
be a human being without having a human nature (without being
human). But Mary's being human is not for her to be human nature.
For Mary might die while other people (other human beings)
continue to live. Her demise does not entail the vanishing of everything that is human.[10]

I take this to mean that Mary and human nature are not one and the
same thing (you will, of course, realize that I am not taking human
nature to be an identifiable thing, like Mary). Mary is an individual of
a kind, and she has a nature precisely as such. But can we think of

God as being like Mary in this respect? It seems to me that we cannot, and basically for the reason given by Aquinas. He writes:

> Things composed of matter and form cannot be the same as their natures or essences. For essence or nature in these things includes only what falls within the definition of a species – as humanity includes what falls within the definition of human being, for this makes us to be human and is what humanity signifies [i.e. what makes human beings to be human beings]. But we do not define the species of anything by the matter and properties peculiar to it as an individual. We do not, for example, define human beings as things that have *this* flesh and *these* bones, or are white, or black, or the like. *This* flesh and *these* bones, and the properties peculiar to them, belong indeed to *this* human being, but not to its nature. Individual human beings therefore possess something that human nature does not, and particular human beings and their nature are not, therefore, altogether the same thing. 'Human nature' names the formative element in human beings; for what gives a thing definition is formative with respect to the matter that gives it individuality.[11]

Aquinas is here talking about material objects, like Mary, which can be thought of as having natures of various kinds. And he is saying that we need to distinguish between these objects and their natures – that, for example, to explain what human nature amounts to is not to make reference to what some actual human being is when it comes to his or her precise physical make-up. In this sense, thinks Aquinas, when it comes to material things in the universe, we can distinguish between what they are and the individuals that they are (in Mary's case, so I think we might put it, between *what* she is and *who* she is). And Aquinas seems to me right here. It follows from this conclusion, however, that where what is in question is not material, not part of the physical world, we have no basis for distinguishing between individuality and nature. Or, as Aquinas says: 'The individuality of things not composed of matter and form cannot derive from this or that individual matter. So, the forms of such things must be intrinsically individual and themselves subsist as things. Such things are therefore identical with their natures.'[12]

Here, of course, one might ask 'How can an individual be identical with its nature?', or 'What would it be for something to be identical with its nature?' My answer to these questions is 'I do not know'. I can make sense of the suggestion that individuals in the material universe are not identical with their natures, for, as I have said, I think that we may, for example, understand and accept the claim that Mary is not humanity. But I have no idea what it would be to be something not like Mary in this respect. Yet neither, I think, does Aquinas. The passages from him which I have just quoted are evidently not designed to convey the impression that we can understand what it is to be something not distinguishable from its nature. They are only intended to indicate why we cannot take God to be something distinguishable from his (divine) nature. They are suggesting that, whatever else we want to say about God, we should not be supposing that God is something distinguishable from his nature. They are examples of negative theology – attempts to indicate what God *cannot* be. As far as I can see, however, they are successful examples. They give us reason to suppose that, without claiming to understand what God is, we would be wrong to think of God as one of a kind, as something like Mary. And, to anticipate what I shall be arguing later, this conclusion is of really serious import when it comes to discussions of God and evil. Confronted by evil, people (whether friends or foes of God) frequently work on the assumption that God belongs to some kind (like Mary) and is to be evaluated accordingly. If, however, we can agree that, when it comes to God, we cannot sensibly distinguish between individuality and nature (between what God is and who God is), that assumption becomes highly questionable.

(c) Essence and existence

That assumption also becomes questionable if we take what is, I think, a further step we need to allow ourselves when seeking to say what God cannot be. Here I am referring to Aquinas's famous claim that there is no distinction (no *compositio*) in God when it comes to essence and existence.[13] In making this claim Aquinas is saying that we cannot think of God as something the existence of which is derived from anything; he is asserting that existence belongs to God by nature. And that, surely, is what has to be said on the assumption that God is what I have so far taken him to be. If existence is not God's by nature, then, presumably, it derives from something other than God. Yet if God makes the difference between there being something rather than nothing, the existence of God cannot derive from something other than God. Nor can it causally derive from God, for that would mean that God, so to speak, causally precedes himself (exists before he exists and brings it about that he exists), which is not a possible scenario (for it is, surely, self-evidently true that something which does not exist cannot cause itself to exist).

One might make this point by saying that God is a necessary being, but I prefer not to do so. Philosophers disagree a lot when it comes to what necessity amounts to, and what I am arguing now can be expressed without reference to these disagreements. I am simply saying that we cannot think of God as created, that we cannot think of him as owing that he is, and, by implication, what he is, to anything other than himself (this is not to be taken as suggesting that God causally owes *that* he is and *what* he is to himself). Philosophers who insist that '___ exist(s)' cannot intelligibly be predicated of anything might reply to my thesis by suggesting that it is false because it seems to be saying that there is something called 'existence' with which God can be somehow identified.[14] I am not, however, saying this. I am merely claiming that for God to be is for God to be uncaused. The claim is a negative one. It holds that whatever God is, he, unlike the universe and everything in it, *cannot* be something the existence of which is derived. Or, as Aquinas says, God's essence includes existing.

Sometimes Aquinas makes this point by saying that God's essence *is* to exist, or that God is *ipsum esse subsistens* (subsistent being itself), and there are philosophers who have challenged that way of talking. Take, for example, Anthony Kenny. According to him, to say that God is *ipsum esse subsistens* is (ludicrously) to suppose that the answer to the question 'What is God?' is 'There is one'.[15] Here Kenny is echoing an argument against Aquinas offered by Peter Geach,[16] one prompted by a passage in Aquinas's *De Ente et Essentia*, 4. In Kenny's translation, the passage reads:

> Every essence or quiddity can be conceived without anything being understood with respect to its *esse*; for I can understand what a human being is, or what a phoenix is, and yet be ignorant whether they have *esse* in the nature of things. Hence it is clear that *esse* is different from essence or quiddity, unless there is something whose quiddity is its *esse*.[17]

As Kenny interprets Aquinas, this text *correctly* maintains that knowing what a common noun means does not amount to knowing that there is anything in reality corresponding to it. But, Kenny continues, Aquinas goes on to speak of something (God) the *whatness* of which is its *existence* (*esse*). And this way of talking is, says Kenny, absurd, implying as it does that the answer to the question 'What is God?' is 'There is one'.

Yet this is not at all Aquinas's position. Nor is it mine. In the *De Ente et Essentia* passage to which Kenny takes exception, Aquinas is only saying that understanding what existing things in the world are (this being an understanding of natures shared by different things) is not to understand that any particular thing having a particular nature exists (that, for example, we can understand what cats are without knowing that there is any such animal as my cat Smokey). It is, of course, absurd to suggest that the answer to the question 'What is God?' is 'There is one'. But I see no reason to suppose that Aquinas is making that suggestion, and I certainly am not doing so. Kenny maintains that when Aquinas identifies God's essence with existence (*esse*) he has in mind a sense of 'exists' which can be referred to as 'specific existence'. By 'specific existence' Kenny means 'what the existential quantifier expresses' – the sense of 'exists' captured by sentences of the form 'There is at least one x such that x is F' or 'Something is F'. This is Frege's notion of existence as a second-level predicate – a predicate of concepts, *not* objects or individuals.[18] For Kenny, one ascribes 'specific existence' to, say, dogs by asserting $(\exists x)(x$ is a dog), not by asserting that '____ exists' is truly predicable of any dog. And yet, Kenny argues, Aquinas, in *De Ente et Essentia*, is (unbelievably) asking us to accept that '____ exists' actually tells us *what* God *is*. In fact, however, Aquinas is doing no such thing, and neither am I. If Aquinas's claim concerning things whose essence can be understood without it being understood that these things cannot but exist means what I have suggested it does, his corresponding claim (and mine) concerning God only means that God is *not* something which can intelligibly be thought of as possibly not existing. It means that, though my actual existence (there being Brian Davies) is not entailed by a true account of my nature, the same is not the case when it comes to God – that in God's case, and in God's case alone, to be what God is includes being not possibly non-actual.[19] If that is so, however, then *De Ente et Essentia*'s teaching that God's essence is *esse* is reasonably construed as a piece of negative theology, as part of an account of ways in which God does not exist.[20]

My suggestion, therefore, is that, considered as a piece of negative theology, the teaching that God's essence is *esse* ought to be taken to be true. It is not (at least as I understand it) asking us to believe too much. Its thesis is remarkably modest. Cast in the terms in which I am recommending it, and to repeat what I have already said, it merely states that the Maker of all things, the reason why there is any universe at all, the reason why there is something rather than nothing, cannot be something caused to exist, cannot be something to which existence does not belong by nature (i.e. it merely states that to be God is to be something that cannot but exist).

(d) God, change, life, and action
To this claim one may, I think, add a further one – that God cannot be something capable of undergoing real change. In much recent literature the assumption has been that God is indeed something undergoing change.[21] Yet it is hard to see how that can be so, given that God accounts for the existence of everything other than himself, and does so for as long as anything other than him exists. For if God indeed does that, then he is the source of all coming to be (and thus of all change in things) and, therefore, cannot himself be something that comes to be (changes) in any way.

It is, of course, obviously true that change can be ascribed to God in one sense. Let us distinguish between 'real change' and what Peter Geach has called 'merely Cambridge change'.[22] By 'real change' I mean 'actual modification of a subject'. Hence, for example, I undergo real change when I become sick, or gain weight, or learn something, or spit, or leave a room.[23] By 'merely Cambridge change' I mean (following Geach) 'change that can be ascribed to something without it being implied that the thing in question has undergone any real change'. Suppose that you fall in love with me. It could then truly be said, 'Davies has come to be loved by someone'. But that statement does not entail that I have undergone any real change. Suppose that a daughter of mine bears a child. It could then truly be said, 'Davies has become a grandfather'. But that statement, too, does not entail that I have undergone any real change. I might, of course, be deeply moved when learning of my grandchild's birth. But 'becoming a grandfather' does not, by itself, signify any modification in the one who becomes a grandparent. Like '____ has come to be loved by *X*', it signifies a merely Cambridge change, change of a kind that can certainly be ascribed to God. Let us suppose that Fred comes to believe that the one, true God exists (assuming that there is such a thing as the one, true God). Then we could truly say that the one, true God has come to be believed in by Fred. Or again, let us suppose that something in the world comes to exist. In that case (and given that whatever exists in the world derives its existence from God) we can say 'God has come to be the Maker of this thing'. And so on for any number of examples. Merely Cambridge changes can, of course, be ascribed to God.

But not, I think, real changes. For when something undergoes a real change it comes to exist (comes to be) in a way in which it was previously not. I come to be fat from having previously been thin. I come to be sick from having been well. I come to be mobile from having being stationary. And so on. Yet, as I have argued, the being of all things other than God derives from him. So how can God himself come to be what he was previously not? You might say that there is no reason to think that God cannot undergo real change while also accounting for the existence of everything other than himself, this including things which undergo real change. But that reply would not really be engaging with the idea that God is what accounts for there being something rather than nothing. It would be sliding over the claim that God, whose essence is to be, makes creatures to be for as long as they exist. For, if God does that, then he accounts for all real change and cannot, therefore, be subject to it.

We might, of course, think that we can imagine or somehow conceive of God being first like this and then like that (as we can imagine or conceive of me as being first fat and then thin, or as being first ignorant and then learned). But to fantasize in such a way would be to suppose that God is just another creature, not the uncaused source of the being that creatures have in their different ways. If God, indeed, accounts for the sheer existence of what is not God, then he must account for the various (and varying) ways in which that which is not God exists. I take this to mean that God must account for there being all things which undergo real changes, from which I conclude that God cannot be something undergoing (or able to undergo) real change (for if he were that, then he would just not be the cause of things undergoing or able to undergo real change). Aquinas at one point speaks of God as 'existing outside the realm of existents, as a cause from which pours forth everything that exists in all its variant forms'.[24] Aquinas here is not, of course, baldly suggesting that God does not exist. He is saying, as I have been trying to say, that we should think of God, not as something in the universe, but as accounting for there being any universe at all. If God does that, however, then he must surely account for variety in the universe, and real change is part of what we have in mind when we talk about there being variety in the universe. Anything undergoing real change cannot, therefore, be divine. You might say that we have no reason to suppose that only God's creatures can really change. But, of course, we do have such a reason. To change is to be first like this and then like that. It is to be actually thus and so while being potentially (able to be) thus and so. To become actually thus and so from being potentially thus and so is to have achieved a new way of being. Yet, so I have argued, the existence of creatures, and all the ways in which they come to be, derive from God, from which it seems to follow that God is not only changeless but unchangeable. If the existence of things that change is derived, it cannot come from what is changeable as they are since, as changeable, they are essentially different from what brings them about.

It has been objected that if that is so, then God has to be conceived of as static or inert and, therefore, not what those who believe in God have traditionally taken him to be. But to say that God undergoes no real change is not to imply that God is static or inert. It is only to say that God undergoes no real change (it is to say what God is *not*, not what God *is*). One might respond to this comment by saying that something has to be static or inert if it cannot undergo any real change, and that response might be thought acceptable if it is things in the universe of which we are talking. We might, for example, think of Mount Everest as undergoing no real changes (though, in fact, it undergoes such changes on a daily basis), and we might, therefore, think of it as static or inert (one does, after all, tend to think of mountains as pretty static or inert). To speak of God as undergoing no real change, however, need not at all be thought of as carrying connotations to do with 'the static' or 'the inert' (notions of which we can surely only make sense, though maybe not a lot, when thinking of what is within the world). If what I am now arguing is correct, then God, who is unchangeable, creatively accounts for the world in all its variety. And, if I am right in what I am saying, it would be wrong to object that God is, therefore, static or inert.

We might think of something like a table as being static or inert. We might also think the same of a rock, or a bottle, or a glass, or a computer. Yet why might we do so? An obvious answer is 'Because we do not think of them as alive'. Something to which life can be ascribed, however, can hardly be thought of as static or inert. Yet might we not think of God as living? If nothing unchangeable can be thought of as alive, then perhaps not. But why should we suppose that being alive (and therefore, so you might think, not being static or inert) entails being changeable? Might we not allow for the thought that something unchangeable could yet be something to which life can be ascribed? Not, perhaps, if we focus on things like rocks, bottles, glasses, or computers. Yet, of course, all of these things, as well as not being alive, are not intrinsically unchangeable. So perhaps we should ask what distinguishes living things from non-living things.

According to Aquinas, 'life belongs to things that have movement and operation through themselves, without being moved by other things'.[25] This seems to me to be correct. One might say that 'living' does not always signify exactly the same thing – that, for example, to be alive as a tulip is not quite the same as being alive as a dog, and that being alive as dog differs from being alive as a human being. Yet all living things have it in common that they move or operate as self-movers (automobiles) and not as things that are pushed around by other things acting on them to cause them to move or operate as they do. A rock needs someone to throw it. A dog, on the other hand, runs around of its own accord. It is a natural unit whose movement and activities are explicable in terms of itself – in terms, for example, of its appetites, its legs, its heart, and so on. I am not here suggesting that living things in the world are wholly and entirely unmoved by what is not them. It should be clear from what I have previously said that I take everything in the universe to have careers or histories which derive from God as the source of the existence of everything other than himself. We can, however, distinguish between what in the world moves and operates *of itself* and what in the world functions as an *instrument* of something else in the world. This distinction, I am suggesting, marks (for us) the primary difference between what is living and what is not living.

Can we invoke it with respect to God? Surely we can. For if God accounts for the being of the universe, he brings it about as an agent-cause. This must mean that action or activity can be attributed to him. Are we to think of this action or activity as deriving from something other than him – as, say, the movement of an arrow through the air derives from the behaviour of an archer? Clearly not. Considered as the source of the existence of everything other than himself, God cannot be passive to the operation or operations of anything distinct from himself. So he acts of himself, which is a reason for attributing life to him.[26] Yet if we can attribute life to God, we have reason for denying that he is static or inert even if we also have reason to suppose that he is not something capable of under-going real change.

Or is that really so? For does not something have really to change in order to act? After all, to speak of a thing as acting is normally to speak of something as going through some kind of process (implying real change). Consider 'The British Prime Minister acted quickly to avoid the threat of a General Election'. We would normally assume that this is true because, for example, the British Prime Minister swiftly wrote certain letters, signed certain documents, phoned up his cabinet and spoke to it, fed certain lines to the media, and so on. We would normally assume that 'John took a shower' is true because John walked into a shower unit, and soaped himself, and so on. We would normally assume that 'Mary murdered her husband' is true because Mary, for example, picked up a gun and pulled its trigger, and so on. In other words, we take ascription of action to individuals as normally to imply that they went through some process or other and therefore underwent real changes.

Yet when 'X has acted' means that X has brought about a result of some kind (if it ascribes agent-causality to X) it makes sense to deny that action *necessarily* involves change in the one who acts. For we need not think of action as a matter of what is going on (what changes occur) in the agent to whom the action is ascribed. Take, for example, the activity we call 'teaching'. How do people manage to teach each other? It seems natural to say that they do it by uttering words, or by writing on blackboards, and so on (and therefore by undergoing various real changes). For that is how teaching is effected by people. But teaching cannot be defined as going through certain motions. I can utter true statements until I am blue in the face. I can fill a thousand blackboards with letters and diagrams. But none of these processes will count as *teaching* unless somebody actually *learns*

something. For this reason it seems necessary to say that, when interested in whether or not I have taught somebody, we are interested,
not in changes occurring in me, but in changes occurring in
somebody else. I cannot (as a matter of fact) teach you except by
undergoing changes of some kind. But my undergoing these changes
does not constitute my teaching you. Unless you actually learn something, they are simply fruitless bits of behaviour on my part. Teaching
occurs *as* learning occurs, when someone changes from a state of
ignorance to a state of knowledge. The activity we call teaching is
not, in fact, definable in terms of changes in teachers, and the same is
true of any activity where we have something achieving an effect in
or on something else. It is true of any activity where there is an agent
and something passive to it, something in or on which the agent is
operative.

One may feel like saying that for an agent-cause to act is always for
it to go through a process of change. Yet it is not obvious that what
has an effect as an agent-cause must itself be something going
through a process of change, and it is not the process of change
through which an agent-cause goes that interests us when we are
ascribing effects to it. What interests us is (a) what is being brought
about (what is being caused) and (b) what it is that this derives from.

Here we can return to the example of teaching. To say that
someone has taught someone something is not to describe or draw
attention to changes in someone called a teacher. It is to register the
fact that someone learned something, and it is to identify someone as
that which helped in the process of learning. One might say that
learning cannot be derived from anything which is not, or which has
not been, in process of change. But to say that would be to miss the
point I am currently making. Learning as effected by a teacher only
occurs as learning comes to be. So teaching depends on and is constituted not by what the teacher undergoes but on what the learner
undergoes. We have no reason, in advance of arguments to the
contrary, for supposing that learning can only be derived from something in process of change. And the same goes for anything we are
pleased to call an effect of an agent-cause. As we may put it, *the
action of an agent lies in the patient.*

Or in the language of Aquinas: 'Action and passion are not two
changes but one and the same change, called "action" insofar as it is
caused by an agent, and "passion" insofar as it takes place in a

patient.'[27] My pulling the curtains might involve all sorts of changes in me. But I pull the curtains only *as the curtains go through changes caused by me,* and that is what is essential to there being curtains whose changing position is ascribable to me. When footballers score goals, their limbs will have moved. But goals get scored by footballers only *as balls go into nets because of footballers.* When teachers teach pupils, they will normally have moved their mouths, their legs, or their hands. But they teach only *as people learn by virtue of them.* Once again: the action of an agent lies in the patient, from which I infer that we have no business concluding that agent-causation always has to involve real changes in agent-causes. I am not for a moment denying that agent-causation (when it comes to agent-causes within the universe) occurs as agent-causes themselves undergo real change. I am, however, suggesting that agent-causation does not have to involve changes in an agent-cause. So I see no reason to think that God, considered as unchanging, cannot be thought of as acting or as living. Considered as an agent-cause, however, God needs to be sharply distinguished from created agent-causes, which leads me to note something else that God, the Creator, cannot be – something which, as we shall later see, has a very special bearing on the topic of God and evil. The thought I have in mind here is that God cannot be something capable of *intervening* in what is created by him.

(e) God and intervention

One might immediately be inclined to object that this thought has to be mistaken because it actually contradicts what theists have traditionally said about God, or because it contradicts what others have understood them traditionally to have said. And, up to a point, I sympathize with this response. The expression 'divine intervention' is, after all, a pretty familiar one. It is especially invoked when it comes to the notion of miracles. Those who believe in God commonly say that God can perform or has performed miracles. But are not miracles instances of divine intervention? Many, for sure, have thought that they are. Or, if they have not explicitly said that they are, they have used language implying that they are, or that they would be if they occurred. Hume (no believer in miracles) famously does so when asserting that a miracle 'may be accurately defined, *a transgression of a law of nature by a particular volition of the Deity, or by the interposition of some invisible agent*'.[28] We find similar definitions in the works of other writers. Take, for example, Richard Swinburne and John Mackie. According to Swinburne, a miracle is 'a violation of a law of nature by a god'.[29] According to Mackie, a miracle is 'a violation of a law of nature' brought about by 'divine or supernatural intervention'. 'The laws of nature', Mackie adds, 'describe the ways in which the world – including, of course, human beings – works when left to itself, when not interfered with. A miracle occurs when the world is not left to itself, when something distinct from the natural order as a whole intrudes into it.'[30]

Yet the thought of God intervening in the created order (or intruding into it) is an exceedingly odd one. It would not be so if we took God to be an agent akin to a human being (albeit an invisible agent) living alongside the world and observing it from outside. Such an agent might well be thought of as able to intervene, just as I can be thought of as able to intervene in a brawl.[31] Yet God, so I have been arguing, is not such an agent. I take God to be the cause of the existence of everything other than himself, and it seems hard to see how God, so understood, can be thought of as literally able to intervene in or to interfere with what he brings about. For something can only intervene by entering into a situation from which it is first of all absent, while God, as I am conceiving of him, cannot be thought to be absent from anything he creates. If God makes the universe to be (at any time), then God is creatively present to everything at all times – as making it to be and to be as it is. From this it seems to follow that God cannot intervene in the world. He is, as creative cause, already in everything at the outset. As Alvin Plantinga puts it, commenting on Mackie's definition of 'miracle', 'on the theistic conception the world is never "left to itself" but is always (at the least) conserved in being by God'.[32] Talk about God as intervening has to presuppose that there is commonly a serious absence of God from created things. Yet if God is (in my sense) indeed the Creator of all things, then he is never absent from any of them (a point to which I shall later return).

You might think that if that is the case then theists should stop believing in miracles (or stop believing that miracles are at least possible). But this conclusion does not follow at all – unless one builds the notions of intervention, interference, or intrusion into the concept of miracle. Yet why should one do that? At any rate, I find it significant that as 'traditional' a 'theist' as one could look for (again I am referring to Aquinas) manages to talk about miracles without

once suggesting that they amount to interventions or acts of interference on God's part.

Thinkers like Hume, Swinburne and Mackie evidently seem to
suppose that a miracle occurs only if something extraneous (i.e. God)
moves into a given way in which something, or several things, are in
the world. For Aquinas, however, miracles only occur when something in the world fails to be acting in some way, or is just not there at
all. In his view, a miracle is an event which cannot be produced by the
powers of anything created. So he takes miracles not to be explicable
in natural terms. What, therefore, brings them about (if they come
about at all)? Aquinas's answer is 'God', but not 'God as intervening or
interfering'. His point is that a miracle is an event which has nothing
but God as its cause. In a rather famous passage he writes:

> God is in everything; not indeed as part of their essence, or as an
> accident, but as an efficient cause is present to that in which its
> action is taking place. For every efficient cause must be connected
> with that upon which it acts and must touch it by its power . . .
> Now, since it is God's essence to exist, created existence must be
> his proper effect, as burning is fire's proper effect. But God causes
> this effect in things not just when they begin to exist but all the
> time they are maintained in existence, just as the sun is lighting up
> the atmosphere all the time the atmosphere remains lit. During the
> whole period of a thing's existence, therefore, God must be present
> to it, and present in a way that accords with the way in which the
> thing possesses its existence. Now existing is more intimately and
> profoundly interior to things than anything else . . . So, God must
> be, and be intimately, in everything.[33]

With thinking such as this in mind, Aquinas concludes that miracles
are not cases of an *absence* of God followed by a *presence* of him.
With this thinking in mind, he effectively denies that miracles are
cases of divine intervention. One can hardly suppose that for God to
create at all is for God to intervene. By the same token, so Aquinas
thinks, one cannot suppose that miracles are instances of divine intervention. They are no more and no less created than anything else
produced by God.

This line of thinking makes sense to me, so I commend it to you.
We should definitely be suspicious of the notion of God stepping in to

tinker with (to act as an outsider on) what is created. Or, as we might put it, God makes no difference to anything. I make a difference to things. I made a difference to Smokey when I fed him this morning. I also made a difference to my dishes when I washed them this evening. But 'making a difference' here means acting on something which does not depend on me for its entire being (as long as it exists). In this sense, I suggest, God makes no difference to anything, and I take this conclusion to be part and parcel of the (traditional) claim that God creates *ex nihilo*. You can certainly see it emerging fairly clearly in what Aquinas says about this claim.

One of the points he emphasizes is that creation is not the bringing about of a change in anything. One changes something, he thinks, if the thing changed pre-exists one's act of changing it. Yet, so Aquinas reasons, nothing pre-exists God's creative act and God, therefore, does not change anything by making it to exist. Or, as Aquinas puts it himself:

> God's action, which is without pre-existing matter and called *creation*, is neither a motion nor a change, properly speaking . . . In the action which is creation, nothing potential pre-exists to receive the action . . . Again, in every change or motion there must be something existing in one way now and in a different way before . . . But where the whole substance of a thing is brought into being, there can be no same thing existing in different ways, because such a thing would not itself be produced, but would be presupposed to the production. Hence creation is not a change.[34]

Note that Aquinas is not here taking God's act of creating to be nothing but the bringing about of the beginning of the universe (though he does, in fact, take God's act of creating to include this).[35] Aquinas is here thinking that for God to create something is for him to make it to exist *period*, and he is saying that for God to do this is not for God to modify or change anything. Here I agree with Aquinas. In my terminology, God makes no difference to anything (which, of course, does not entail that God cannot bring it about that things undergo change).[36]

The oddness of God

There is a strong biblical tradition according to which one is ill advised to try to second-guess God. A famous place in which it surfaces is St Paul's first letter to the Corinthians. Here Paul talks about the apparent foolishness of God and goes on to declare that God has worked in ways that many would never have anticipated.[37] Though I shall be returning to such thoughts later in the present volume, I am not, for the moment, concerned to argue that Paul is right in what he says here. At this point, however, and on the basis of what I have argued in the present chapter, I do think it worth drawing attention to what we might call God's oddness, an oddness that we can hardly ignore or gloss over as we try to reflect on the topic of God and evil.

For think what we should be saying if what I have been arguing above is cogent. We should be saying:

(1) God is the source of the existence of absolutely everything other than himself.

(2) God is not an item in the universe.

(3) God acts in or on what is not divine not as something external but as a source of existence.

(4) God is not something the nature of which can be distinguished from the individual that it is.

(5) God's nature is to exist (or, God exists by nature).

(6) God does not undergo (and cannot undergo) any real change.

If 1–6 here are true (and it is worth stressing that they are all pretty much part of what most theists have meant by 'God' for centuries), then God, I should say, is pretty odd.[38] He is not like anything we know (or think we know). Indeed, it makes sense to regard him as incomprehensible. For what we primarily know are things in the universe and truths about them expressed in propositions. You might say that we know abstract objects (e.g. numbers) and ethical truths, neither of these being items in the universe (so one might think). Abstract objects and ethical truths, however (whatever else is to be said about them, which might include the suggestion that they do not exist), are not alive, as I have argued that God is. If my position is correct, then, God is a living thing – but not an individual (not something distinguishable from its nature) and not material.[39] Such a being does not seem to fall easily within human powers of comprehension.

Admittedly, a lot here depends on how one construes 'comprehend'. For can we not be said to comprehend God if we can know that it is true to say certain things of him? If we take our lead from the *Oxford English Dictionary*, we might do so, since there is a sense of 'comprehend' where it means 'to grasp with the mind' and since it does not seem particularly odd to say that one comprehends God if one can know that it is true to say certain things of him. But 'to comprehend' can also mean 'to understand fully or adequately', and it seems fair to say that nobody comprehends God (on my account of God) in that sense. Full or adequate understanding of something is (is it not?) what we take ourselves to have when we arrive at a scientific account of it, when it is something in the world that we can single out, analyse, compare and contrast with other things in the world, and end up defining (even if we subsequently wish to revise our definitions). Given what I have argued, however, God is nothing in the world and is not one of a kind among others of the same kind. For this reason it surely makes sense to call him incomprehensible and, therefore, seriously odd. Aquinas makes the point by saying that when it comes to God we cannot know what he is (*quid est*). Aquinas does not mean that we cannot take ourselves to be able to make many true statements with God as their subject. As is well known, of course, he claims to be able to establish the truth of many statements of the form 'God is ____'. He does not, however, think that we are able to develop a science of God as, for example, we have already developed a science of cats, which is what he has in mind in saying that we cannot know what God is. We can, Aquinas thinks, know what Smokey is, for Smokey belongs to the universe and is something we can single out while going on to compare and contrast him with things of his kind and with things of other kinds. Yet God, thinks Aquinas, is not like Smokey in any of these respects.

You will realize that I side with Aquinas here. I think that if we take God to be the Creator of the universe, the source of the existence of everything not divine, we should be very struck by the notion that God is seriously hard to fathom. I also think that we should keep this notion firmly to the foreground when approaching the topic of God and evil. To start thinking about this topic while presuming that we know what God is seems to me misguided. Yet discussions of God and evil frequently proceed on the contrary assumption. They often begin by supposing that we do have a pretty good understanding of God. This supposition usually takes the form of regarding God as something familiar to us. It reaches its peak in the claim that God, if he exists, is a moral agent, so I shall now turn to that suggestion.

Notes

1. You might say that you could accept that, for example, the explanation of someone's having some disease is a genetic malfunction, something you might understand little about and therefore know less about than what you invoke it to explain. You would not, however, have an explanation here yourself. You would be believing people who tell you about what actually is an explanation, something that they must take to be more understandable than what is explained.

2. For more on this see Philip Dixon, *Nice and Hot Disputes: The Doctrine of the Trinity in the 17th Century* (T&T Clark: Edinburgh, 2003).

3. For more on all this see J. N. D. Kelly, *Early Christian Doctrines* (5th edn, Adam and Charles Black: London, 1980) and G. L. Prestige, *God in Patristic Thought* (SPCK: London, 1952), esp. chs 8 and 9.

4. René Descartes, *Meditations on First Philosophy* (Meditation II). I quote from *The Philosophical Writings of Descartes*, vol. 2, tr. John Cottingham, Robert Stoothhoff and Dugald Murdoch (Cambridge University Press: Cambridge, 1984), p. 19. Much that Descartes says about people shows him to be acutely aware of the fact that people are not just to be thought of as, so to speak, angels – things whose histories are unaffected by what is material. He does, however, strongly suggest that the bodies of people, though influencing what they essentially are, cannot be identified with them. On his account, therefore, I could be what I essentially am even if there is no material world.

5. Hence, for example, in *The Coherence of Theism* (revd edn Clarendon Press: Oxford, 1993) Richard Swinburne spends time (in ch. 7) arguing that there could be an incorporeal spirit (a person) by defending certain views about personal identity when it comes to human beings.

6. See Gilbert Ryle, *The Concept of Mind* (Hutchinson: London, 1949), Ludwig Wittgenstein, *Philosophical Investigations*, 2nd edn, tr. G. E. M. Anscombe (Basil Blackwell: Oxford, 1968), J. J. C. Smart, 'Sensations and Brain Processes', *Philosophical Review* 68 (1959), and David Armstrong, *A Materialist Theory of Mind* (Humanities Press: New York, 1968).

7. It has been said that God is a person on the basis of Genesis 1:26, in which people are described as being made 'in' God's image and 'after' his likeness. That text, however, provides no justification for thinking of God

as being seriously like people in any particular respect. In fact, it is far from clear what that text is saying, as you might infer from, for example, Gerhard von Rad, *Genesis: A Commentary*, tr. John H. Marks (Westminster Press: Philadelphia, 1961), pp. 55ff.

8. For a superb treatment of Aquinas on this question see Gregory P. Rocca, *Speaking the Incomprehensible God* (Catholic University of America Press: Washington, DC, 2004).

9. I think that we might well be able to imagine such circumstances (even though I am somewhat uncomfortable with thought experiments invoked for the purposes of philosophical argument). For we can surely imagine there being only one cat, since we can imagine there being people determined to exterminate all cats, people unsuccessful only because they missed one.

10. I am not, of course, suggesting that there is some sort of entity rightly referred to as 'human nature'. All I am saying is that a particular human being can be distinguished from (cannot be identified with) the nature that he or she shares with other human beings.

11. Aquinas, *Summa Theologiae*, Ia.3.3 (my translation).

12. Ibid. (my translation).

13. Cf. ibid., Ia.3.4.

14. For someone seeming to argue along these lines see C. J. F. Williams, 'Being', in Philip L. Quinn and Charles Taliaferro (eds), *A Companion to Philosophy of Religion* (Blackwell Publishers: Oxford, 1997).

15. Anthony Kenny, *Aquinas on Being* (Clarendon Press: Oxford, 2002), p. 41.

16. See G. E. M. Anscombe and P. T. Geach, *Three Philosophers* (Basil Blackwell: Oxford, 1961), p. 89.

17. Kenny, *Aquinas on Being*, p. 34. The Latin reads: 'Omnis autem essentia vel quidditas potest intelligi sine hoc quod aliquid intelligatur de esse suo: possum enim intelligere quid est homo vel phoenix, et tamen ignorare an esse habeat in rerum natura; ergo patet quod esse est aliud ab essentia vel quidditate. Nisi forte sit aliqua res cuius quidditas sit ipsum suum esse.'

18. Frege thinks that if I say that Smokey is grey, then I am using a predicate to say what Smokey (a particular individual cat) actually is. So he takes '____ is grey' to be a predicate which might tell us what something actually is. Consider, however, '____ is numerous'. We can hardly say sensibly that Smokey is numerous. But we can sensibly say that cats are numerous. In doing so, thinks Frege, we are saying something about the concept 'cat' and not talking about any particular cat. We are saying that '____ is a cat' is truly predicable of many individuals.

19. What I am now attributing to Aquinas does not conflict with his claim (to be found, for example, in *Summa Theologiae* Ia.2.2) that we cannot demonstrate God's existence from an understanding of the meaning of the word 'God'. That claim maintains that one can consistently accept that the word 'God' has a certain meaning and that there is no God.

Aquinas's assertion that God's essence is *esse* is saying that, given that God exists and is not something the essence of which can be understood, something cannot be true of God without it also being understood that it actually exists.

20. I develop these points in 'Kenny on Aquinas on Being', *Modern Schoolman* 82 (2005).

21. Richard Swinburne, for example, argues for this assumption. See *The Coherence of Theism*, ch. 12.

22. Peter Geach, *God and the Soul* (Routledge & Kegan Paul: London, 1969), pp. 71f.

23. Do we undergo a real change when we die? It seems to me that we do not, because as soon as we are dead we do not exist, and so cannot be described as having undergone what I mean by a real change. When I die, my corpse will be there for people to view. But my corpse is hardly me and is, therefore, not *me as modified*. There is surely a vast difference between dying and, say, coming to appreciate the music of Puccini. Wittgenstein famously said, 'Death is not an event in life. Death is not lived through' (*Tractatus Logico-Philosophicus*, tr. C. K. Ogden (Routledge & Kegan Paul: London, 1922), 6.4311). It is not hard to see what Wittgenstein is driving at here, even if one hopes for a life to come, which may, indeed, come.

24. Thomas Aquinas, *Commentary on Aristotle's 'De Interpretatione'*, I.14 (my translation). The Latin here reads: 'extra ordinem entium existens, velut causa quaedam profundens totum ens et omnes eius differentias'.

25. Thomas Aquinas, *Commentary on Aristotle's 'De Anima'*, I.14, tr. Robert Pasnau (Yale University Press: New Haven, Conn. and London, 1999), p. 113.

26. Cf. Thomas Aquinas, *Summa Contra Gentiles*, I.97: 'It is supremely true of God that He does not act from another, but through Himself, since He is the first agent. Therefore, to live belongs to him in a supreme way.' I quote from *Saint Thomas Aquinas: 'Summa Contra Gentiles', Book One*, tr. Anton C. Pegis (University of Notre Dame Press: Notre Dame, Ind. and London, 1975), p. 294.

27. Thomas Aquinas, *Commentary on Aristotle's 'Physics'*, III.5. I quote from *Aquinas: Selected Philosophical Writings*, tr. Timothy McDermott (Oxford University Press: Oxford and New York, 1993), p. 84.

28. David Hume, *An Inquiry Concerning Human Understanding*, ed. Tom L. Beauchamp (Clarendon Press: Oxford, 2000), p. 87.

29. Richard Swinburne, *The Concept of Miracle* (Macmillan: London and Basingstoke, 1970), p. 11.

30. J. L. Mackie, *The Miracle of Theism* (Clarendon Press: Oxford, 1982), pp. 19f.

31. Many philosophers, of course, would object to the notion of an invisible human being; but I leave that point aside for now.

32. Alvin Plantinga, 'Is Theism Really a Miracle?', *Faith and Philosophy* 3 (1986), p. 111. Plantinga's understanding of God differs significantly from

mine. In this quotation, however, he seems to me to hit an important nail on the head. One might well, however, challenge his phrase 'the theistic conception', for people calling themselves theists have disagreed about what God is. In the sense that there is something we can rightly call 'the Eiffel Tower', there is nothing that we can similarly call 'the theistic conception'. That fact, indeed, is something that accounts for my writing the present volume.

33. Aquinas, *Summa Theologiae*, Ia.8.1 (my translation).
34. Aquinas, *Summa Contra Gentiles*, II.17. I quote from *Saint Thomas Aquinas: 'Summa Contra Gentiles', Book Two: Creation*, tr. James F. Anderson (University of Notre Dame Press: Notre Dame, Ind., 1975), p. 54. See also *Summa Theologiae*, Ia.45.1.
35. For Aquinas on creation and the beginning of the universe, see *Summa Theologiae*, Ia.46.
36. Aquinas famously argues that a reason to believe in God lies in the fact that things in the world undergo change – this being something that Aquinas believes to derive from God as the first cause of all change (see *Summa Theologiae*, Ia.2.3 and *Summa Contra Gentiles*, I.13). So he does not deny (and neither do I) that God brings it about that there are things which are different at some times from what they are at others. What Aquinas denies (and what I deny) is that God's making something to exist at any time (God's being its Creator) is the action of God *on* anything, a changing or modifying of something.
37. See I Corinthians 1:18–31.
38. By 'what theists have meant by "God" for centuries' I am simply alluding to the fact that, as you can quickly verify, what I am saying about God now would have been taken to be axiomatic by most theists from the patristic period to around the beginning of the nineteenth century.
39. I take the word 'individual' here to mean what we have in mind when we say that an individual is one of a kind of which there could be more than one. So I take Smokey to be an individual cat (even if he is the last surviving member of his species). I do not, however, take God to be an individual anything (a position for which I have argued above).

Four

God's Moral Standing

In *The Coherence of Theism* Richard Swinburne (who takes himself to be speaking on behalf of theism) writes as follows:

> In claiming that God is by nature perfectly morally good, I suggest that the theist be interpreted as claiming that God is so constituted that he always does the morally best action (when there is one), and no morally bad action. For God, as for us, there is often no one best action, but a choice of equal best actions, only one of which can be done . . . Perfect moral goodness includes doing both the obligatory and supererogatory and doing nothing wrong or bad in other ways . . . Perfect moral goodness surely involves fulfilling one's moral obligations . . . 'Morally' good actions are those which it is of overriding importance to do, which are overall better than other ones . . . I suggest that in our sense of 'moral' all theists hold that God is perfectly good, and that this is a central claim of theism.[1]

Note what Swinburne seems to be assuming here. He appears to be taking it for granted that to commend God as good is to commend him for doing what he ought to do – implying that God has moral duties or obligations just as we do (note his phrase 'For God, as for us'). Swinburne evidently allows that we might think of God as good because he does what goes over and above the call of duty, and because he never does what he ought not to do. But his focus is clearly on the idea that the core of God's goodness is a matter of obedience (God's obedience to moral laws).[2] And Swinburne retains this focus in *Providence and the Problem of Evil*.[3] Quoting me as saying that 'theologians have taught that God is good without holding that his goodness is moral goodness', he replies: 'Western religion has always held that there is a deep problem about why there is pain and other suffering – which there would not be if God were not supposed to be morally good.'[4]

'God is morally good' and the problem of evil

The idea that God is morally good is a commonplace among contemporary philosophers of religion.[5] Hence, for example, William Rowe also writes:

> Since God is unsurpassably good, he has all the features that unsurpassable goodness implies. Among these is absolute *moral goodness* . . . God's moral goodness has long been thought to be in some way the source or standard of what it is for human life to be moral . . . Clearly, given his absolute moral perfection, what God commands us to do must be what is morally right for us to do. But are these things morally right because God commands them? . . . The dominant answer in religious thinking concerning God and morality is that what God commands is morally right independently of his commands.[6]

From other things that he says, it is clear that Rowe believes that there must be more to God's goodness than moral goodness. But, equally clearly, Rowe takes God's goodness to include this, and he suggests that those who believe in God predominantly think of his moral goodness as a matter of conformity to moral demands which are somehow independent of him (just as my moral goodness might be thought of in terms of my conformity to requirements over and above me). And there are many who line up with Rowe on this matter. According, for instance, to Stephen T. Davis, 'God is good' means 'God never does what is morally wrong; all his intentions and actions are morally right. If it is always morally wrong, say, needlessly to break a promise, this is something God never does. If it is always morally wrong to cause needless suffering, this too is something God never does.'[7] Davis goes on to add that God's goodness also consists in the fact that he could do what is morally bad but does not. He writes: 'God is also laudable for being morally good, and I cannot see how a being who is unable to do evil can be laudable for being good.'[8]

The idea here seems to be that God is someone trying to be good (and succeeding) while confronted by moral claims of various kinds (not to mention various options for acting).[9] The idea seems to be that God is good because he manages, in spite of alternatives open to him, always to be *well behaved*.[10]

This notion of divine good conduct comes much to the surface in contemporary discussions of the problem of evil, in which it is regularly assumed that if God exists, and if God is good, then God is morally good. So God's friends often explain how God is *morally justified* for allowing the occurrence of various evils. And God's foes often tell us why this is not so. They tell us that any impartial jury would find God morally guilty when confronted with evils that he has allowed to come to pass, and they therefore conclude that God is morally bad – though, in fact, they almost always conclude that there is no God (on the supposition that if God exists, then God is morally good). In this discussion, the issue, time and again, seems to turn on whether or not God acts morally, where 'to act morally' means to act like someone we commend morally – someone confronted by, and acting in accordance with, moral duties, obligations, or laws. Hence, for example (and as I noted in Chapter 1), friends of God will say things like (a) 'Much evil is a means to a good end which God cannot bring about without allowing (or risking) the evil in question', or (b) 'God might have good reasons for allowing the evils that exists, though we (perhaps because of our limited information) cannot know what those reasons are'.

When it comes to (a), the basic idea is that, just as one might morally exonerate surgeons for cutting people open in order to save their lives, one can morally exonerate God for permitting various evils. So, for example, it is commonly argued that evil actions freely engaged in by people are no indication of God's moral badness. This is the Free Will Defence (also noted in Chapter 1), according to which: (i) it is good for people to have freedom of choice; (ii) God, being good, wants the good of human freedom; (iii) but this means that God cannot prevent all evil human choices (not to mention their consequences), since this would undermine their character as free; (iv) so God is morally justified in allowing people freely to act badly.

With respect to (b), the basic idea is that, just as morally good parents might act in ways that baffle their children, so God, being very knowledgeable and very moral, might be morally justified in allowing the evils that exist – evils the moral justification of which is not now apparent to us. Or, as William Alston says:

> The fact that we cannot see what sufficient justifying reason an omniscient, omnipotent being might have for doing something [does not provide] strong support for the supposition that no such reason is available for that being . . . Being unable to estimate the extent to which what we can discern exhausts the possibilities, we are in no position to suppose that our inability to find a justifying divine reason is a sufficient ground for supposing that there is none.[11]

If we take this at face value, Alston seems to be suggesting that God is morally good (by human standards) and that, though (by human standards) we might incline to fault him on moral grounds, we might yet end up exonerating him (by human standards) should we come to know as much as he does (presumably concerning the entire history of the universe and the ways in which bits of it connect with each other).

In response to thinkers like Plantinga and Alston (and to others who attempt moral justifications of God given the evil that we know of) one might argue that the justifications do not succeed – that they do not give us reason to suppose that, given evil as we know of it, there is any God who can defend himself morally. I shall return to this line of thinking later (in Chapters 5 and 6). For the moment, however, the question I want to raise is 'Why should we suppose that God's goodness *is* moral goodness?' My reading of those who think we should suggests to me that they do so for one major reason. Their big idea seems to be that belief in God's moral goodness is *traditional*. More specifically, they tend to argue (or, more often, to imply or take for granted) that it is part and parcel of what we find said about God in the Bible and in the writings of (mostly Christian) post-biblical religious authorities.[12] But is that really the case?

God's moral goodness

Before I tackle this question head on, let me make it clear that in taking issue with the proposition 'God is morally good' (as you will realize that I am), I am not denying that one can ever truly say (albeit with suitable qualifications) that God is what morally good people are. What moral goodness amounts to in people is, of course, a big question, and not one for me to comment on here, although I shall be touching on it later.[13] But many would, for example, say that we might morally commend someone for helping those in need, or for telling the truth. And I am not suggesting that it is remotely inappropriate (whether one believes in God or not) to say that God is good in that he (sometimes, at any rate, though *manifestly* not always) helps those in need, or in that he tells the truth (or even that he *cannot but* tell the truth).[14] Nor am I suggesting that (whether one believes in God or not) it is right to say that God ever does what might be held to be morally impermissible. I think most of us would say that it is morally impermissible to torture someone to death just for the fun of it. And I can see no reason to object to the claim that God does not (or does not have it in him to) torture people to death just for the fun of it. And, I might add, I am not denying that God (whether you believe in him or not) commands what is morally good. Indeed, the opposite seems true. At any rate, given what the Bible says, God commands much that many would take to be morally good (think of what we find given out in God's name by Old Testament prophets like Amos and Micah). And he prohibits much that many would take to be morally bad (think of most, even if not all, of the prohibitions contained in the Ten Commandments). People sometimes say that God's commands and prohibitions as depicted in the Bible express his moral character, and I have no objection to that way of talking if it means that many of God's commands and prohibitions as depicted in the Bible are commands and prohibitions which lots of people today would find morally congenial.

But to say all this is not really to say very much. And it does not serve to support the claim that God is morally good. For it is all perfectly compatible with the view that God is not a moral agent subject to moral praise or censure. Yet why should one want to support that view? I want to do so on two grounds. The first has to do with the notion of God as Creator. The second has to do with things that are said of God in some primary theistic sources.

A morally good creator?

Should we take seriously the suggestion that God the Creator is a moral agent subject to moral praise or censure? Much, of course, depends on what one takes 'God is the Creator' to mean, and here we need to note that this assertion has been construed in different ways (or that there are grounds for saying that it has been so construed).

Take, for example, the familiar notion that God creates *ex nihilo* – that he makes things to be, though not out of anything. This notion of creation is classical, and you can find it expounded and defended by writers like Augustine and (as I have noted) Aquinas. Is it biblical, however? There are certainly biblical texts which might be cited in its defence. Examples include Romans 4:17, Romans 11:36, I Corinthians 8:6, Colossians 1:15–16, and Hebrews 11:3. These (taken in order) read as follows and seem to be teaching, albeit in a non-philosophical manner, that God creates *ex nihilo*:

(1) '... as it is written, "I have made you the father of many nations" – in the presence of the God in whom he believed, who gives life to the dead and calls into existence the things that do not exist.'

(2) 'For from him and through him and to him are all things. To him be glory forever.'

(3) 'Yet for us there is one God, the Father, from whom are all things and for whom we exist, and one Lord, Jesus Christ, through whom are all things and through whom we exist.'

(4) 'He is the image of the invisible God, the firstborn of all creation; for in him all things in heaven and on earth were created, things visible and invisible, whether thrones or dominions or rulers or powers – all things have been created through him and for him.'

(5) 'By faith we understand that the worlds were prepared by the word of God, so that what is seen was made from things that are not visible.'[15]

Yet there are other biblical texts dealing with the topic of God as Creator which (arguably) do not seem to express a belief in creation *ex nihilo*. Genesis 1:1 is a famous case in point. Here, a 'formless void' covered by water seems to precede God's creative act.[16]

Then again, should we take God to be continuously creating, or should we think of him as having created only in the past? Here also we find conflicting (or possibly conflicting) understandings (or ways of talking). As we have seen, according to Aquinas, for example, there is a serious sense in which what God did by bringing it about that the universe began to exist is something he continues to do in so far as he makes things to be for as long as they exist. For Aquinas, the Genesis narrative of creation is an account of creation *ex nihilo*, and it prohibits us from saying that God makes 'new creatures'.[17] But Aquinas also holds (a) that for God to create is for God to make something to exist, and (b) that creatures need God in order to exist at any time.[18] As far as I can gather, however, the biblical scholars seem to agree that the account of creation in Genesis 1 views it as over and done with in a matter of days – even though other biblical passages seem to be supposing that God is continually creating.[19] And, so I suspect, many religious believers would find it odd to think of creating as an activity to be continuously attributable to God. Simply going by what I have heard a lot of them say, they often agree that God continues to 'sustain' his creation. But I do not think that they mean what, for example, Aquinas has in mind when he speaks of God making everything to exist for as long as it exists (this, for him, and rightly in my view, marking the first difference between God and creatures). I suspect that they mean that God props up (and sometimes tinkers with) things he has somehow set up in advance – this not implying their total dependence on God as an agent-cause (something which Aquinas always has in mind when he writes about God as Creator). And, so I might add, there are contemporary Christian philosophers of religion who seem to think that something might exist which is not created by God. Hence, for example, explaining what it means to believe in God as Creator, Richard Swinburne tells us: 'The main claim is that God either himself brings about or makes or permits some other being to bring about (or permits to exist uncaused) the existence of all things that exist.'[20] What Swinburne says here arguably coheres with some biblical texts, but it is very far removed from anything we find in mainstream Christian writers, hardly any of whom would ever have spoken of anything other than God as existing uncaused.

Now my view is that such authors can be credited with drawing out the drift of what biblical texts say about God as Creator. But I also think that they do so by rightly reading them with philosophical eyes. And, one might ask, how else can one read the Bible? The Bible does not interpret itself. People need to interpret the Bible, and they certainly cannot do so simply by citing biblical texts taken at their face value (or interpreted literally, as we might say). As far as I can work out, neither the Old nor the New Testament ever come out with a precise teaching to the effect that God is incorporeal.[21] But both of them often seem strongly to want to distinguish between God and various creatures so as to suggest that God is no inhabitant of the physical world. In the Old Testament, for instance, God is frequently referred to as lacking certain needs and limitations found in human beings and other creatures.[22] Yet, as I have noted, the Old Testament is also full of talk about God which depicts him in thoroughly human terms.

How are we to deal with these apparent discrepancies? If our interest in biblical texts merely extends to noting what they appear literally to say verse by verse, then we can do just that and have no problem of interpretation. But we might think of the Bible as helping us to some understanding of God and ourselves – in which case we have to introduce what I can only call philosophical reasoning. Is God a body or not? There are biblical texts which can be cited on both sides here. So what if we say that God is a body? Then we presumably need non-biblical arguments (in my current terminology, 'philosophical arguments') for supposing that God is indeed corporeal and that anything in the Bible which suggests otherwise should be regarded as metaphor or something like that. Or again, what if we think that God is not a body? Then we presumably need non-biblical arguments (in my current terminology, 'philosophical arguments') for supposing that God is indeed incorporeal and that anything in the Bible which suggests otherwise should be regarded as metaphor or something like that.

In a parallel way I now want to suggest that we have philosophical reason to deny that God is a moral agent. For given what I argued in Chapters 2 and 3, we would be wrong to think of God as, so we might put it, an existent among others – wrong to suppose that 'God and the universe should add up to make two'.[23] The claim that God is the source of the universe implies that 'God is to be thought of as existing outside the realm of existents, as a cause from which pours forth everything that exists in all its variant forms'.[24] And that, I think, is what we have to say if we take God to account for there being any universe at all. An existent among others is one of a kind, or something unique, occupying a world where things can be classified. But the source of the universe as a whole, the cause of its sheer existence, cannot be any such thing. Nor can its existence be derived. Since it accounts for the being of what we call the universe, it certainly cannot owe its existence to anything within the universe. And, as I have argued, since we are invoking it as accounting for what exists but might not, it cannot be something whose existence is distinguishable from its nature – as, for example, the existence of my (actual) cat (Smokey) is distinguishable from its nature (to know what felinity is, considered as a nature had by various cats, is not to know that there is any such thing as my actual cat).[25]

Notice that none of the above suggestions amount to an attempt to describe God. I am only drawing attention to what God *cannot* be if he is indeed the Creator. I am engaging in negative theology. But it is negative theology with what we might think of as positive results. For it rightly puts up 'No Entry' signs (positive, you might say) at the beginning of certain roads down which one might be tempted to stroll and explore the details. And one of these roads is called 'God is a moral agent'.

For how do we typically think of moral agents? Primarily, we think of them as people living in the world and capable of acting well or badly. Philosophers, of course, have disagreed about the key concepts to invoke when it comes to good and bad action. Some focus on 'duty' and 'obligation'. Others make much of 'virtue' and 'vice'.[26] But they are all talking about people and what makes them to be (morally) good or bad (and what it therefore is for them to be moral agents). Yet God is not a human being. And if what I have said above has anything to recommend it, we have to think of God as radically different from anything created.[27]

As I have also argued, we need, in addition, to think of him as radically incomprehensible. We can get our minds around Smokey. We can examine him, compare and contrast him with other things, note his progress and character, and even note how well or badly he is doing (considered as a cat). Can we do the same when it comes to God? Not if what I have been saying above is correct. There can be no laying hands on the source of the universe's being, and no way of comparing and contrasting it with other things on which hands can be laid (i.e. God, as I have argued, is not remotely subject to scientific analysis, as Smokey is). And if there is time only because there is a universe in which things change, God makes no progress and has no character (taking character to be something displayed over time). And what sense can it make to talk of how well or badly God is doing? Such talk seems to suppose that God has a life-span in which he is now like this and now like that – one in which he might change from being better to worse or from worse to better. Yet how can one intelligibly conceive the Creator (the source of the universe's being) as having a life-span or as lurching from one state to another? Something with a life-span has a beginning and end. Can we, however, make sense of the claim that the Creator has a beginning and end?

You might say that there are moral laws of which any decent God needs to take account – this making God a moral agent. After all, is it not commonly said that God is a person? And are persons not subject to moral laws (or duties, or obligations)? And are not such laws (or duties, or obligations) binding on all persons – even divine ones? And does this not mean that God is a moral agent? And, focusing on moral goodness with an eye on virtues and vices, are not persons either virtuous or vicious? So is not God (if he exists) either virtuous or vicious?

As I have noted, the formula 'God is a person' is (given the history of theistic thinking and writing) a relatively recent one. It has, however, stuck with many who take themselves to be expressing orthodox Christian belief. What do people who endorse it tend to mean by it? As I have also noted, by 'person' they seem to mean what Descartes thought he was when ruminating on himself in his *Meditations*. They believe that a person is essentially an incorporeal substance who reasons, believes, and knows (in a private world, as if nothing else existed).[28] And they presume that God is just such a person. In doing so, they are, of course, taking sides on a series of philosophical debates that I can hardly begin to enter into here. So I am now just going to have to show my hand and move on – saying that the notion of person just mentioned (grounded as it is only on reflection about *people*) has been blown out of the water by philosophers such as Wittgenstein (not to mention Aristotle). And with this thought in mind, I suggest that 'God is a person' is not the best slogan to invoke in defence of the claim that God is a moral agent. It would not be a good one to invoke even on the supposition that Descartes's basic understanding of himself is right. For let us grant Descartes all that he says about what he is in the *Meditations*. As I noted earlier, it still remains that the essentially incorporeal thing that he takes himself to be belongs to a world containing other such things (things of a kind, all of them members of a world). So Descartes, on his own admission (to which he seems to hold), is, on my count, a creature. And why should we suppose that God is a creature?

Note also that the formula 'God is a person' does not fit easily with biblical accounts of God. These, as I have said, vary. But while there is plenty of biblical language suggesting that God is very like a human being,[29] the Bible, as I have already observed, also contains texts which discourage the supposition that God is really like anything of which we can conceive. It makes much, for example, of God's hiddenness.[30] And it makes much of his holiness – certainly not a moral category, but one used (in the Old Testament anyway) sharply to distinguish between (a) God as an awe-inspiring mystery distinct from creation, and (b) created things (familiar, understandable, manipulable, and responsible to something or other).[31] And, as I have said, the Bible sometimes explicitly warns against comparing God with anything creaturely.

One might, of course, reply that biblical texts implying a serious likeness between God and creatures (especially people) should be deemed to trump texts implying a radical difference between them. But whether or not this line of thinking is defensible on purely philosophical grounds, it seems to me that, taken as a whole, the Bible stresses the incomparability of God more than it does the similarity between God and any creature. I also think that the very concrete descriptive language it often uses when talking of God favours this conclusion. If you try to compose anything that we might call a picture of God from what the Bible says about him, you will fail precisely because of the diversity of its depictions of God. The Bible portrays God as a man who can walk in a garden, but also as surveying the created order and as being distinct from it.[32] It tells us that he is a warrior and a king.[33] But it also tells us that he is a woman who cries out in childbirth, that he is various kinds of non-human animals, and is also an instance of dry rot.[34] And he *appears* in forms that *hide* him rather than show him forth. So Ezekiel sees only 'the appearance of the likeness of the glory of the Lord', and Moses sees only the 'glory' of God's backside.[35] Arguably, it is not an accident that the

Bible does not settle for any clear image or picture of God. Arguably, also, many of its various authors are of Aquinas's mind when he says that crude imagery used when talking of God is appropriate, since it conveys something to us in terms we can do something with, and since it obviously cannot be taken literally.[36]

Yet (and at this point I put the formula 'God is a person' behind me) it might still be said that biblical texts present us with the notion of God as a moral agent. For does not the Bible continually speak of God as being righteous? And is it not thereby teaching (a) that God acts in accordance with the requirements of morality and (b) that God is therefore a *good* moral agent? And is this not the picture of God that comes to us in post-biblical Christian texts – ones which we might think of as embodying 'the Christian tradition' when it comes to God's moral status?

The Bible certainly says that God is righteous. So far as I can gather, however, it never conceives of God's righteousness along moral lines – by which I mean that it never takes God to be righteous because he does what is (morally) the right thing for him to do (as someone might commend me for doing what it is morally right for me to do).

In the Old Testament, God's righteousness seems to consist in his acting in accordance with his covenant with the people of Israel (all the terms of which are drawn up by him).[37] So it amounts to the notion that God can be relied upon to do what he has said he will do (with respect to Israel).[38] Righteousness, in this context, clearly does not mean 'moral goodness which accords with standards of goodness binding on all who seek to be morally good'.[39] And Old Testament texts *never* suggest that God is good because he conforms to some code or other (which I take to mean that they never suggest that God is good as a good moral agent is good).

The Old Testament notion of God's righteousness carries on into New Testament writings and is clearly displayed in, for example, what St Paul has to say in Romans 9. Here he is worried about his fellow Jews. They, he says, were given promises, the law, and the covenant. They were also given the patriarchs and the assurance of a Messiah. But they do not seem to have turned to Christ (whom Paul takes to be the Messiah). So what shall we say about all this?

We cannot, replies Paul, claim that God's word has failed. For some Israelites are not *true* Israelites. And yet, Paul adds, some people are God's chosen regardless of what they have done in their lifetimes. For what about Jacob and Esau? Their fates, says Paul, were settled 'even before they had been born or had done anything good or bad' (v. 11). There is, says Paul, a matter of God's *election* to consider here. God, he adds, does not always deal with people on the basis of what they do. He deals with them as he sees fit. 'As it is written, "I have loved Jacob, but I have hated Esau"' (v. 13).

But, so Paul then asks, does this not mean that God is not just? His answer (emphatic in its Greek) is 'By no means' (v. 14). This answer, however, is clearly not intended to stress that God is just by (say) Aristotelian views about what it is for people to be just. Paul's point seems to be that we have to deal with God on the basis of what he does – that God's justice is what God takes it to be (not something conforming to standards to which he ought to conform). Not surprisingly, therefore, Paul can add (in v. 20), 'Who indeed are you, a human being, to argue with God?' (a question which strongly echoes what we find at the end of the book of Job, which is another good example of a biblical text refusing to think of God as an agent subject to moral requirements and, therefore, as intelligibly defensible or impugnable with reference to them).

At this point in his discussion Paul invokes some familiar Old Testament imagery – that of God being a potter making what he wants from the clay on which he works.[40] We might think that God ought to make things to be thus and so. But, says Paul, we should not do so. He writes: 'Has the potter no right over the clay to make out of the same lump one object for special use and another for ordinary use?' (v. 21). It should, I think, be obvious that St Paul is not here conceiving of God as an individual who needs to justify himself in the light of moral canons to which he is bound or obliged. And, so I might add, notions of God's righteousness in the Bible seem pretty much to accord with what St Paul says in Romans 9.[41]

Once again, therefore, I suggest that (whether or not we believe in God) we have reason for fighting shy of the formula 'God is a moral agent'. To do so seems to accord with biblical ways of thinking. And, so I have argued, it accords with what follows from the notion of God as Creator.[42] As I have noted, Richard Swinburne thinks that mainstream religious traditions conceive of God's goodness in moral terms since they think of there being a problem as to why there should be pain and suffering. But Swinburne's inference here is open to question. *Of course* religious people have asked why there is pain and suffering. But it is not obvious that they have always done so as posing a question about God's moral integrity. This is not, for example, how Old Testament writers proceed. They sometimes worry about what causes pain and suffering. And, when believing that it comes from God, they sometimes ask how *some* pain and suffering can be inflicted by a God who, in a covenant, has promised *some* people certain goods on condition that they act in accordance with his decrees.[43] But they never engage in a general moral defence or attack on God because of the existence of pain and suffering.[44] And this is especially so if we take 'pain and suffering' to mean 'pain and suffering as such, not just that of those who take themselves to be faithful to God's covenant with Israel'. Someone like Swinburne might say that morality requires that, so far as is possible, everyone should be treated as equals. But this is clearly not a position ascribed to the biblical God. He is incredibly partisan, electing some and wreaking havoc on others without providing anything like a moral defence of himself for what he brings about, and without being *required to* by any biblical author.

Then again, consider the way in which Aquinas (a classical example of someone in a mainstream religious tradition, and someone held up by many religious believers as a classical representative of it) discusses pain and suffering. If Swinburne is right, you would expect his various treatments of these topics to home in at once on questions of the form 'Is God morally justified in . . .?' But he never raises any such question (and the same can be said of almost all Christian authors from New Testament times to around the eighteenth century).[45] He asks whether God can be thought of as causing evil (his conclusion, grounded in metaphysical views about causation and privation of *esse*, is always 'No', though he does say that God causes the act of sin).[46] He asks whether God can bring good out of evil (his answer being 'Yes'). But he never makes God's moral integrity something to consider given the existence of pain and suffering, and his silence here (one that, so to speak, can be heard in the writings of any number of Christian theologians) seems to me yet another reason for supposing that Swinburne is wrong in his inference concerning the 'problem' of pain and suffering to which he refers.[47]

God and morality

Notice, however, that this conclusion does not entail that one can in no sense speak of morality (i.e. being moral) as somehow being in what it is to be God. Nor does it entail that we cannot think of God as good.

I defended many of the points I am now advocating in an earlier book of mine, in a chapter called 'The Problem of Evil'.[48] Commenting on my claim in that chapter that God is not a moral agent, Brian Shanley subsequently attacked me for not being faithful to the writings of Aquinas.[49] He had three main charges to level:

(1) that my claim is not consonant with texts of Aquinas since 'Aquinas argues that the moral virtues can be attributed to God in the form of exemplar virtues';[50]

(2) that my claim conflicts with Aquinas's teaching on God's justice; and

(3) that (so a Thomist might say) moral goodness (which Shanley calls a 'spiritual perfection') can be ascribed to God analogically.

Elaborating on (3) Shanley says that goodness 'fundamentally means perfect actuality in being' and that 'that is precisely what the achievement of moral goodness is in a rational creature'.[51] Perhaps my position might become clearer if I respond to these criticisms.

To begin with, Shanley is right to say that Aquinas attributes moral virtues to God in some sense. Hence, for example, in *Summa Theologiae*, Ia2ae,61.5 we read: 'The exemplar of human virtue must needs pre-exist in God, just as in him exist the patterns of all things.'[52] Aquinas is here working on the principle (to which I shall return later) that the effects of efficient causes resemble their causes (which causes must therefore somehow have in them what they produce). So he is thinking that moral virtues in people somehow reflect what God is (just as he thinks that other human perfections – like being able to do a crossword puzzle in ten minutes – reflect what God is, and just as he thinks that what I am when I am the victim of a virus reflects what the virus is, this being something the nature of which is shown forth in its effects on me because it is acting in me).[53]

But this line of thinking is far removed from what I am presently targeting (from what I am objecting to in the claim that God is a moral agent). Aquinas certainly does not think of God as an individual who is subject to duties and obligations, or as something displaying Aristotelian virtues, as Aristotle took good people to do. If Aquinas takes moral virtue to exist in God, it is only because he thinks that nothing God produces can fail to have some grounding in God's nature. It is not because he takes God to be morally virtuous in any sense that we can fathom and adjudicate on (or in any sense that we ought to try to fathom and adjudicate on). In the passage from Aquinas just quoted, his basic idea is: moral goodness as it exists in people must derive from God and must therefore reflect what he is. I do not want to quarrel with that conclusion here, but it does not seem to me that the most perspicuous way of expressing it is to say that God is morally good. At any rate, given ways in which people commonly think of moral goodness, it is misleading to say that God is morally good if we are thinking of God along the lines that Aquinas does. Aquinas thinks that cats derive from God and therefore reflect what he is. But he never suggests that we should embrace the slogan 'God is feline' (albeit he is certainly committed to the conclusion that felinity is somehow in God).[54]

Again, Shanley is right to observe that Aquinas says that there is justice (*justitia*) in God. But consider what that claim amounts to – as elaborated in, for example, *Summa Theologiae*, Ia.21. Here Aquinas says: (1) God is in no sense anything's debtor, so we cannot associate (Aristotelian) commutative justice with him; (2) God can be said to indulge in distributive justice since he gives what is owed to various things. But notice how Aquinas explains what it is for God to give what is owed. He clearly does not think that God is (distributively) just because he provides for things what some moral law to which he is subject says that he should (and is, therefore, a good and just God). He says that God is distributively just by being the Creator who, by his providence, makes things to be what they deserve to be in so far as they are creatures fashioned by him (e.g. he provides hands and feet for human beings). He also says that God gives what is owed in so far as he brings about what is owed to him. Yet this is not the justice that people usually have in mind when commending God for being just (or denying that he is just). It is not the justice of one who ought or needs to act in certain ways in order to be deemed to be morally respectable. And it is surely significant that in *Summa*

Theologiae, Ia,21, Aquinas can say: 'Since the object of will is an understood good, God can only will what falls under his wisdom. For his wisdom is, as it were, the law of justice by which his will is right and just. So he does justly what he does according to his will (as we do justly what we do according to law). But we, of course, do things according to the law of someone superior to us, while God is a law unto himself.'[55]

With respect to analogical predication, I agree with Shanley that (and shall later be arguing that) goodness is a matter of actuality (that to say that *X* is good is to say that it has succeeded in being in some way – that, for example, a good cat is one which actually has what you look for in healthy cats).[56] But being good as a human being is not, for Aquinas, to be what God's goodness is (even though it is a reflection of that). In talking about analogical predication (defending the view that we can apply some terms to creatures and God analogically) Aquinas argues that terms signifying perfections (in creatures) can be applied to both creatures and God so long as we realize that nothing essentially creaturely can be literally attributed to God. Now we might think that 'being morally good' (being well behaved) is a perfection in a creature. So we might therefore say that God is morally good. But I see no reason to think that Aquinas would have said so. His basic line seems to be that the moral goodness of creatures (the fact that there are creatures who are morally good) derives from God. But he never seems to suggest that their goodness (be it moral or otherwise) should be taken as a model for God's goodness (except in the sense that, for Aquinas, all goodness is a matter of actuality). I take him to be saying (or firmly implying) that being well behaved is not a perfection ascribable to God (any more than being able to ride a bicycle is).[57]

Shanley attacks me on Thomistic grounds. What I am saying now is that he is not really engaging with what I was saying when claiming that God is not a moral agent (or not morally good). And, so I should add, what I am currently saying is not intended to deny that God is good. For why not say that God is good? Isn't that a biblical teaching? And might it not even be defended without reference to biblical texts?

Actually, and contrary to what one often finds suggested, that God is good is not a teaching the Bible emphasizes. Most biblical sentences directly ascribing goodness to God (and there are not very many of them) occur in the Psalms.[58] But, in these sentences, 'God is good' seems regularly to mean that God is faithful to the terms of the covenant he (freely and without any obligation) has established with Israel (and *only* with Israel). In Jeremiah 33:11 we also have 'God is good'. But the meaning seems to be the same as that in the Psalms, as it also seems to be in Nahum 1:7 ('The Lord is good, a stronghold in a day of trouble; he protects those who take refuge in him'). In the New Testament we find 'God is good' only in two verses: Mark 10:18 and Luke 18:19 (in both of which Jesus says 'Why do you call me good? No one is good but God alone').[59] Of course, there is plenty of biblical talk about goodness. People are told to do good or are said to have done good; they receive good things (often from God); various kinds of human behaviour are said to be good in God's eyes; and so on. But, apart from the verses just mentioned, the Bible does not push the idea that God is good. What it typically says is that he is holy, or righteous, or just, or faithful, or merciful, or loving.[60] In doing so, however, it does not seem to be commending God for conforming to moral standards (or to what we might call 'universal moral requirements'). There are, of course, the verses from Mark and Luke. But it is not obvious what they are driving at. Their main function seems to be to say that 'good' should *only* be predicated of God (not a typical biblical view, just as it is not a typical view in general) – but in what sense is not explained. The notion that God is good really only comes into its own in post-biblical theological and philosophical reflection (maybe because of the influence of St Augustine, who, at one point in his life, had real problems with evil considered as a power alongside God). Notice, however, that until relatively recently, and in spite of what authors like Swinburne say, the notion that God is good has not been construed in moral terms.[61]

To illustrate this fact I shall again focus on Aquinas, who several times over asks whether God can be said to be good. His answer is 'Yes', but only (I repeat, *only*) because God is the source of the being of everything created. Or, as Aquinas writes in the *Summa Theologiae*:

> We should especially associate goodness with God. For something is good in so far as it is desirable. But everything desires its perfection, and an effect's perfection and form consists in resembling its efficient cause (since every efficient cause produces an effect like itself). So an efficient cause itself is desirable and good, what

is desired from it being a share in resembling it. Clearly then, since God is the first efficient cause of everything, goodness and desirability belong to him. That is why Dionysius ascribes goodness to God as to the first efficient cause, saying that we call God good 'as the source of all subsistence'.[62]

Aquinas is here working in terms of Aristotle's claim that good is what everything desires.[63] Aquinas thinks that we do not call something good unless we take it to be desirable. He also thinks that effects of efficient causes reflect their causes' natures and that the good desired by an effect is first of all in its cause. So he reasons that all creatures desire (though not necessarily consciously) what is in the first cause of all (i.e. God) and that God is therefore good.

You may not like this argument (to which I shall later be returning). What you cannot say, though, is that it is an argument for God being morally good (i.e. well behaved). And, quite generally, and in spite of what Brian Shanley says against me, Aquinas has no concept of God as being good in the sense implied by the philosophers of religion to whom I referred above when introducing the notion of God's moral goodness. He does not, of course, want to say that, for example, God can determine by fiat whether or not it is right to torture children (though there have been some who seem to have embraced this position). But neither does he want to say that God's law forbidding such a practice comes from one who has first checked on what is right and wrong and then decreed accordingly. His position is that God cannot effect (bring about) anything bad, since for God to create is for him to bring about what is real, and therefore (at least to some extent) good. For Aquinas, it makes no sense to conceive of God as producing (and therefore as willing) evil. He also wants to say that being perfectly actual, God cannot be thought of as lacking in any way.

As philosophers know well, in debates about God's goodness it is often asked whether God wills something because it is good or whether something is good because God wills it. Aquinas, who never directly tackles this question (so far as I know), can, I think, be said to hold that the answer must be: (a) God wills us to do what is good because it is good, and (b) what is good for us to do depends on the way in which God has made creatures to be. In terms of this account, Aquinas would say that God could never command us to torture children because, in effect, that would involve him in contradicting himself, or going against his nature as the source of creaturely goodness. And this, of course, is not to suggest that God's goodness consists in him acting in accordance with moral norms to which he responds in any sense.

Is Aquinas right when it comes to ascribing goodness to God? I shall return to this question later. For the moment, however, let me just register the fact that I think that what he says makes sense. If you can swallow the notion that the goodness of creatures reflects what is in God before it is in them, then you might be able to agree (as I do) that in seeking what is good for us we are seeking what lies in God – which gives us a reason for saying that there is goodness in God. Furthermore, if, like Aquinas, you take 'X is perfect' to mean 'X cannot be improved' (and if you are happy to take 'good' and 'perfect' as possibly interchangeable, in some contexts anyway), then, like Aquinas, you will think that God is good (perfect) since (being immutable, being something that cannot undergo real change) he is not something of which it makes sense to say that it is capable of improvement (to be God is to be all that it takes to be divine, with no possibility of improvement).[64] In agreeing with Aquinas on these matters, though, you will not (as I hope should seem obvious) be conceding that God is well behaved and, for that reason, is a moral agent or is morally good.

Moving on

As D. Z. Phillips says, much contemporary discussion of God and evil (the present state of the art on it, so we might say) reads like an end-of-term report on God's performance.[65] Foes of God deny that he has done as well as he should from the moral point of view. God's friends, on the other hand, make moral excuses for him. I have been arguing that it is wrong to suppose that God is morally good. I have also been arguing that an end-of-term report on his moral standing (whether favourable or unfavourable) would simply fail to engage with what he is. It would be confusing the Creator with some of his creatures. It would be grounded in a category mistake, since it would take God to be something that he could not be. Suppose I complain that a particular tennis player is not scoring many goals. You would rightly reply that tennis players are not in the business of scoring goals. That is what football players are about. By the same token, so I am arguing, we have reason to deny that God should be thought of as morally good or bad and we therefore have reason to deny that God is a moral agent. Or as R. F. Holland nicely puts it:

> It makes sense for *us* to have or fail to have moral reasons for our doings and refrainings because as human beings we are members of a moral community. We have been born and brought up in a shared form of life in which there are, as there would be in any other form of human life, customs and traditions; ideas, more than one set of them perhaps, about what it is for instance to keep or break faith with another, what ways of behaving incur ignominy, what it is to treat someone well or badly, what justice and injustice are . . . But God is not a member of a moral community or of any community. To be sure there are small 'g' gods who have been conceived in that way, like those of the ancient Greeks: such gods are like fairies. To credit the one true God with having a moral reason for doing anything is to conceive Him in the manner of Greek popular religion as a being among beings instead of the absolute being who is the Creator of the world. When 'God' is conceived as a one among many he becomes subjectable to moral judgement; and within a moral community of course it would make perfectly good sense for the one by whom, or let us say the chief one by whom we are judged, to be submitted to our moral judgement.[66]

One might, I suppose, take issue with Holland's claim that God is not 'a being among beings'. One might argue that God must be a being if he exists, and that, if there are beings other than God, then God is a being among beings. Yet this would be to miss the point that Holland seems to be making. He is not, I am assuming, denying God's existence. He is concerned with what divine reality amounts to. And he is suggesting that it does not amount to being an item in the universe. As I have already argued, that is a plausible suggestion. Holland is therefore right, I think, to press it so as to challenge the notion that God is 'a member of a moral community' – or, in my language, a moral agent.

If that challenge is cogent, something of considerable importance follows when it comes to how we should approach the topic of God and evil. As I have tried to explain, people often turn to this topic on the supposition that God, if he exists, is morally good. These people see 'the problem of evil' as (among other things) calling on us to take sides on the question of God's moral integrity. If that view is based on a category mistake, however, then there simply is no problem of evil as they conceive it to be. Whether we believe in God or not, we need no more worry as to whether or not he is well behaved than we need worry as to whether or not tennis players score goals.

Yet suppose that we wish to insist on defending God's moral integrity. Can we do so in any cogent way? As I noted in Chapter 1, friends of God have often argued that his moral goodness can be defended in spite of the reality of evil since there are valuable things which God might not be able to bring about without allowing or risking certain evils. So let me now turn to some versions of that line of thought.

Notes

1. Richard Swinburne, *The Coherence of Theism*, revd edn (Clarendon Press: Oxford, 1993), pp. 184–87.
2. Swinburne regards moral laws ('necessary moral truths' as he sometimes calls them) as akin to laws of logic. He thinks that they are analytic and that they hold entirely independently of God. See Richard Swinburne, 'Duty and the Will of God', *Canadian Journal of Philosophy* 4 (1974).
3. Richard Swinburne, *Providence and the Problem of Evil* (Clarendon Press: Oxford, 1998).
4. Ibid., p. 7.
5. It can be found in earlier writers, however. It is present, for example, in Ralph Cudworth's *Treatise Concerning Eternal and Immutable Morality* (1731). Cudworth, I believe, had an influence on Kant's early moral thinking. See Manfred Kuehn, *Kant: A Biography* (Cambridge University Press: Cambridge), p. 470.
6. William L. Rowe, *Philosophy of Religion: An Introduction*, 3rd edn (Wadsworth: Belmont, Calif., 2001), p. 9.
7. Stephen T. Davis, *Logic and the Nature of God* (Macmillan: London, 1983), p. 86.
8. Ibid., p. 95. For a similar conclusion see Nelson Pike, 'Omnipotence and God's Ability to Sin', *American Philosophical Quarterly* 6 (1969).
9. In *New Perspectives on Old-Time Religion* (Clarendon Press: Oxford, 1988), George N. Schlesinger speaks of what he calls 'the sensible assumption that ethical rules which apply to human beings are also the rules by which to judge of Divine actions' (p. 50).
10. According to Peter van Inwagen, that God is morally perfect is a 'non-negotiable' element of theism. See 'The Argument from Evil' in Peter van Inwagen (ed.), *Christian Faith and the Problem of Evil* (Eerdmans: Grand Rapids, Mich., and Cambridge, 2004), pp. 59f.

11. William Alston, 'Some (Temporarily) Final Thoughts on Evidential Arguments from Evil', in Daniel Howard-Snyder (ed.), *The Evidential Argument from Evil* (Indiana University Press: Bloomington, Ind. and Indianapolis, 1996), pp. 317, 321.

12. Another position sometimes advanced by those who take God to be a moral agent is bound up with what is sometimes called 'perfect being theology'. I shall have something to say about this position in Ch. 8.

13. Perhaps I should have mentioned this before, but I am here presuming that sentences like 'X is morally good' and 'Y is morally bad' express true propositions and are not, for example, expressions of feeling. It certainly seems to be the case that those (whether believers in God or not) who take God's goodness to be moral goodness are adopting this position. A possible exception is J. L. Mackie. In 'Evil and Omnipotence', *Mind* 64 (1955), Mackie argues that there cannot be a good omnipotent God given the evils that exist. His argument in that paper seems to make little sense unless we read it as supposing that '—— is good' tells us (at least sometimes, and certainly when it comes to 'God is good') what something is in and of itself and regardless of our tastes or opinions. In other writings, however, Mackie seems to endorse what we might call a subjectivist approach to the notion of goodness. Cf. *Ethics: Inventing Right and Wrong* (Penguin Books: Harmondsworth, 1977).

14. I do, however, wonder what someone might have in mind when saying that God tells the truth. What does 'tell' mean here? Sounds coming from the sky? One might, of course, say that God tells the truth as he reveals himself in the Bible or the teachings of Jesus Christ. For present purposes, I have no wish to argue with that claim even though I think it raises loads of questions.

15. For discussion of the extent to which these texts support a notion of creation *ex nihilo* see Paul Copan and William Lane Craig, *Creation out of Nothing* (Baker Academic and Apollos: Grand Rapids, Mich., 2004), ch. 2.

16. See John Barton and John Muddiman (eds), *The Oxford Bible Commentary* (Oxford University Press: Oxford, 2001), pp. 42f. Some philosophers might say that to speak of a 'formless void' as preceding creation is as good as saying that God creates *ex nihilo*. And I can sympathize with that view. But it seems to me (as it also seems to many biblical commentators) risky to attribute that conclusion to the author of Genesis 1:1 – not to mention the authors of other biblical passages such as Psalm 74:13–14 or Isaiah 51:9 in which there appear to be echoes of a notion of creation which sees it as following a conflict between God and other agents. For a contrary view see Copan and Craig, *Creation out of Nothing*, ch. 1.

17. Thomas Aquinas, *Summa Theologiae*, Ia. 73.2 ad 2.

18. See ibid., Ia.44.1 and Ia.45.1 – but also many other places in Aquinas's writings.

19. See John L. McKenzie, 'Aspects of Old Testament Thought', in Raymond E. Brown, Joseph Fitzmyer and Roland E. Murphy (eds), *The New*

Jerome Biblical Commentary (Geoffrey Chapman: London, 1968), esp. pp. 1293f.

20. Swinburne, *The Coherence of Theism*, p. 131.
21. Isaiah 31:3 says 'The Egyptians are men, and not God; their horses are flesh, and not spirit'. But I gather that Old Testament scholars commonly read this text as making a distinction between power and weakness, not immateriality and materiality. John 4:24a says 'God is spirit'. But this, in context, does not seem simply equivalent to 'God is incorporeal'. Taken in conjunction with the rest of John 4:24 ('and those who worship him must worship in spirit and truth') it seems to be an allusion to what God imparts to people, this being something to do with his very being (with echoes of Old Testament talk about the 'spirit of God', conceived of as life, force, power, and so on). For more on the lack of Old Testament teaching on God's incorporeality, see Walther Eichrodt, *Theology of the Old Testament*, tr. J.A. Baker, vol. 1 (Westminster Press: Philadelphia, 1961), pp. 210ff.
22. See ibid., pp. 213–20.
23. Herbert McCabe, *God Matters* (Geoffrey Chapman: London, 1987), p. 6.
24. Thomas Aquinas, *In Peri Hermeneias*, I.xiv.22.
25. This, I think, is what Aquinas is arguing in *De Ente et Essentia*, 4 (and in other places also). I defend this reading of Aquinas against Anthony Kenny in 'Kenny on Aquinas on Being', *Modern Schoolman* 82 (2005). Note that neither Aquinas nor I take it to follow from 'God's nature is to be' that 'God does not exist' can be proved in some abstract sense to be logically contradictory. Our point is that, given the appropriateness of asking 'How come the universe as opposed to nothing?', one cannot reply by referring to something to which the same question equally applies. So neither of us are endorsing some of the most familiar versions of the so-called 'Ontological Argument' for God's existence (in various texts Aquinas rejects a version of this argument). All the same, though, both of us are noting what cannot be true of God given that there is a God (we are saying that God cannot be something the existence of which is derived). This might be thought of as a 'grammatical' observation – see D. Z. Phillips, *The Concept of Prayer* (Routledge and Kegan Paul: London, 1968), ch. 1.
26. I associate 'duty' and 'obligation' talk with writers working within a Kantian tradition, and with ethical intuitionists such as H. A. Prichard (1871–1947). I associate 'virtue' and 'vice' talk with writers working within a broadly Aristotelian tradition, recent exponents of which include Peter Geach, Alasdair MacIntyre and Philippa Foot. I am not assuming that reference to virtue and vice has no place in Kantian and similar treatments of ethics. Nor am I assuming that Aristotelian-inspired moralists have no room for talk about duty and obligation. (Aquinas, for example, though Aristotelian in his general philosophical approach to ethics, certainly allows for there being duties and obligations generated by contracts made between people.)

27. As noted earlier, Genesis 1:26 tantalizingly speaks of people being made in God's 'image' according to his 'likeness'. There is, however, no reason to suppose that this verse is licensing the suggestion that God seriously resembles human beings, even morally good ones. It seems basically to be comparing God and people on the ground that, like God, people have a kind of sovereignty. Note that Genesis 1:26 in its entirety reads: 'Then God said, "Let us make humankind in our image, according to our likeness; and let them have dominion over the fish of the sea, and over the birds of the air, and over the cattle, and over the wild animals of the earth, and over every creeping thing that creeps upon the earth."' And Genesis 1:27 begins: 'So God created humankind in his image'.

28. In so far as they do so they are, at any rate, subscribing to a position verbally at odds with Christian orthodoxy. This tells us that God is three persons in one substance, not that God is a person (or three persons in one person). And, of course, and as I noted above, 'person' in classical trinitarian discussions does not mean what, for example, Descartes took himself essentially to be.

29. I take it that when philosophers say that God is a person they are taking human beings as paradigm examples of persons – as, for example, Richard Swinburne does in ch. 7 of *The Coherence of Theism*. (Swinburne does not take God to be all that human persons are; he believes that there are differences between them. Nevertheless, his defence of the coherence of 'God is a person' starts with an account of what he takes people to be.)

30. See Samuel Balentine, *The Hidden God: The Hiding of the Face of God in the Old Testament* (Oxford University Press: Oxford, 1983).

31. See Eichrodt, *Theology of the Old Testament*, vol. 1, pp. 270ff.

32. Genesis 3:8; Isaiah 40:28.

33. Psalm 24:8; 44:4.

34. Isaiah 42:14; Deuteronomy 32:11; Hosea 5:12.

35. Ezekiel 1:28; Exodus 33:18–23.

36. *Summa Theologiae*, Ia.1.9.

37. See Eichrodt, *Theology of the Old Testament*, vol. 1, pp. 339ff. See also Edmond Jacob, *Theology of the Old Testament*, tr. Arthur W. Heathcote and Philip J. Allcock (Harper and Brothers: New York, 1958), pp. 94ff.

38. To say that one shall do such and such is, among people, to make a promise. And people able to make promises are, surely, moral agents. But when biblical authors talk of God's righteousness they are clearly not taking him to be a human being making a promise. They are obviously taking him to be one who has declared what he shall do.

39. See K. L. Onesti and M. T. Brauch, 'Righteousness', in Gerald F. Hawthorne and Ralph P. Martin (eds), *Dictionary of Paul and his Letters* (Inter-Varsity Press: Downers Grove, Ill., 1993), p. 829: 'Righteousness [sc. in the Old Testament] is not primarily an ethical quality; rather it characterizes the character or action of God who deals rightly within the

covenant relationship and who established how others are to act within that relationship.'
40. See Isaiah 29:16.
41. See the article 'Righteousness in the New Testament' in *The Interpreter's Dictionary of the Bible* (Abingdon Press: New York and Nashville, 1962): 'If, as has been stated, righteousness is to be understood basically as a relational term, then it is also true that it cannot mean basically "conformity to a (moral) norm" . . . Aside from the fact that righteousness as meaning conformity to a moral norm would mean that God too conforms to this norm, since God is called "righteous" (an idea incompatible with the NT view of God's sovereignty), such an understanding makes it difficult to see how the term "righteousness" can so often be applied to God's saving act on behalf of those who are supremely unrighteous and thus morally delinquent (Rom. 5:8, among others) . . . The clear statement of Paul that no man is counted righteous before God on the basis of works should be enough to eliminate moral conformity from consideration (Gal. 3:11 etc.).'
42. If we take a moral agent to be subject to duties, then it is perhaps worth noting that Immanuel Kant can be invoked as denying that God is a moral agent. In, for example, 'Toward Perpetual Peace' he explicitly asserts that God 'is the only being to whom the concept of duty is inapplicable'. See Immanuel Kant, *Practical Philosophy*, ed. and tr. Mary J. Gregor (Cambridge University Press: Cambridge, 1996), p. 323.
43. I stress 'some' here because Old Testament worries about people who suffer do not extend to non-Jews. In Old Testament texts there is no concern raised when it comes to suffering people overseas (so to speak).
44. For more on all this see James L. Crenshaw (ed.), *Theodicy in the Old Testament* (Fortress Press: Philadelphia, 1983). Pain and suffering is, of course, the major concern of the book of Job. As I have noted, however, that work is clearly not endorsing a view of God as subject to moral demands. Quite the contrary, as should be obvious even from a casual reading of it.
45. My knowledge of Jewish and Islamic discussions of God is limited, but I would be surprised to find classical post-biblical Jewish authors, or Islamic authors in general, having any time for the suggestion that it makes sense to ask whether or not God is morally justified for doing, or not doing, *X*, *Y*, or *Z*.
46. For Aquinas on God and the act of sin (*actus peccati*) see *Summa Theologiae*, IaIIae.79.2: 'The act of sin not only belongs to the realm of being but it is also an act. And from both these points of view it somehow comes from God.' I quote from vol. 25 of the Blackfriars edition of the *Summa Theologiae* (Eyre and Spottiswoode: London and McGraw-Hill: New York, 1969).
47. Aquinas wrote a commentary on the book of Job: *The Literal Exposition on Job*, tr. Anthony Damico (Scholars Press: Atlanta, 1989). As you will see if you read it, however, he does not there engage in the task of

morally exonerating God. For more on this see Eleonore Stump, 'Aquinas on the Sufferings of Job', repr. in Eleonore Stump (ed.), *Reasoned Faith* (Cornell University Press: Ithaca and London, 1993).

48. In Brian Davies (ed.), *Philosophy of Religion: A Guide to the Subject* (Cassell: London, 1998).

49. Brian Shanley, *The Thomist Tradition* (Kluwer Academic Publishers: Dordrecht and London, 2002), ch. 5.

50. Ibid., p. 115.

51. Ibid., p. 116.

52. I quote from vol. 23 of the Blackfriars edition of the *Summa Theologiae* (Eyre and Spottiswoode: London, and McGraw-Hill: New York, 1969).

53. Elementary, my dear Watson. You can always deduce something about causes from their effects.

54. See Aquinas, *Summa Theologiae*, Ia.15.3.

55. Ibid., Ia.21.1 ad 2 (my translation).

56. Here I am simply assuming that 'good' is an attributive adjective as applied to things in the world and that it can be used when talking of all sorts of things (not just moral agents). So I take it that there can be good meals, good washing machines, and good cats – meaning healthy, fit, thriving ones. And so on. More on this later.

57. Can God ride a bicycle? If we suppose that 'God is omnipotent' means that 'God can ——' might be filled in by any phrase which captures what can be done by people, then Aquinas would say 'No'. On his account, God is omnipotent because he can bring about the existence of anything of which it makes sense to say that it exists. More on this later.

58. See Psalms 34:8; 54:6; 69:16; 86:5; 100:5; 106:1; 107:1; 118:1; 119:29; 135:3; 136:1.

59. What are these verses asserting? Nothing, it seems to me, in defence of the proposition 'God is morally good' as I am construing it. And I find little to contradict this conclusion in what contemporary biblical critics have to say about them. Hence, for example, in *The Gospel of Luke* (Liturgical Press: Collegeville, Minn., 1991) Luke Timothy Johnson suggests that 'Jesus's response is the reflex deflection of human praise in favor of God as source of all being or goodness' (p. 276). Suppose that Johnson's exegesis (a fairly common one) is right. We still do not have a clear statement to the effect that God is morally good (in my sense). On Johnson's reading, if I interpret it rightly, Jesus is effectively saying, 'Stop flattering me; focus on God and start from there.' For a reading of 'No one is good but God alone' which compares with Johnson's, see I. Howard Marshall, *The Gospel of Luke* (Paternoster Press: Exeter, 1979), p. 684.

60. It is sometimes said that, for the Bible, God's love is an ethical attribute of him. But I cannot imagine why anyone should think that. Talking of God's love as recorded in Hosea (a book big on God loving), Walther Eichrodt (rightly to my mind) observes: 'This demonstration of the way in which the concept of love is worked out in history is far removed from any attempt to reduce the love of God to a rational principle, to turn it

into some sort of "ethical law of the universe". This is ruled out first by *the strong emphasis on the inexplicable and paradoxical character of God's love*, which is portrayed in terms of the wooing of a wanton – an absolutely grotesque proceeding, flying in the face equally of morality and of justice' (*Theology of the Old Testament*, vol. 1, p. 252).

61. Maybe lots of religious believers from the time of the New Testament to the modern period have actually construed God's goodness in moral terms. And if that is the case, then I look forward to seeing the evidence supporting it. But I am not aware of any serious evidence to support it.

62. Aquinas, *Summa Theologiae*, Ia.6.1 (my translation).

63. Aristotle, *Nicomachean Ethics*, I.1, 1094a3.

64. See Aquinas, *Summa Theologiae*, Ia.6.2–3. I have defended these ways of thinking in *Philosophy of Religion: A Guide to the Subject*, pp. 185ff.

65. D. Z. Phillips, *The Problem of Evil and the Problem of God* (SCM Press: London, 2004), p. 149.

66. R. F. Holland, 'On the Form of "The Problem of Evil"', in R. F. Holland, *Against Empiricism* (Blackwell: Oxford, 1980), pp. 237f.

Five

How Not to Exonerate God: I

It sometimes happens that in order to obtain something we take to be good we have to put up with what we really do not like. For example, if I want a holiday in Hawaii, I shall have to endure a plane trip, and I truly hate flying. Then again, a dentist who wants to relieve you of your toothache (a good end, presumably) may have to drill or extract one of your teeth (not very desirable, so most people would think), and a doctor who wants to save your life may have to arrange for you to undergo surgery with very unpleasant after-effects. We are, indeed, often the victims of means when it comes to our ends – a thought which, as I have noted, has struck some of God's friends who are anxious to defend him in the face of evil. We do not suppose that surgeons are bad when they hack into people, because we take them to be trying to save lives (or to improve lives) in the only way they can. Might we not, therefore, correspondingly think that God's goodness is not compromised by evils in the world since they can be viewed as used by him, or as permitted by him, in order to bring about goods which cannot exist without them?

In response to this question one might first be tempted to say that God can hardly be bound by means in order to arrive at an end. People, certainly, are often so bound. But God is not a limited human being, so can he not (in Monopoly™ fashion, as it were) go directly to ends without passing through means? Is not his being able to do this actually entailed by the traditional claim that he is omnipotent? The right answer to this question is, I think, 'No', though to explain this I must now say something about the notion of God's omnipotence.

Omnipotence, means and ends

When thinking of God's omnipotence it is not a good idea to start with the notion that 'God is omnipotent' means that God can do anything that can be done. For there are obviously things that can be done which God cannot do. Since he is incorporeal, he cannot, for instance, ride a bicycle. Nor can he walk to work, take a bath, dig a trench, or scratch himself.[1]

When thinking of God's omnipotence it is also not a good idea to suppose that God can produce what is logically impossible – that he can, for example, make a cat which is also an elephant, or arrange for it to be false that a whole is greater than any of its parts. If they are to make any sense at all, statements of the form 'God can bring it about that _____' need to be followed by strings of words which do not cancel themselves out given their meaning. I take it that what we mean by 'cat' and 'elephant' cancel themselves out in 'Some cat is an elephant'. I also presume that what we mean by 'whole' and 'part' cancel themselves out in 'Some whole is smaller than any of its parts'. These last two sentences do not report anything that could possibly be true (given the meanings of the terms that occur in them). So it would seem ludicrous to suppose that God could bring it about that they actually manage to do so.

It does not follow from this, however, that we cannot attach sense to the claim that God is omnipotent. If God is the Maker of all things, then he can also make what is not but can be. So he can bring it about that whatever can be thought without contradiction to exist actually does exist. Or as Aquinas says:

> Everyone confesses that God is omnipotent. But it seems hard to explain just what his omnipotence amounts to, since one might wonder about the meaning of 'all' when someone says that God can do all. Yet looked at aright, when we say that God can do everything we are best understood as meaning this: since power is relative to what is possible, divine power can do everything that is possible, and that is why we call God omnipotent.
>
> According to Aristotle [*Metaphysics* IV.2, 1019b34] there are two senses of 'possible': one relative, and the other absolute. We use the first sense with an eye on some particular power. Thus, for example, we say that what falls under human power is possible for

us. But we should not say that God is omnipotent because he can do everything that created natures can do, for his power extends to many more things. Yet if we say that God is omnipotent because he can do everything possible to his power, our explanation of omnipotence goes round in a circle – stating nothing more than that God is omnipotent because he can do all that he can do.

So, employing the second sense of 'possible', we should conclude that we call God omnipotent because he can do everything that is absolutely possible. We judge something to be absolutely possible or impossible from the implication of terms: absolutely possible when a predicate is compatible with a subject (as in 'Socrates is seated'); absolutely impossible when it is not so compatible (as in 'Human beings are donkeys').

Consider this: since every agent produces an effect like itself, every active power has a possible objective corresponding to the nature of the activity which the active power is for. Thus, for example, the power of heating supposes that things can be heated. But God's being, on which the notion of his power is based, is infinite existing, not limited to any kind of being, but possessing in itself the perfection of all existing. So, whatever can have the nature of being falls within the range of things that are absolutely possible, and we call God omnipotent with respect to these.

Nothingness, and only that, contradicts the real meaning of being. So, whatever implies simultaneous existing and non-existing is contrary to what is absolutely possible and subject to God's omnipotence. For that which is contradictory is not subject to God's omnipotence – not because of a lack of power in God, but because it simply does not have the nature of being something achievable or possible. So, whatever does not imply a contradiction is included in the class of possible things with respect to which we call God omnipotent. But nothing implying a contradiction falls within God's power, since all such things are impossible. The best thing to say, however, is that they cannot be brought about, not that God cannot bring them about. Nor is this against the angel's saying, 'No word shall be impossible with God.'[2] For a contradiction in terms cannot be a word, since no mind can conceive it.[3]

Aquinas is here effectively denying that 'God is omnipotent' means that God can ride a bicycle or engage in comparable feats. He is also denying that God can bring it about that what is logically impossible is actually the case. Aquinas is saying that, as Creator, God can bring about anything which can be thought to have been brought about. His basic idea is: if it can be thought to be, then God (as Creator) can make it to be.

Yet this account of omnipotence, with which I agree (for reasons that should be clear from what I have said in previous chapters), does not entail that God can bring every X about without also bringing about some Y. It does not entirely release God from a dependence on means when it comes to ends. I cannot get myself to Hawaii without a plane trip (or without a means of getting there which I might think to be as awful as a plane trip). So I am subject to a constraint when it comes to ends and means. Yet God must, in a similar way, be subject to comparable constraints. For consider the following questions:

(1) Can God bring it about that the offspring of a cat is a cow?

(2) Can God bring it about that I am a hero without having brought it about that I once faced danger?

I suggest that the answer to both of these questions is 'No'.

Perhaps God can create a cow which has no parent cows. This would be a cow which came to be by the direct action of God and by the action of nothing else. It would be a cow which came about by virtue of what Aquinas would have called a miracle.[4] But it would not be the offspring of a cat. Cats are things with a particular biological make-up, one which does not allow them to give birth to cows. So if, without working a miracle, God aims to get offspring from cats, he is going to have to settle for offspring that are feline. In this sense, he needs cats as a means to there being kittens, and he needs something other than cats for there to be bovine offspring.

God will also have to put me in a dangerous situation if he is going to make me a hero. Perhaps God can miraculously bring it about that there is someone (call him Fred) who is brave and courageous from the moment he is created. Fred, however, cannot be a *hero* if he has not faced danger and risen to the occasion. There is a conceptual connection between 'being a hero' and 'having faced danger'. People cannot be actually heroic unless they have first been placed in a context calling for courage. So if God aims for there to be heroes, he needs danger as a means. Similarly, he needs cancer for there to be people who die gracefully from it, and he needs genocide for there to be people who repent of having committed it. Even an omnipotent God cannot bring it about that Mary died gracefully of cancer if Mary did not have cancer. Even an omnipotent God cannot bring it about that those who repent of genocide have nothing of which to repent.

The Free Will Defence

So God is clearly (and in general) at least to some extent constrained by means, ones which we might think of as necessary for him given that he aims to produce certain outcomes. But can we use this thought in order to exonerate God when it comes to evils that exist in our world? As I noted in Chapter 1, many have said that we can. Working on the assumption that God is morally good, they have said that evils in the world serve good purposes which God cannot achieve without them. In particular, they have said that moral evil is something that God might have to put up with in a good cause. Here we come to the Free Will Defence, according to which: (a) freedom is highly desirable; (b) if God creates free creatures he blamelessly runs the risk of them acting badly; (c) the evil freely perpetrated by creatures is no indication of God's moral badness.

Few, I suppose, would quarrel with (a). Of course there are people who seem hell-bent on curbing the freedom of others. Even these individuals, however, value their own freedom, and most of us would regard them as misguided in some way for wanting to suppress the freedom of their fellows. One might, perhaps, suggest that freedom as such is not intrinsically desirable – that it is not something we should want to be present in all things at all costs. And this seems a sensible kind of view. Our world would become pretty horrific if everything suddenly developed the ability to make choices – if desks, for example, could suddenly decide to jump on us, or if planets could choose to engage in a cosmic version of football. Yet freedom in people is surely a good thing, even though it might be hard to say why.

For present purposes I am assuming that people have freedom if they are able to make choices which reflect their goals or intentions. On my account, Peter has freedom if he is able to choose between alternative courses of action, if his behaviour can (at least some-times) reflect his purposes. In my view, therefore, Peter has no freedom at time t if someone is coercing him at t. In my view, also, Peter has no freedom at t if, at t, his behaviour is forced on him by what (apart from people) acts on him so as to bring it about that he cannot but do what he does (as would be the case, for example, if Peter vomits because of some noxious substance he has swallowed).

Yet why is it good that people should be free in this sense?[5] A problem here is that we (or, at least, most of us) would not value people less if we came to believe that human freedom is an illusion of some kind. There are philosophers who, for various reasons, argue that we are not, in fact, free and that everything we do is what we cannot but do.[6] I doubt, however, that such thinkers love their families and friends any less than those who dispute their position. With this thought in mind one might well wonder why human freedom should be invoked in defence of God given what people get up to. Suppose that God made a world containing people whose behaviour was determined by him – behaviour that never resulted in harm or pain or suffering. Should such a world be less valued than one in which people acting freely wreak all sorts of havoc? If, having philosophically concluded that people have no freedom, we can still love our families and friends, then arguably not.

Yet we do, it seems, rate human freedom highly. The best justifica-tion I can come up with for doing so goes like this:

(1) X is better than Y if X is able to do more than Y can.
(2) Something having freedom can do more than something lacking freedom.
(3) So X is better than Y if X has freedom and Y does not.

With respect to (1) I am thinking that, for example, a cat should be deemed superior to a desk since it can run around, enjoy food, and procreate. With respect to (2) my idea is that something able to act with purposes of its own (e.g. a free human being) is superior to something incapable of this (e.g. a desk). What I am saying at this point, however, clearly depends on value judgements which not everyone might share, and I do not think that these judgements can be justified in any kind of knockdown fashion. It is not, I think, hard to argue that, given two things of the same kind, one of them is better than the other. We might well be able, I think, to justify the conclusion that, for example, Sara is a better cook than Robert, for we have standards when it comes to cooking and can evaluate Sara and Robert with respect to them. Yet it seems to me that we flounder somewhat when we try to explain why things of one kind are better than things of another – that, for example, things which have freedom are better than things which lack it.

Be that as it may, I shall not now dispute the claim that it is good for there to be people who have freedom. I do, however, want to deny that God is to be morally exonerated for the reason that, willing the good of human freedom, he has to put up with what people freely choose to do. That is because I dispute the reasoning that leads up to this conclusion. Typically, it runs as follows:

(1) If people act freely, then what they choose to do is up to them only.

(2) So if God wants to create freely acting people, he has to create things that can choose to do what is up to them only.

(3) If God wants to create freely acting people, he therefore has to put up with what they choose to do.

Here are some representative examples of philosophical writings which display this pattern of argument (the first of which I also quoted in Chapter 1):

(1) 'Of course, it is up to God whether to create free creatures at all; but if he aims to produce moral good, then he must create significantly free creatures upon whose cooperation he must depend. Thus is the power of an omnipotent God limited by the freedom he confers on creatures.'[7]

(2) 'It is not logically possible for an agent to make another agent such that necessarily he freely does only good actions. Hence if a being *G* creates a free agent, he gives to the agent power of choice between alternative actions, and how he will exercise that power is something which *G* cannot control while the agent remains free. It is a good thing that there exist free agents, but a logically necessary consequence of their existence is that their power to choose to do evil actions may sometimes be realized. The price is worth paying, however, for the existence of agents performing

free actions remains a good thing even if they sometimes do evil. Hence it is not logically possible that a creator create free creatures "such that necessarily they do not do evil actions".[8]

(3) 'It is a great good that humans have a certain sort of free will which I shall call free and responsible choice, but . . . [i]f they do, then necessarily there will be the natural possibility of moral evil . . . A God who gives humans such free will necessarily brings about the possibility, and puts [moral evil] outside his own control whether or not it occurs. It is not logically possible – that is, it would be self-contradictory to suppose – that God could give us such free will and yet ensure that we always use it in the right way.'[9]

(4) 'In a world inhabited by significantly free persons, whether there is moral evil or not depends upon these free persons. It is up to them whether they will choose to do right or wrong in a morally significant situation. If they are capable of doing right, at the same time they are capable of doing wrong. If they choose to do wrong, God cannot prevent them from doing that wrong, or even choosing it, without removing their significant freedom.'[10]

As I say, I am not in sympathy with this line of thinking, so let me now try to explain why.

To begin with, let me stress that I do not wish to deny the reality of human freedom. Since philosophers have offered conflicting accounts of what that involves, to say so might seem somewhat uninformative. So let me flesh out my position a little, drawing on what I wrote earlier in this chapter.

We can, I think, distinguish between behaviour and action. If my leg goes into a spasm and causes me to knock a chair over, then behaviour of a kind is ascribable to me. By 'behaviour' here I mean any bodily process which we go through. So inadvertently knocking a chair over is, on my count, a piece of behaviour. The same would be true of rolling over in bed while asleep, sweating, or shifting one's position slightly while concentrating on a novel by Jane Austen. Yet none of these examples involve behaviour undergone with a purpose. I take a purpose to be ascribable to someone who can answer the question 'With a view to what did you do that?' Hence, for example, I would say that if John can say something like 'Because I wanted to get my hands on his money' in reply to 'Why did you break into Fred's house?', a purpose can be ascribed to John. He is acting for reasons that he has. He is acting intentionally. Such action is readily distinguishable from the examples of behaviour just given. If my leg goes into a spasm and causes me to knock a chair over, it would be silly of you to ask 'With a view to what did you do that?' It would be equally misplaced to wake sleepers up and ask them why they rolled over in bed, or to ask people why they shifted position slightly while intent on something else. Aquinas, for example, distinguishes between 'acts of a human being' (*actiones hominis*) and 'human acts' (*actiones humanae*). This distinction matches my contrast between 'behaviour' and 'action'.[11]

Now I take it that being able to act for reasons of one's own, to be able to act intentionally, is to be able to act freely. We do not always act in this way. We do not do so when, for example, we fall asleep because someone has given us an anaesthetic, or when our hand moves an object because someone is manipulating our hand. Sometimes, however, we act without being caused to do what we do by anything else in the world. The explanation for what we do sometimes lies in ourselves, not in the nature of causal properties of things other than us. Some philosophers have argued that there are no free actions in this sense. They have suggested that everything we do is comparable to everything a computer does given its make-up and the action on it of other things (mostly ourselves). Yet this is a position than can hardly be *argued* for. If everything we say comes from our mouths in the way that words appear on computer screens, then it is difficult to see how any dialogue between people could occur. As Herbert McCabe writes: 'If your words come from your mouth as automatically as the sounds come from a tape-recorder, then two people apparently engaged in discussion are in no different position from two tape-recorders playing simultaneously: they are both contributing to the noise that is being made but cannot be said to be engaged in communication *with* each other.'[12]

So I am not denying that people have freedom (at least in one commonly understood sense of 'freedom'). Not everything they do is freely chosen by them (e.g. rolling over in bed while asleep). Yet, so I am happy to agree, they can sometimes (by choosing to do so) act independently and without being constrained by other things in the world. I am even willing to offer an argument for the conclusion that people are free in this sense. It runs thus:

(1) Things which lack freedom are constrained in the sense that what they can do is limited to what they are by nature. Thus, for example, stones are at the mercy of gravity, and balloons filled with helium can only rise upwards.

(2) People, like stones and balloons, are constrained in various ways. Like stones, they fall when dropped from a height. Like balloons, they rise when flying on an aircraft.

(3) Unlike stones and balloons, however, people can recognize alternatives. For they can view objects under different descriptions. A healthy and hungry dog confronted by a steak will see it only as something to be eaten. Human beings, however, can view steaks differently – e.g. as 'things which I ought to avoid given my heart condition', 'things which I ought to tuck into given that I want to look like a muscle god', 'things which I want to see abolished given my beliefs about animal rights', 'things which I should avoid on Good Friday given my religious beliefs', and so on.

(4) So people can act with a view to alternatives. They can choose between doing this and doing that given the beliefs and desires that they have to start with.

(5) So people are (at least sometimes) able to make free choices since, because they can recognize alternative ways of thinking about things. They are not (like stones and balloons) forced into only one way of moving onwards.

My view is that our ability to understand the world under many different descriptions constitutes a ground for thinking that people can act with reasons of their own and can, therefore, be thought of as things to which freedom can be ascribed.

However, whether I am right or wrong here does not for my present purposes matter when it comes to the Free Will Defence. What really matters is what the Defence argues on the presumption, however it might be justified, that people are able to act freely. For, having insisted on the reality and value of human freedom, all forms of the Free Will Defence proceed to speak about human freedom as though it existed independently of God's causal action. They all argue that when people actually act freely they are somehow acting outside of God's causality. Supporters of the Free Will Defence nearly always agree that the world is continually sustained by God. Yet they also want to say that when I make a choice, God is not causally operative in my choosing as I do. They lay responsibility for my choices on me while suggesting that God adopts a 'hands-off' attitude to them – as some kind of observer or onlooker. And here, it seems to me, lies the most serious objection to the Free Will Defence.

For exponents of the Defence are forgetting that God is the Creator, the source of the existence (the continued and total existence) of everything other than himself. If God is this, however, then my making a choice has to be something that God is *making to be*. If everything that exists owes its existence to God, then God must be the source of my free actions, not someone who merely observes them, permits them, or somehow merely supports (what could that mean?) a context in which they are caused by me and not by God. To think otherwise, it seems to me, can only stem from the conviction that God is really an item in the universe, something able to distance itself from its fellows so as to let them act independently of its causality. Yet God, I have argued, is not an item in the universe. As making the world to be, his causality extends to everything that exists, and free choices are as real as anything else in the world. If you think that Mount Everest needs God to account for its being as opposed to not being (for as long as it is), then you ought to think that all human choices need God to account for them being (and therefore being what they are) as opposed to not being. There can be no such thing as a creaturely reality which is not produced or creatively made to be by God.

Someone who brings this point out well is Antony Flew. Referring to what he calls 'the essential theist doctrine of Divine creation', he contests the Free Will Defence by suggesting that it has to be misguided if God is indeed the Creator. The claim that God is, he says,

> apparently requires that, whether or not the creation had a beginning, all created beings – all creatures, that is – are always utterly dependent on God as their sustaining cause. God is here the First Cause in a procession which is not temporally sequential.[13]

In proceeding as though this were not the case, the Free Will Defence is worthless as a piece of theistic apologetic. In saying so, I am not denying everything its defenders seem concerned to insist on. I am not saying that there is no such thing as human freedom. Neither am I denying its value.[14] I am, however, insisting that, whatever human freedom amounts to, it cannot be causally independent of God as making it to be even as it is exercised.[15] If it were, then it would not exist at all. Or, as Aquinas writes:

> Just as God not only gave being to things when they first began, but is also – as the conserving cause of being – the cause of their being as long as they last . . . so he not only gave things their operative powers when they were first created, but is also the cause of these in things. Hence, if this divine influence stopped, every operation would stop. Every operation, therefore, of anything is traced back to him as its cause.[16]

As Aquinas also argues, God 'causes everything's activity in as much as he gives it the power to act, maintains it in existence, applies it to its activity, and in as much as it is by his power that every other power acts'.[17] For Aquinas, since 'the very act of free choice goes back to God as its cause, whatever people freely do on their own must fall under God's providence'.[18] This conclusion strikes me as inescapable given that God is the source of the existence (and continued existence) of everything in the universe. Belief in God as Creator seems plainly incompatible with the way in which God is conceived of by adherents to the Free Will Defence. Viewed in terms of this belief, the Defence looks positively idolatrous.[19] As Rowan Williams says:

> Plenty of theologians have pointed out that, if God is conceived as acting in a punctiliar way, the divine action is determined by something other than itself; likewise if God is conceived as 'reacting' to anything. If either of these conceptualities gets a foothold in our thinking about God, we ascribe to God a context for God's action: God is (like us) an agent in an environment, who must 'negotiate' purposes and desires in relation to other agencies and presences. But God is not an item in any environment, and God's action has been held, in orthodox Christian thought, to be identical with God's being – that is, what God does is nothing other than God's being actively real. Nothing could add to or diminish this, because God does not belong to an environment where the divine life could be modified by anything else. God is the empowering source of anything other than God being real, that is, the ultimate 'activator' of all particular agency.[20]

Does it not therefore follow, however, that freedom really is an illusion? Does not my rejection of the Free Will Defence amount to an argument for philosophical (or theological) determinism? Exponents of the Free Will Defence would presumably say that it does. On their account an action of mine cannot be free if what is not me causes it to be (and therefore causes it to be as it is – since something can only be by *being as it is*). And it is easy to see why one might think this. Indeed, it seems to be generally true that what I do cannot be freely chosen by me if my choosing is caused by what is not me. If I hit a table because you are gripping my wrist and forcing my arm to the table, then I am surely not freely hitting the table. If I lunge from the left to the right because a drug is acting on me, then I do not freely move from left to right. Yet is it so obvious that if God causes me to do something, I am thereby unfree in what I do?

If God were an item in the universe acting on me so as to produce a change in me, then the answer to this question would presumably be 'Yes'. As I argued in Chapter 3, however, God is not an item in the universe, and he does not effect changes in creatures by acting *on* them so as to *tinker* with them or *modify* them. As bringing it about that created things undergo various changes, God cannot be thought of as *interfering* with them or as *intervening* in their careers. Yet I undergo a change when I make a free decision. So it seems to follow that, even though my doing so is caused by God, it is not the case that God is therefore interfering with me or intervening in my career. Even though God is the cause of my freedom, it does not follow that he is thereby a threat to it.

Here, once again, I find Aquinas illuminating. In his commentary on Aristotle's *Peri Hermeneias* he asks whether all that happens must happen. Along the way he notes the following argument: 'If God's providence is the cause of everything that happens in the world, or at the very least all good things, it seems that everything *must* happen the way it does . . . because he wills it and his will can't be ineffective, so everything he wills, it seems, must necessarily happen.'[21] This argument, says Aquinas, erroneously depends on thinking of the working of God's will on the model of this activity in us. He continues:

God's will is to be thought of as existing outside the realm of exis-tents, as a cause from which pours forth everything that exists in all its variant forms. Now *what can be* and *what must be* are variants of being, so that it is from God's will itself that things derive whether they must be or may or may not be and the distinction of the two according to the nature of their immediate causes. For he prepares causes that must cause for those effects that he wills must be, and causes that might cause but might fail to cause for those effects that he wills might or might not be. And it is because of the nature of their causes that some effects are said to be effects that must be and others effects that need not be, although all depend on God's will as primary cause, a cause which transcends the distinction between *must* and *might not*. But the same cannot be said of human will or of any other cause, since every other cause exists within the realm of *must* and *might not*. So of every other cause it must be said either that it can fail to cause, or that its effect must be and cannot not be; God's will, however, cannot fail, and yet not all his effects must be, but some can be or not be.[22]

Aquinas is saying here that God is not anything in the universe and that all such things, however they differ from each other, derive from him as Creator. Within the world we can distinguish between what happens of necessity (given the causal action of various things) and what does not so happen. Aquinas takes human choosing to be an example of something that is not causally necessitated by anything in the universe. Yet he does not therefore conclude that human choosing is not caused by God. His point is that it is not causally necessitated by any creature. The big thought here is that the free/determined distinction applies only within creation and does not carry over into worries about God's making created things to be. Aquinas's position is that we are free not *in spite of* God but *because of* him. He thinks that if there are people making free choices, that is because nothing else in the world is having its way with them, not because God is not creating them as acting freely. And in this I agree with Aquinas.

Philosophers arguing in favour of philosophical determinism rarely bring God into their arguments. They generally try to explain how people cannot be free given the way the world is. Exponents of the Free Will Defence tend to reason along similar lines. Alvin Plantinga, for instance, says that human actions can only be free if 'no causal laws and antecedent conditions determine' that they occur or do not occur.[23] I take 'causal laws' to refer to codifiable ways in which unfree bits of the world behave of necessity, and I take 'antecedent conditions' to mean 'the state of the world prior to a human choice'. And on that reading of Plantinga's words I take him to be right. But Plantinga is wrong to speak as though divine causality is something subject to causal laws or is something exemplifying them somehow, and he is wrong to think of it as an antecedent condition of anything that happens. If we are thinking of God as the cause of the whole universe, if God is what makes things to be (whenever they are), then God (to use Rowan Williams's language) 'cannot be fitted into the same space' as causal laws and antecedent conditions. He is not 'an element' in 'any picture' – including that of determining causes having their inevitable way with things to which they connect.[24]

In this context we need very seriously to recognize that 'cause' is a term which does not always have the same meaning, even though its meanings on given occasions might well be related to each other. Plantinga and other exponents of the Free Will Defence are clearly using the word 'cause' to signify what I mean by the expressions 'agent-cause' or 'efficient cause'. Yet there is no reason to suppose that these phrases should always signify realities of exactly the same kind. If Henry pushes Bill over, then he is an agent-cause (or an efficient cause) of Bill's falling. Does it follow that if Henry pushes Bill then Bill cannot but fall? Perhaps not, for something might intervene so as to prevent him falling even though Henry has pushed him, and, for this reason, we might argue that it is wrong to equate causation with necessitation.[25] Confronted by caused events, however, we commonly explain them in terms of causes which, given their natures and the natures of things on which they act, account for them in a way that leads us to say that their effects come about of necessity. If I swallow a lot of arsenic, and if nobody interferes with me, then I shall certainly die. So we have a sense of 'cause' in which it means 'something in the world which inevitably produces a certain effect (barring interference)'. Yet we do not have to confine the meaning of 'cause' to just this. For we can speak of God as a cause, and God's causation clearly has to differ in certain ways from the causation of things in the world.

If what I have previously argued is correct, God's causation is not the causation of something the choice of which to cause is different from the thing itself. That is because (a) there is no distinction in God (none that we can get our minds around, anyway) when it comes to individuality, nature, and existence, and (b) there is no real change in God. Then again, God's causation, unlike all agent-causation within the world, cannot be a case of acting on what pre-exists it (as I said earlier, God's making things to be should not be thought of as a case of interference or intervention). Finally, God's act of causing cannot exemplify any causal law or count as any antecedent condition of anything. Causal laws, as we normally take them to be, are exhibited over time by things that undergo change. As I have argued, however, we ought not to ascribe real change to God. And the notion of antecedence surely has no place when thinking of what transcends and accounts for the universe. How can what is not part of the universe be antecedent to anything in it? If X is antecedent to Y, then X precedes Y in time. Yet how can what is not part of the universe precede anything in time? Is not the notion of temporal precedence one that applies only to things within the world?

You might say that before the world began to exist (assuming that the world ever had a beginning) God pre-existed it for times without beginning. I have to reply, however, that this suggestion seems to me unintelligible. If we take God to be unchanging, we have no way of making sense of the idea that, before the existence of the universe, God lived through times. We distinguish between times by virtue of real changes, by changes as they succeed each other. If there were nothing but something wholly unchanging, there would be no ground for talk about times succeeding or preceding each other.

Hence, once again, I commend Aquinas's thinking on God and human freedom. If God brings it about that I do something as you might bring it about that I do something, or as something else in the universe might, then he and his omni-causality would be a threat to my freedom. Yet, so I am arguing, that is not how God makes it to be that I act freely. He does so simply by making me to be a freely acting person. Or as James F. Ross nicely puts it:

> The being of the cosmos is like *a song on the breath of a singer*. It has endless internal universal laws, and structures nested within structures, properties that are of *the song* and *not* of the singer or the voice or the singer's thought, though produced by them and attributively predicated of them . . . The universe is continuously depending, like a song or a light show ... Its being is its own, yet it is from a cause, everywhere, and at no *including* time . . . God

produces, for each individual being, the one that does such and such (whatever it does) throughout its whole time in being . . . God does not make the person act; he makes the so acting person *be* . . . The whole physical universe, all of it, is actively caused to be. Still, to say that freedom or human agency is thereby impeded is absurd. Nothing can be or come about unless caused to be by the creator. So the fact that God's causing is necessary for whatever happens cannot impede liberty; it is a condition for it. Similarly, in no way is our liberty impeded by the fact that God's causing is sufficient for the being of the very things that do the very things that we do. Nothing possible can be impeded by its necessary conditions . . . God did not make Adam to be the first man to defy God; God made Adam, who was the first man to defy God, to be. God made Adam, who undertook to sin . . . God makes all the free things that do *as* they do, instead of doing otherwise as is in their power, by their *own* undertaking. So God does not make Adam sin. But God makes the sinning Adam, the person who, *able* not to sin, does sin. It follows logically that if Adam had not sinned, God would have made a person who, though able to sin, did not. And, surely, God *might* have made a person who, though able to sin, did not . . . It is the whole being, doing as it does, whether a free being or not, that is entirely produced and sustained for its time by God.[26]

Ross here well echoes the reasoning of Aquinas's commentary on the *Peri Hermeneias* to which I referred earlier (and more than once). His thinking, like that of Aquinas, seems a cogent rebuttal to the claim that if God causes what we do, then we cannot act freely.

An implication of this reasoning is, as Ross says, that God might have made a sinless person.[27] This thought has been used to attack belief in God. As we saw in Chapter 1, J. L. Mackie has argued that God might have made free agents who never did anything bad, from which (given that lots of people do what is bad) Mackie concludes that God cannot be good. Mackie is here assuming that God's goodness is moral goodness, so, given what I said in the previous chapter, you will realize why I do not accept his conclusion. But I do accept his premise – that God might have made free agents who never did anything bad. This premise has been rejected by some theists. They have argued that God cannot ensure that people freely act well, or that it is possible that no world createable by God contains people who never freely choose to do wrong.[28] The arguments of these theists, however, rest on the supposition that it is impossible for a free human action to be made to be as it is by God – a supposition which, as I have said, we have strong reason to challenge. As Mackie observes: 'It would, no doubt, be incoherent to say that God makes men freely choose the good: if God had made men choose, that is, forced them to choose one way rather than the other, they would not have been choosing freely. But that is not what was suggested [sc. by Mackie, and, I might add, by me], which was rather that God might have made – that is, created – beings, human or not, *such that* they would always freely choose the good; and there is at least no immediate incoherence or self-contradiction in that.'[29]

Other means and ends arguments

So we can forget about the Free Will Defence as an exoneration of God with respect to moral evil. The notion of human freedom which is central to this defence (freedom independent of God's causal activity) is a mirage given that God is the Maker of all things, the source of their being for as long as they exist. God cannot be thought to need human freedom as the Free Will Defence construes it, as a means to an end (whether good or bad). Yet might there be other (non-moral) evil which God *does* need in order for there to be certain goods? As we also saw in Chapter 1, some, notably Swinburne and Hick, have maintained that there is.[30]

Swinburne's main idea in this connection is that naturally occurring evil provides us with opportunities to perform good actions and develop morally. Does it? To some extent it surely does. If there were no famines, for example, nobody could be moved to struggle on behalf of their victims. There is a logical connection between virtue in the face of famine and the occurrence of famines as such. The first necessarily depends on the second. One might ask whether huge amounts of naturally occurring evil are needed so that goods of various kinds might come about in their wake. As Swinburne argues, however, it is not difficult to see why they might be so needed.[31] Dramatic heroism depends on extreme danger. Large-scale and costly attempts to help others depend on there being a lot of people in difficult circumstances to help. Fortitude in the face of life-threatening illness requires the existence of such illness. And so on. There are undoubtedly goods which could not come about were it not for a great deal of naturally occurring evil.

Should this fact be thought of, however, as providing a moral exoneration of God? As I have said, I think that the whole project of evaluating God morally is confused. For the moment, however, let us work on the opposite assumption and consider whether the line of thinking just noted manages to provide a moral exoneration of God on the supposition that he is a moral agent. A difficulty in doing so is that discussion of moral justifications immediately raises complex ethical questions which I have no space to consider in this book. Yet we do not, I think, need to wade through ethical tomes in order to pursue our present enquiry to some effect.

We can start by asking why it should be thought that logical connections between certain goods and evils could provide a basis for a moral justification for the occurrence of actual naturally occurring evils. Suppose we accept the conceptual point (with which I do not quarrel) that, for example, there could be no dedicated care of cancer patients if there were no such thing as cancer.[32] Does that justify God in inflicting cancer on Mary, or for setting things up so that she and others contract it? Regardless of the benefits to others when it comes to opportunities to do good and so on, what are we to make of an agent who *arranges* for people to contract cancer? I should have thought that most moralists would regard such a person as simply vicious.

Hick tells us that we need a world of pain and suffering in order to develop morally. Swinburne takes the same line. Yet even if we accept that moral development depends (at least sometimes) on there being various kinds of naturally occurring evils, what are we, with an eye on a God we are seeking morally to justify, to say to the victims of these evils when it comes to the moral development of others? I suppose we would have to say something like, 'You died so that I and others might live and engage in character formation, and we thank God for letting things be this way.' But what sort of a God would we be thanking here? It would be one who helps us by wasting others. And such a God could be criticized on at least two counts. First, because he would be acting so as to get us to concentrate on ourselves at the expense of our fellows (this, surely, not a good thing). Second, because he would be acting as if someone being able to do good is a morally justifiable state of affairs simply because there is some bad

situation in which that person is able to act well. It is, of course, true
that we cannot choose to help people unless they are in need. It
seems odd, however, to suggest that one is morally justified to put
people in need so that others can help them. To do that would be to
render them nothing but opportunities for others to gain advantages.
Suppose that the Good Samaritan, on coming across the man beaten
by robbers, had said, 'Thank you, God, for another opportunity to be
responsible and well behaved.'[33] Would we respect him or his God? I
think that most of us would not. We might, of course, learn from the
afflictions of others. But to try to justify God for allowing us to do so
would amount to saying that he is prepared to make people tools
when it comes to the well-being of others, and one might surely
wonder about the moral propriety of treating people in this way,
treating them as means to an end, treating them as *instruments*.

It has been suggested that naturally occurring evils (without
involving others) can help people to improve themselves, and, at a
purely conceptual level, perhaps there is nothing to quarrel with
when it comes to this idea. My cancer might successfully give me the
opportunity to become a better person than I was before it was diag-
nosed. Yet physical misfortune can lead people to less than admirable
actions. Indeed, it can sometimes leave them incapable of doing any
good. It can sometimes result in them being utterly broken. Are we to
say that God might be morally justified in allowing for or intending
natural evil in particular concrete instances? I think that we would
normally say that someone who implemented a policy *designed* to
result in situations in which people end up (or possibly end up)
broken is hardly a moral mentor. Once again, I am not denying that
we may be improved in various ways by the natural evils that afflict
us. I do, however, find it hard to believe that God can be morally justified for dealing with real people according to what D. Z. Phillips
calls 'the logic of economic management, the calculus of gain and
loss'.[34] Good often comes out of evils. But what are we to make of
someone who *organizes* evils so that goods might arise from them? I
think that most people would take such a person to be less than
morally justifiable, and their verdict would not, I think, change if they
were told that God is the person in question. With an eye on the Free
Will Defence, someone who believes in God's moral integrity might
argue that naturally occurring evils always give us opportunities to do
good or to improve ourselves. As I have noted, however, naturally

occurring evils can leave people wasted, unable to act in what we might take to be a morally responsible manner. Admittedly, we cannot always be certain whether people have ended up in a state which leaves them unable to act freely and to choose between good and evil. Sometimes, however, we can surely conclude that they have indeed ended up like this, and if we are right so to conclude, then we can hardly morally justify bringing it about that they are in such a situation. I take this point to be made, in its own way, by a poem ascribed to God in Kingsley Amis's novel *The Anti-Death League*:

To a baby born without limbs

This is just to show you who's boss around here.
It'll keep you on your toes, so to speak,
Make you put your best foot forward, so to speak,
And give you something to turn your hand to, so to speak.
You can face up to it like a man,
Or snivvel and blubber like a baby.
That's up to you. Nothing to do with Me.
If you take it in the right spirit,
You can have a bloody marvellous life,
With the great rewards courage brings,
And the beauty of accepting your LOT.
And think how much good it'll do your Mum and Dad,
And your Grans and Gramps and the rest of the shower,
To be stopped being complacent.[35]

As I noted in Chapter 1, it has been argued (especially by William Alston) that we should not take evil to count against God's existence, since we do not see all the picture, since we do not have a God's-eye view of how things stand and relate to each other. I have considerable sympathy with this line of thinking. It seems to me positively comical that someone should (a) insist that he or she can comprehend how all things are as known to God and (b) make judgements for or against God on that basis. If, however, this 'We Cannot See All the Picture' Argument is used to suggest that God might be morally justified in the face of evil as we know it, then it seems to me that the argument needs to be resisted. Considered as having an eye on God's moral status, it appears to amount to the claim that what we take to be bad might be thought of as good in the long run. Considered as such, it holds that there are means which God might justifiably employ in order to bring about various goods. Yet are there not certain means which cannot be morally justified even though they might lead to various goods arising? As we have seen, authors like Swinburne and Hick tell us that there are evils which can be morally justified. They tell us, for example, that God is morally justified in making a world in which a great deal of evil occurs. He is justified, so they say, because these evils are needed for certain goods to come about. Yet, so I am arguing, many of these evils are not justifiable in terms of some abstract notions of how certain kinds of good depend on certain kinds of evil. We may not know how things fit together as God does, but we can be pretty sure when someone is in agony, and we can sensibly resist the suggestion that anyone (even God) is morally justifiable for *arranging* this, however it fits in with the entire history of the universe (whatever that is and regardless of our ignorance concerning it). This is pretty much the position advanced in the famous speech of Ivan to Alyosha in Dostoevsky's novel *The Brothers Karamazov.*[36] Ivan cites actually occurring examples of evil and cannot make sense of the view that they are justified in anything that we might call a moral sense. Whatever your good purposes, he reasons, we cannot take you to be morally justified in using certain means so as to bring about what you intend. He therefore washes his hands of God, considered as one who intends various evils as a means to some 'higher harmony'.

Yet suppose that our end lies in union with God. Might it not be said that we cannot achieve that union without there being naturally occurring evils? According to John Hick, the answer to this question is 'Yes'. But why? Here is Hick's argument:

(1) We can distinguish between the existence of human beings as such and the existence of people who enjoy a personal relationship with God.

(2) People cannot be created ready-made in a personal relationship with God. They need to grow into such a relationship by choices that they make over time.

(3) For people to grow into a personal relationship with God they need a 'vale of soul-making' in which to become mature. They need obstacles, challenges, and temptations to overcome.

(4) They also need to be placed at an 'epistemic distance' from God – they need to be in an environment in which God's goodness is not overwhelmingly evident (an environment containing various evils).[37]

It seems to me, however, that this line of thinking hardly suffices to justify God in any moral sense. For it allows for there being people who end up as mere victims of pain and suffering and not as 'matured' into a personal relationship with God. It allows for people being *used* as instruments for the well-being of others. It presents us with the picture of a God who is prepared to plan for there being what we might call 'victims of the system' – human victims who have no chance to exercise choice, an example being babies who have died in the course of natural disasters. Hick is telling us that God can be excused for setting up a world in which such babies have met their end – excused because of what their deaths might prompt others to be (i.e. well-behaved students in God's finishing school). I find this line of thinking seriously hard to swallow. I do not deny that much that we admire in people (whether we are theists or not) would not be there to admire were it not for evils in the world. It is one thing to say this, however, and quite another to say that someone (call him 'God') is morally justified for setting up a context in which pain and suffering are there as *intended* to bring certain (unspecified) people to some desirable state. It is easy to think of cases in which we might commend someone for arranging (or allowing) that someone else is, say, in psychological or physical pain – cases in which the pain leads to a good which seems to depend on the pain. Hence, for example, we might value teachers who force their unwilling and suffering students to write and rewrite their essays. Or we might sympathize with dentists. Hick, however, is asking us *morally* to commend one who intentionally sets up a cosmic obstacle course which benefits some and destroys others, a course which is strewn with corpses and casualties. In doing so, he seems to be ignoring the actual and particular suffering that seems to be required for the benefit of those who run the race successfully. In doing so he seems to be *excusing* God for reasons that most of us would never employ when trying to excuse our fellow human beings. It is famously part of Hick's view of things that nobody is lost in the end. According to Hick, all will be saved since justice demands this. If not in this life, then how? As a conse-

quence of lives to come, says Hick. In other words, Hick thinks that
people can continue to grow after death, or in a series of lives after
death. God, he says, 'will eventually succeed in His purpose of
winning all men to Himself in faith and love'.[38] Yet this strand in Hick's
thinking (not an orthodox Christian one, I might note) does nothing
to nullify what seem to be Hick's moral commitments as noted above.

To my mind Hick also makes a mistake when it comes to the need
for the obstacle race that he takes to justify God's permission of evil.
Hick thinks that we could not be in a proper relationship with God
unless he played a game of hide-and-seek – hence the stress Hick puts
on 'epistemic distance'. To be created with a clear knowledge of what
God is would, he thinks, paralyse us morally. But this seems a very
odd view to espouse. Good moral agents, I am presuming, are things
which are attracted to what is good. They are instinctively attracted
to that. Now we often find it hard to work out what is really good. So
we may dither when it comes to making decisions about what to do
on various occasions. But suppose we fully realize what is truly good
for us to aim for in some situation. Then we shall just home in on that
without a second thought. This will be because it is what we want,
and is therefore something we move to willingly or voluntarily. So
loving a good need not be something with respect to which we have
to deliberate. Hick, however, tells us that a knowledge of God as he
is would render us unfree. His basic line is 'See God and you have to
love him, and are therefore not free to develop a right relationship
with him'. I have to say that this way of thinking seems to me pretty
unreasonable. To see and know God as he is might render a human
being unable not to love God. But it does not follow that the human
being in question has been deprived of freedom. This person has been
presented with what he or she most *wants* (given that God is a good
to be prized above all others), and in going for it he or she is not being
deprived of freedom. We are surely free in so far as we home in on
what we want. Being presented by what we see as absolutely, and
without qualification, desirable, and instinctively being drawn to it,
can hardly represent a threat to our freedom. That, of course, is why
Christians have traditionally said that the blessed in heaven, though
free agents, cannot be thought of as sinning.

Conclusion

In this chapter I have discussed certain ways of morally justifying God with an eye on means and ends. I have concluded that none of them give us reason to believe that, given evil, God is truly well-behaved. Philosophers and theologians have offered many moral justifications of God based on a means and ends approach. I have not been able to refer to all of them (though I have had something to say about the best-known among them). I hope, however, that what I have argued gives you pause for thought when presented with any claim to the effect that God is morally justified (because of a necessary relationship between means and ends) in bringing about, or allowing, the evils we encounter in the universe. The Free Will Defence is a nonstarter since it proceeds on the assumption that God is not the Maker of all things. Different (albeit related) attempts morally to justify God with an eye on means and ends always seem to end up making God to be a less than respectable individual (if not a moral monster).[39] Yet, as I noted in Chapter 1, defenders of God have offered other arguments for concluding that evil does not show him to be morally culpable – arguments which do not attempt to exonerate him on a means and ends basis. So let me now say something about these.

Notes

1. If you believe in the orthodox Christian doctrine of the Incarnation, then you will want to say that God can indeed do these things since Jesus could do them. On the orthodox Christian account what is predicable of God is predicable of Christ, and vice versa. On this account, therefore, from 'Jesus scratched his nose' we can infer 'God scratched his nose'. Notice, however, that this account (laid down by the Council of Chalcedon) also stipulates that Jesus (the Word Incarnate) has two natures (human and divine) which are not to be confused with each other. So it is not claiming that if Jesus scratched his nose it follows that the divine nature (whatever it is to be God) did so. The most orthodox of Christologies allows me to say that God (meaning the divine nature) cannot walk to work, take a bath, dig a trench, or scratch himself. More on this below.
2. The reference here is to Luke 1:37.
3. Thomas Aquinas, *Summa Theologiae*, Ia.25.3 (my translation).
4. For Aquinas on miracles see *Summa Theologiae*, Ia.110.4.
5. Notice that I am not here concerned to offer a detailed discussion of the claim that people actually have no freedom. If that claim is true, then the

Free Will Defence is clearly broken-backed. I offer some argument for human freedom later in the chapter, and in all that follows I assume that freedom can truly be ascribed to people. It goes beyond the scope of the present book, however, to engage in a full-scale attack on philosophical determinism.

6. For examples of philosophers arguing in this way (authors endorsing what, in the last note, I called 'philosophical determinism'), see Robert Kane (ed.), *The Oxford Handbook of Free Will* (Oxford University Press: Oxford, 2002).

7. Alvin Plantinga, 'God, Evil, and the Metaphysics of Freedom', repr. in Marilyn McCord Adams and Robert Merrihew Adams (eds), *The Problem of Evil* (Oxford University Press: Oxford, 1990), p. 106.

8. Richard Swinburne, 'The Problem of Evil', in Stuart Brown (ed.), *Reason and Religion* (Cornell University Press: Ithaca, NY and London, 1977), p. 85. Swinburne is here only summarizing the basic thrust of what he takes to be the Free Will Defence. But he clearly seems to agree with that defence.

9. Richard Swinburne, *Is There a God?* (Oxford University Press: Oxford, 1996), p. 98.

10. Bruce R. Reichenbach, *Evil and a Good God* (Fordham University Press: New York, 1982), p. 64.

11. For Aquinas's distinction see *Summa Theologiae*, IaIIae.1.1. Aquinas takes *actiones humanae* to be actions performed with particular ends or goals. He takes *actiones hominis* to be unreflective bits of behaviour such as unthinkingly stroking one's cheek while talking (cf. *Summa Theologiae*, IaIIae.1.3 and IaIIae.18.9).

12. Herbert McCabe, *God Matters* (Geoffrey Chapman: London, 1987), p. 12.

13. Anthony Flew, *The Presumption of Atheism and Other Essays* (Elek/Pemberton: London, 1976), p. 88.

14. See above, pp. 119–21.

15. We might say that Fred has freedom to choose even though he is doing nothing (even though he is, for example, asleep). So we can distinguish between something that has freedom and something that exercises its power to act freely on given occasions.

16. Thomas Aquinas, *Summa Contra Gentiles*, III.67. I quote from Vernon J. Bourke's translation of this text (University of Notre Dame Press: Notre Dame, Ind. and London, 1975), p. 221.

17. Thomas Aquinas, *De Potentia*, III.7. I quote from Timothy McDermott (ed.), *Aquinas: Selected Philosophical Writings* (Oxford University Press: Oxford, 1993), p. 304.

18. Aquinas, *Summa Theologiae*, Ia.22. 2, ad 4 (my translation).

19. I take idolatry to be adherence to a conception of God which takes him to be less than the Creator of all things.

20. Rowan Williams, 'Redeeming Sorrows', in D. Z. Phillips (ed.), *Religion and Morality* (St Martin's Press: New York, 1996), p. 143.

21. Thomas Aquinas, *Commentary on Aristotle's 'Peri Hermeneias'*, 1.14. I

quote from McDermott (ed.), *Aquinas: Selected Philosophical Writings*, p. 281.

22. Aquinas, *Commentary on Aristotle's 'Peri Hermeneias'*, 1.14, quotation from McDermott, *Aquinas: Selected Philosophical Writings*, p. 283.
23. Alvin Plantinga, *The Nature of Necessity* (Clarendon Press: Oxford, 1974), p. 166.
24. Williams, 'Redeeming Sorrows', p. 145.
25. For more on this thought see G. E. M. Anscombe, 'Causality and Determination', in G. E. M. Anscombe, *Collected Philosophical Papers*, vol. 2 (Basil Blackwell: Oxford, 1981).
26. James F. Ross, 'Creation II', in Alfred J. Freddoso (ed.), *The Existence and Nature of God* (University of Notre Dame Press: Notre Dame, Ind. and London, 1983), pp. 128–34.
27. For what it is worth, I would note that the Roman Catholic doctrine of the Immaculate Conception teaches that God has indeed done this in the case of Mary, the mother of Jesus. Catholics also seem committed to believing that Jesus never sinned.
28. For argument along these lines, see, for example, Alvin Plantinga, *The Nature of Necessity*, ch. 9. In *Evil and the God of Love* (2nd edn, Macmillan: London, 1985) John Hick maintains that though God could have made people who always freely choose the good, he cannot make them such that they always 'freely respond to Himself in love and trust and faith' (p. 272).
29. J. L. Mackie, *The Miracle of Theism* (Clarendon Press: Oxford, 1982), p. 165.
30. As I noted in Chapter 1, it has been argued that there cannot be good without at least some evil. You might think of this as a means and ends argument in defence of God. It does not seem to me, however, to merit much discussion. There is no reason to suppose that there cannot be good without evil – as theists seem committed to believing in so far as they are prepared to think that, God's act of creating being free, there might have been nothing but (a wholly good) God.
31. Swinburne develops his position in ch. 9 of *Providence and the Problem of Evil* (Clarendon Press: Oxford, 1998).
32. It should, I hope, be obvious that what I am saying here is not falsified by the fact that we might connect the occurrence of some cancer with what people freely choose to do (e.g. smoke).
33. Happily, in this parable (Luke 10:25–37) the Good Samaritan does not say anything like this.
34. D. Z. Phillips, *The Problem of Evil and the Problem of God* (SCM Press: London, 2004), p. 71. I am considerably indebted to ch. 3 of this book for much that I say in the present chapter.
35. Kingsley Amis, *The Anti-Death League* (Harcourt, Brace & World: New York, 1966), pp. 128f.
36. Fyodor Dostoevsky, *The Brothers Karamazov*, bk 5, ch. 4. The text of

Ivan's speech is reprinted in Nelson Pike (ed.), *God and Evil* (Prentice Hall: Englewood Cliffs, NJ, 1964), pp. 6ff.

37. John Hick, *Evil and the God of Love*, esp. chs 12 and 15.
38. Ibid., p. 342.
39. I say 'albeit related' since, as you will probably deduce from what I have previously said, various means–ends defences of God frequently seem to presuppose that the Free Will Defence is correct and treat its conclusion as a supposition for what they argue.

Six

How Not to Exonerate God: II

In the previous chapter I argued against certain lines of thinking designed to defend God's moral integrity given the reality of evil. These lines of thinking all make use of what I call a means and ends approach to the problem of evil. They all suggest that evils of various kinds can be viewed as means which God legitimately employs so as to bring about or foster varieties of goodness. As I noted in Chapter 1, however, defenders of God who seem to be arguing with an eye on his moral standing have not always employed a means and ends approach. They have, for example, argued for at least one of the following alternatives:

(1) The universe is better with some evil than no evil.

(2) There actually is no evil, so God cannot be blamed for it.

(3) Evil as we know it is justly inflicted punishment.

(4) There might be a moral justification for God allowing evil but we may not be in a position see what that amounts to.

I might also add that defenders of God's goodness (though not necessarily defenders of God's moral goodness) have pleaded on his behalf along one or more of the following lines:

(5) People are not always as happy as they could be. But this is no reason to criticize God.

(6) Our world, with its various evils, is, in fact, the best possible world.

(7) God also suffers.

These are the positions that I want to consider in this chapter.[1]

Better some evil than no evil

Suppose that the world contained nothing but good. Would such a world be better than one which contained at least some evil? You might think so, since good and evil seem to be opposites and since a wholly good world would just have to be better than one containing evil. Yet, so it has been argued, evil can indeed contribute to the goodness of the universe. Why? By being part of a whole which is better for the evil it contains than it would be without it. One sometimes finds discord in great works of music. The discord contributes to the value of the works taken in their entirety. Bits of certain paintings might strike one as ugly taken in isolation. As parts of the works they comprise, however, they are essential to an overall effect. Similarly, it has been said, evil in the world renders it more valuable than it would be without it. It contributes to a product which is better as a whole because of it.[2]

In defence of this line of thinking we can surely concede (at least when thinking in terms of aesthetics) that what is disagreeable taken on its own, might, in a given context, make a great contribution. When Scarpia makes his entrance in *Tosca* the orchestra emits a horrid noise, one which, taken as a piece of sound plucked from the musical score of the opera, might simply be written off as an offence against our ears. But it is not an offence in its context. As opera buffs seem to agree, it fits in perfectly there, and also when it is echoed while the opera continues. Then again, a blob of black paint is not, by itself, especially lovely (or so you might think). There are paintings, however, in which a patch of black is part of something which, as a whole, we admire. That which, taken on its own, can be thought of as undesirable, might, together with other things, strike us as contributing to a product that is good.

Yet this line of reasoning seems pretty weak if intended, with an eye on evil, as a moral justification of God, or even if not so taken. For why can there not be a state of good, or even infinite good, without the presence of anything evil? Let us agree that what is disharmonious or ugly taken in isolation might contribute to an effect that is overall good. It does not follow from this that evil is necessary for good to exist, even if we allow, as I do not see that we should, that disharmony and ugliness count as evils (they are hardly evils in the sense that wicked actions and physical suffering are). We can sometimes appreciate goods because we have encountered badness of various kinds. I often do so when I return home from being away. Given what I have encountered on my travels, I often end up valuing what I have at home more highly than I did before I left there. Yet 'good' and 'bad' are not terms that register what, as a matter of fact, I do or do not appreciate. They look remarkably like adjectives which describe how things are regardless of the reactions to them that particular people might display.[3] To say that X is good is to say what X is, and it seems far from obvious that something cannot be good unless it is also somehow bad. So why must the existence of goodness depend on the presence of badness? Certain sorts of good states may depend on the existence of certain sorts of bad states. It does not follow from this, however, that what actually exists could not be anything but good. Theists, at any rate, have no reason for supposing that it does. Those who believe in God have traditionally taken him to be perfectly good. They have also commonly said that God did not have to create. So traditional theism supplies us with a reason for supposing that there can be goodness without badness. So does common sense. My cat Smokey is currently in the peak of condition. He is as fit and well as any cat can be. Would it not be ludicrous to suggest that I could add to his well-being by injuring him somehow?

You might say that the world as a whole is better for the evil in it than it would be without it. But what are we to take that idea to mean? I can understand what people would mean if they said, for example, that Mary would be better than she is if she lost her cough. Mary is an individual of a certain kind who is better for being in some states rather than others. So when she has lost her cough, and when people ask her how she is, she can say 'I'm better now'. But what might 'better' signify when applied to the universe as a whole? The universe is not a distinct kind of item within itself. So it seems hard to see what 'would be better as a whole if . . .' could mean when predicated of the world as a whole. One might, perhaps, argue that the real world, with its various evils, is better than some imaginary world containing no evil. But it can hardly be better considered as a *world*. It can only be *different* from some world we might fantasize about. And there still remains the point that there can certainly be good without evil.

Evil is not real

As I said in Chapter 1, the 'Unreality of Evil Argument' (as I called it) takes two forms: (a) the thesis that evil is an illusion, and (b) the claim that evil is an absence or privation of a due good. Here I want to argue that (a) should be rejected while (b) should be accepted.

With respect to (a) one could, of course, demand that those who challenge it need to provide a full-scale epistemological treatise showing (among other things) that there are hard and fast ways to distinguish between reality and illusion and that evil can be proved to be illusory in terms of these ways. Someone might even demand a proof that there is any reality at all or that there is such a thing as a world distinct from our minds. In other words, a serious rebuttal of (a) might be taken to require answers to some of the historically central questions of philosophy (especially those concerned with the relative merits of realism versus idealism). I clearly cannot hope to satisfy these demands in this book, so I shall simply make a few points concerning (a) and trust that you will be indulgent with me as I engage in the vice of epistemological brevity.

First, if you want to say that evil is truly an illusion, you will also have to concede that you have no business making value judgements involving such terms as 'good' and 'bad'. Or, at least, you have no business making such judgements on the supposition that they actually are *judgements* – i.e. statements purporting to note what in fact is the case. You will not, for example, be able to say such things as that Jesus of Nazareth was a good man while Hitler was a bad one, or that John's operation has brought him back to a good state of health while Mary's disease has left her in a bad way. Judgements like these make no sense unless they are taken to mean that there is genuine goodness and badness to be noted in the world. So if you embrace (a), you pay a heavy price for doing so.

Second, the notion that evil is an illusion is arguably self-contradictory. If I am mistakenly convinced that something is bad, then I am deluded, which is surely a bad state in which to be. Or, as Peter Geach says, picking up on the language of Mary Baker Eddy, 'if my "mortal mind" thinks I am miserable, then I am miserable, and it is not an illusion that I am miserable'.[4] One may, of course, suppose that evil pales into insignificance when set beside some known or hoped-for good. In this vein, so I take it, St Paul says, 'I consider that the sufferings of this present time are not worth comparing with the glory about to be revealed to us.'[5] Yet Paul is not here saying that evil is an illusion. Indeed, given his views about right and wrong, and given his belief that Christ endured a passion, he could not consistently do so.

If (a) seems highly dubious, however, the same is not, I think, true of (b). For (b) is not asserting that evil is an illusion or that in no sense does it exist. It is making a claim about the meaning of what we are saying when we call something bad (in whatever way we take it to be bad), a claim which I think can be defended. I should immediately note that this claim is wholly indefensible if it is true that statements like 'X is good' and 'Y is bad' do not really tell us what X and Y are in themselves. If, for example, 'X is good' only means something like 'I approve of X', then (b) is plainly false, since it relies on an understanding of 'X is good' which is just not compatible with that which takes 'X is good' only to mean something like 'I approve of X'.[6] Most people, however, do take themselves to be describing things in calling them good or bad, and, if we think that they are not completely mad to do so (as I will assume we should), then the way is open for a defence of (b).

Perhaps 'describing' in the last sentence is a wrong word for me to have used. For a description gives one a fairly precise sense of what something is. Descriptions tend to picture things or to make it clear how they differ from other things. Sometimes they identify things precisely. The police may ask a victim 'Can you describe your attacker?' Here they are looking for an account which might help them to arrest a particular suspect. Yet to say that something is good or bad (and to say only this of it) is not, in this sense, to describe. Suppose I say (a) 'These are good strawberries', (b) 'He's a good parent', '(c) 'Paris is good for a holiday', or (d) 'She's in good health'. If you ask me to justify my statements here, I shall have to describe what I am talking about in each of them. But my accounts, taken together, will not add up to a coherent description of anything. I take strawberries to be good in so far as they are sweet and juicy. I take parents to be good in so far as they look after their children and provide what they need. I take good holiday places to have decent hotels, lots of amusements, an agreeable climate, and plenty of interesting things to see. But now imagine me saying that X is sweet, juicy, looks after its children and provides what they need, has decent hotels and lots of amusements, has an agreeable climate, and has plenty to see. You could make no sense of this. So saying that something is good is not to use 'good' as an ordinary descriptive term, one which explains what something, to be contrasted with other things, is actually like. Assuming, however, that 'X is good' says something about X, '____ is good' here is in a sense describing, for it is somehow telling us what X is.

What, though, is it telling us? Given what I have just said, I am assuming that goodness is not a particular property had by all good things – as, say, yellowness is a particular property had by all yellow things, or as being plastic is a property common to all plastic things, or as being valid is a property had by all good arguments. Following an analysis offered by Peter Geach, let us say that 'in a phrase "an AB" ("A" being an adjective and "B" being a noun) "A" is a (logically) predicative adjective if the predication "is an AB" splits up into a pair of predications "is a B" and "is A". Let us also say that, if such is not the case, "A" is a (logically) attributive adjective'.[7] On this account, 'big' and 'small', for example, are attributive adjectives while 'red' is predicative. As Geach puts it:

> 'X is a big flea' does not split up into 'X is a flea' and 'X is big', nor 'X is a small elephant' into 'X is an elephant' and 'X is small'; for if these analyses were legitimate, a simple argument would show that a big flea is a big animal and a small elephant a small animal . . . On the other hand, in the phrase 'a red book', 'red' is a predicative adjective . . . For 'is a red book' logically splits up into 'is a book' and 'is red'.[8]

Now my present point is that 'good' can be thought of as *something* like a logically attributive adjective. True, 'X is a good man' splits up into 'X is good' and 'X is a man', so 'good' is not logically attributive in precisely Geach's sense. But just as we cannot fully understand (and can be deeply misled when it comes to) what is being said by the use of 'big' and 'small' without knowing what they are being applied to, so we cannot get a sense of what is being said by the use of 'good' unless we know what it is being applied to. Or at least, when told only that X is good we have no serious description of X (one which allows us to pick it out as different from other things – as in 'Describe the person who attacked you'). 'Good' works more like 'big' and 'small' than it does like 'red'. The fact that wine can be made from good grapes has no tendency at all to suggest that wine can be made from good desks.

Yet it does not therefore follow that there is no common meaning to 'good' as we use it to say what different things are. Indeed, there does seem to be just such a common meaning. For (and forgetting about God for the moment) when we call something good we are surely saying that it succeeds in some way. We are saying that it matches up to what we expect it to be given the kind of thing it is. A good computer is one which functions as we want a computer to function. A good doctor is one who succeeds in performing as we require doctors to perform. A good human being is one who behaves as we expect human beings (*qua* human beings) to behave. Of course, people have different expectations when it comes to what should be found in computers, doctors, people, or whatever. The computer I love may strike some as antique. The doctor I value might seem inexpert to certain medical specialists. Someone I take to be a good human being might be thought by others to be anything but that. My point, however, remains. To call something good, regardless of how we go on to justify our judgement, is to commend it for having what we are looking for in things of that kind. Things we call good are things that we find desirable in some way, and we call them good because they have what we find desirable in things of the kind they are.

If this is so, however, we can make a corresponding point about the meaning of 'bad'. If 'X is good' means (roughly) X has what we are looking for, then 'X is bad' means (roughly) that X does not have what we are looking for. We call something a bad X (e.g. a bad computer, doctor, or human being) when it does not come up to our expectations considered as what it is. As is the case with 'good', 'bad' does not signify a property common to everything to which it is applied. What we take a bad computer to be is bound to be very different from what we take a bad doctor to be. And what we take to amount to badness in some things might not be taken by us as indicating badness in others (we might say, for example, that a chair is bad because it collapses when sat on, but not that a piece of fruit is bad because it collapses when sat on). Badness, like goodness, is relative (though not therefore subjective). Whether or not someone or other thinks so, such and such might be bad (a view which I suspect almost everyone accepts in practice). Yet understanding what badness amounts to depends on knowing what it is that is supposed to be bad. Be that as it may, however, understanding that something is bad is to understand something about it, albeit something negative. It is to understand that it is failing to be what we are looking for.

This is what the claim that evil is an absence or privation of a due good amounts to (a claim embraced, as I noted in Chapter 1, by writers like Augustine and Aquinas). So I now suggest that this is a claim to endorse. You might reply that badness is not something negative since it can arise because of the presence of something positive. And that is true enough. I recently wrecked a laptop computer by inadvertently spilling some port into it (thereby rendering it a defective or bad computer by virtue of the wine inside it). Or, as McCabe observes, 'a washing machine may be bad not only because it has too little, as when there is no driving belt on the spin drier, but also because it has too much, as when someone has filled the interior with glue'.[9] It remains, however, that to call something bad is to say that it does not measure up to desires or expectations and, in this sense, always displays an absence. Critics of this view have accused its proponents of asserting that badness is simply unreal – meaning, I suppose, that it is a figment of our imagination or 'an error of the mortal mind', as Mary Baker Eddy said it was. As I noted in Chapter 1, however, this is not the attitude of people like Augustine and Aquinas (and many others that I could quote). They take badness (or evil) very seriously. They are convinced that there are lots of things that are bad in the world around us. They are also convinced that there are lots of bad people. And they accept that bad things and people can, in virtue of their badness, have real or positive effects. But they do not therefore conclude that badness (or evil) is some kind of thing (as Smokey is some kind of thing). Their main point is that badness amounts to a particular lack in certain particular things, that it is not the name of a stuff (like milk) or even the name of a quality (like redness). As McCabe says, their position is:

> Things really are bad sometimes, and this is because the absence of what is to be expected is just as real as a presence. If I have a hole in my sock, the hole is not anything at all, it is just an absence of wool or cotton or whatever, but it is a perfectly real hole in my sock. It would be absurd to say that holes in socks are unreal and illusory just because the hole is not made of anything and is purely an absence. *Nothing* in the wrong place can be just as real and just as important as *something* in the wrong place. If you inadvertently

drive your car over a cliff you will have nothing to worry about; it is precisely the nothing that you will have to worry about.[10]

On this account, 'badness' (or 'evil') is a word we use to signify a gap between what is *actually* there and what *could be* there (and *should be* there) but is *not*. There are people, but, so authors like Augustine and Aquinas think, there are no 'baddities' (actual things or positive properties whose nature is captured simply by saying that they are bad).

So, to repeat, I think that the claim that evil is a privation or absence of some kind is a credible one. Yet what could be its relevance to the problem of evil? As I noted in Chapter 1, Aquinas thinks it relevant to discussions of God and evil since he takes it to imply that evil cannot be thought of as something created by God. My view is that Aquinas is right here, but I would like to postpone further discussion of the matter until the next chapter. For the moment, let me proceed to consider the other views noted at the start of the present one.

Evil as justly inflicted punishment

In Albert Camus's 1947 novel *La Peste* (*The Plague*) a priest prepares to preach in a town ravaged by disease. The priest, Fr Panneloux, looks at the people assembled in front of him and tells them that they deserve the calamity that has fallen on them.[11] As Camus makes clear, Fr Panneloux sees a direct connection between suffering and punishment. He makes sense of what his flock is experiencing by taking it to amount to what God rightly inflicts on them. And people in real life have shared Panneloux's perspective. They have said that evil is basically deserved and therefore casts no slur on God.

These people might have a point. By this I mean (and only mean) that we can often justify pain and suffering with an eye on the notion of justly (or reasonably) inflicted punishment. We certainly often try to do so at any rate. People sent to jail are hardly enjoying themselves, but society (western society anyway) takes the view that a jail (considered as punitive) is something to which people might be rightly committed. Philosophers have differed when it comes to how the use of punishment can be justified. I know of none who hold that it should never be engaged in, but they certainly disagree when it comes to why it should be administered. Should it be handed out on purely retributive grounds?[12] Should it be engaged in only with an eye on reform or deterrence?[13] Different answers have been given to these questions, but the point I am drawing attention to now is that defending the occurrence of suffering with an eye on the notion of punishment is not an unusual practice. Nor does it seem obviously wrong, as I would suggest by means of a simple example. Suppose that you rob me of money. You are caught by the police and a judge asks me what I want him to do to you. I tell the judge that I do not want him to send you to prison and that I do not want him to force you to pay me back the sum of money that you stole from me (let us say that I realize that if you have to do this, your family will suffer from a lack of basic needs). But I know that you own something, valueless in the eyes of most people, which I value as much as the money of which you robbed me and which you love very dearly. So I tell the judge to oblige you to give me this item. That would certainly leave you feeling pretty miserable. It would be positively punitive. Would it, however, be wrong for the judge to comply with my request? I doubt that many would say that it would, so I take it that suffering can, in principle, be defended in terms of punishment.[14]

I therefore have no general objection to the suggestion that there might be evil (in the form of pain and suffering) which might justly be inflicted by God. I do not, however, see how all evil or badness can be categorized in these terms, and that for the following reasons.

First, appeal to justly inflicted punishment does not cope with evil or badness as it affects non-rational things. When my video recorder breaks down I end up with an example of badness (a bad, defective video recorder). But my video recorder is hardly a justly punished individual. When a blight hits cornfields lots of corn becomes bad. Yet corn is not something of which it makes sense to say that it is (or that it is not) justly punished. The other animals we share the world with are victims of evil just as (though, perhaps, not as much as) we are.[15] Yet, so I assume, they never make conscious choices, deliberating between alternative courses of action and selecting one for reasons of their own. I therefore suggest that what they endure cannot be sensibly thought of as punishment they deserve. In this connection it is, perhaps, worth noting that the number of non-human animals who have been victims of evil (many of them preceding our emergence) far exceeds the number of human ones.[16]

Second, it seems implausible to hold that all human beings suffer because of what they deserve. Babies and very young children often suffer. This cannot be because of offences they have committed. Babies and very young children have not had a chance to develop to the point at which they might be deemed culpable of (and therefore justly punished for) anything. It has been said by certain Christians that victims of AIDS are being punished by God for their sin of engaging in homosexual relations. Yet there are victims of AIDS (including babies) who have never had a homosexual thought in their lives.[17] I recently watched a television programme in which someone was saying that the tidal waves which have afflicted people in Asia was God's punishment for them not being Christian. Yet many of the people who suffered from these waves had little or no contact with Christians and precious little knowledge of what Christianity amounts to. So they can hardly be held to have been culpable for not being Christian. And, in general, there seem to be lots of instances of human suffering which cannot be written off as 'justly inflicted punishment'.

For what it is worth, this seems to be a conclusion embraced by some biblical texts. To be sure, the book of Proverbs appears to be wedded to the notion that people suffer because they have misbehaved. So in that book we read

> The LORD's curse is on the house of the wicked,
>   but he blesses the abode of the righteous.[18]

We find other biblical passages, however, which pull in a different direction. Many of these can be found in the book of Job. This tells us about an innocent man, Job, who is afflicted by drastic misfortunes. Some of his friends, thinking along the lines of the book of Proverbs, suggest that he must have done something wrong. Job, however, insists that he has always done his best to abide by what God commands. He ends up saying,

> I am blameless; I do not know myself;
>   I loathe my life.
> It is all one; therefore I say,
>   he destroys both the blameless and the wicked.
> When disaster brings sudden death,
>   he mocks at the calamity of the innocent.[19]

Then again, we find the prophet Jeremiah (clearly not assuming a correlation between wrongdoing and suffering) saying,

> Why does the way of the guilty prosper?
> Why do all who are treacherous thrive?[20]

In the New Testament there is an *explicit* denial of a connection between misfortune and guilt. In the Gospel of Luke Jesus asks, of some Galileans whose blood Pilate had mingled with their sacrifices, 'Do you think that because these Galileans suffered in this way they were worse sinners than all other Galileans? No, I tell you'.[21] In the Gospel of John Jesus meets a man born blind. His disciples ask him whether the man is blind because he sinned or because his parents sinned. The answer given by Jesus rejects the assumption of the question: 'Neither this man nor his parents sinned; he was born blind so that God's works might be revealed in him.'[22]

That comment ascribed to Jesus manifestly denies that the suffering of *X* is necessarily to be attributed to wrongdoing committed by *X*. Yet what of the Christian doctrine of original sin? Some would say that this allows us happily (or unhappily) to view much suffering as deserved – deserved because of wrongdoing committed by those who preceded us. Christian discussions of God and evil often stress that the topic cannot be seriously addressed without allowing for original sin, so perhaps I should now say something about it, albeit that, in trying to do so briefly (as I am), I shall be treading over a number of minefields where explosions can be expected to occur frequently (at least in the minds of my readers).

A traditional line on original sin goes like this: In the distant past there were people who committed the first sin ever. For doing so, God punished them. And his punishment extended to all of their offspring, who consequently came to endure most of the miseries that we now take to be part and parcel of the world in which we live (i.e. physical suffering and psychological anguish).

You can find what looks like the origin of this account in Genesis 1–3. Here people (Adam and Eve) are said to have been created by God in a world that they controlled and by which they were not crushed (Genesis 1:26–31; 2:8–9, 15–16). Here we are also told that, though the first human beings lived in a state of contentment, they disobeyed God and were punished by being placed in a world of pain and death (Genesis 3:14–19), a world in which their heirs came to birth.

Then again, consider what St Paul says in Romans 5. Here we read:

> . . . just as sin came into the world through one man, and death came through sin, and so death spread to all because all have sinned – sin was indeed in the world before the law, but sin is not reckoned when there is no law. Yet death exercised dominion from Adam to Moses, even over those whose sins were not like the transgression of Adam[.][23]

What Paul calls 'death' here might reasonably (though not, I think, necessarily) be equated with all that eats away at our humanity and, in this sense, might be thought of as basically equivalent to the naturally occurring evil that people draw attention to when insisting that there is a theological problem of evil (or when insisting that theism flounders in the face of evil). And Paul seems to be taking this naturally occurring evil as some kind of punishment – a punishment inflicted on the descendants of Adam.

The same theme emerges in what the Council of Trent (1545–63) has to say at one point. We read:

> If anyone declares that the sin of Adam damaged him alone and not his descendants, and that the holiness and justice received from God, which he lost, he lost for himself alone and not for us; or that, while he was stained by the sin of disobedience, he transmitted only death and bodily pains to the whole human race, but not that sin which is the death of the soul: let him be anathema.[24]

Trent immediately goes on to cite Romans 5. So its position seems to be that naturally occurring evils should be viewed as a penalty for Adam's sin. Trent also seems to be taking human wrongdoing after Adam (or a propensity to do wrong, or guilt of some kind) somehow to be a consequence of what Adam did when first acting wrongly.

Now suppose we take note of the views I have just reported. Might we not go on to say that naturally occurring evil in the world is indeed a matter of justly inflicted punishment? Might we even say that moral evil is somehow a legitimate inheritance when viewed against the wrongdoing of humans committed a long time ago?

Some would say that we should not think in these terms since it is not plausible to suppose that there ever was a first human sinner – a historical Eve, for example.[25] Yet even if we do not take the Genesis account of Adam and Eve to be historically accurate, it seems perfectly reasonable to say that there must have been a first occurrence of moral evil or sin. If people have not always existed (as everyone seems to assume to be the case), then human history is finite and it has to have been the case that wrongdoing (or sin) emerged at some point in time and in the action of some historical human being (or in the simultaneous actions of a number of human beings).[26]

Other critics of belief in original sin as I am currently understanding it would say that we should not accept it because it seems to imply that X's being in a bad way can never be rightly thought of in terms of justly inflicted punishment unless it is punishment inflicted on X for what X has done. Yet that line of thinking seems somewhat simplistic. Of course it is true that most people would not think it right to inflict what is bad on X because of what Y has done. Hence, for example, I think that it would be generally agreed that it would be wrong to send me to prison for a crime that you have committed. Justly inflicted punishment, however, can certainly have bad effects on individuals (whether human or non-human) who are not themselves the doers of what is wrong.

Let us suppose that I am a married man with children who freely chooses to murder someone so as to benefit in some way. If I am arrested and convicted, you might think it right for me to be punished. But my punishment (a just one, let us say) might well, so to speak, carry through to and affect my family. As a consequence of my sentence, my wife and children (though not because of what those who have convicted me do) might be immediately deprived of certain goods (e.g. my income and what that does to help my family). Here we can even go on to imagine a truly horrendous scenario: my wife goes to pieces and turns to prostitution (to make money) and to drink (to console herself). My children, in due course, are introduced to all sorts of undesirable characters who cause them much pain – pain which leaves them physically and psychologically damaged. On the supposition that people can sometimes act freely, the bad free choices of human beings are, presumably, attributable to them and can hardly be thought of as punishment on them for what they have chosen to do. Human free choices, however, obviously proceed from human desires and one might reasonably argue, as many have done, that people have the desires they have because of what they have come to be over time and as a consequence of justly inflicted punishment. Let us suppose that because her parents were justly imprisoned Jane ended up as the sort of person who wants to take drugs. Jane's drugging herself on some occasion is attributable to her, if we take her to be doing what she wants to do, and if we assume that there is nothing outside her coercing her. But her desires might be explicable in terms of what happened following the incarceration of her parents. In this sense it might turn out to be explicable in terms of justly inflicted punishment.

In other words, justly inflicted punishment may well have very bad consequences in the lives of those who are not wrongdoers as well as in the lives of those who are. To concede as much is not, however, to say that we can morally exonerate God in the face of evil by appealing to belief in the notion of justly inflicted punishment in the context of belief in original sin. I say this for the following reasons.

First, this belief, as I sketched it above, cannot account for all evil. Assuming that there were suffering animals on Earth before people came on the scene, there has been evil in God's world which cannot remotely be linked to human wrongdoing. If we are determined to indulge in theodicy, if we insist that God, considered as a moral agent, is morally justified in allowing the occurrence of evil, then we need more than what the doctrine of original sin seems to offer (and assuming we believe in that doctrine). You might hold, as some do, that there was no suffering before people sinned. Or you might suggest that the suffering of non-human animals does not count as evil. The first position is one I associate with biblical fundamentalists, who take the Genesis narrative to be (or to be basically) historically accurate – thereby ruling out the thought of there being suffering sentient creatures before people came on the scene. Both for reasons of space and a lack of competence, this is not a position with which I can engage in this book. At this point, therefore, I shall have to content myself lamely with saying that it seems contrary to what the mainstream scientific community seems to espouse. The second position, however, is one that I think I can decisively refute even in two sentences. Here are the sentences: (a) If X, whatever it is, is suffering, then X is not as good as it could be and is therefore in some way deprived; (b) For any X to be deprived is for X to be deficient or lacking in some way and, therefore, to display, or to be a victim of, badness or evil.

Second, though one might argue (as I have) that one might be able to account for lots of suffering (even that of the innocent) in terms of justly inflicted punishment, one cannot plausibly hold that God, thought of as someone morally excusable, is morally justified with respect to all of it. I do not see, for example, how one can morally exonerate a genuine moral agent who plans for there to be suffering prior to the emergence of people. Such suffering, it might be said, is something that we can learn from so as to be able to choose between good and evil. It is, however, *planned* suffering, the deliberate bringing about of evil so that good might arise – something on which I commented adversely in the previous chapter. You might say, with an eye on the notion of original sin, that there is none the less evil which can be accounted for in terms of a just decree by a morally good person. If this person is God, though, then he is surely someone who either inflicts preventable pain and suffering on people or who tolerates it. The judge who rightly sends me to prison is in no position to avert the bad consequences to my family to which his judgement might lead. Yet a morally good God, if we take him to be omniscient and omnipotent, can presumably figure out a way of averting bad consequences. And even if that is not the case, it remains that such a God, if we take him to be morally justified for allowing or accounting for the evils that affect us following some supposed primeval human fall, is allowing or causing evil to be suffered when it comes to those who are not themselves guilty. It is one thing to say that the suffering of innocent people might be explicable in terms of justly inflicted punishment on someone *other* than them. It is another thing to say that the sufferings of the innocent can be thought of as justly inflicted on *them*. Some defenders of belief in original sin (St Augustine, for instance) have said that the sufferings of all people are justly inflicted on them since they actually sinned when the first sin was committed. I have to say that I can make absolutely no sense of this suggestion.[27] If anything is self-evident, it is that people cannot do wrong before they are born.

Evil and our ignorance

Something we normally regard as bad without qualification might yet contribute decisively in the coming about of a good. This is the thought running through the 'We Can't See All the Picture' Argument (as I called it in Chapter 1). Can we be sure that there are instances of evil that are, so to speak, undefeated by good, instances with respect to which God can be morally blamed? Leaving aside the issue of whether or not God is to be thought of either as morally culpable or as morally praiseworthy, it seems to me that a case can be made for saying that we cannot be sure when it comes to this question, though some have suggested otherwise.

William Rowe is a case in point. As I have noted, he finds it hard to believe that there are no instances of suffering which God could have prevented without the loss of a greater good or the coming about of something just as bad, and here I am in sympathy with Rowe. I can think of cases of suffering which strain my credulity as Rowe says that his credulity is strained. Yet the fact that people find something hard (or easy) to believe is surely neither here nor there when it comes to what is actually the case. We may find it hard to believe that Fred is a serial killer. He may be, however, and, given enough information, we may readily concede that he is. By the same token, so it seems to me, the fact that nobody can see how certain instances of suffering could have been prevented by God without the loss of a greater good or the coming about of something just as bad is no good reason to suppose that they could have been so prevented. The fact of the matter is that we just are ignorant of many things, and especially of how historical realities relate to each other in the past and in the future. We may hit on what we take to be an instance of evil with no compensating or defeating good, an instance which we might think could easily have been prevented by a God intent on goodness and intent on minimizing badness. Since we lack a thorough understanding of how the elements in our world fit together when considered from a perspective which is not merely ours, might it not be suggested that we are simply not entitled to say that we know that this or that instance of evil is what we take it to be – i.e. that it does not play a part in the coming about of a compensating good or the prevention of something more evil?

Yet to concede all this is not to agree that the 'We Don't Know All the Picture' Argument serves as a defence of God's moral integrity. To be fair to exponents of the argument, they commonly do not say that it *shows* God to be morally good. They take it as a reason for supposing that we should be rash to conclude that God is morally bad.[28] In spite of what I have just said, however (general remarks, and only intended as such), I think that we *can* think of examples of actual evils that are preventable by God without blocking a great good and without leaving something worse in their place.

I trapped my thumb in a door some years ago. That was a painful experience for me. Have I reason to suppose that my pain on that particular occasion contributed to some good? Let us seriously try to consider to what good it might have contributed.

You might say that it helped me to learn where and where not to put my thumb. But I knew that before I trapped it.

You might say that my pain helped to make me a better person. If you say this, however, I am going to retort that it did nothing of the kind. It simply gave me a wounded thumb.

You might say that my bearing of my pain served as an example to others. But it did not, since I was on my own when I was suffering and I told nobody about what happened.

Did my experience prevent something as bad or worse than it? Here I shall reply 'No', since the trapping of my thumb had a causal effect only on me (there were, for example, no terrorists in my house who, moved by my pain, refrained from going on a shooting spree).

I want to say that the pain I suffered when I trapped my thumb in the door brought about no good and prevented no worse evil. This, I think, is something that I know. Should people in two thousand years' time read the words I am writing now they may well (God knows why) be moved to acts of great virtue and they may strive to remove many evils. Of course, I do not know whether that fantasy will ever become reality since I cannot see all the picture. But I think it pretty implausible to suppose that it will. If we are reasonable in believing anything, we are reasonable in believing that there are instances of evil (I have just given you one) which are not morally justifiable in terms of good brought about or evil prevented.

It is certainly true that we do not know all the picture. There may well be evils on which we can look without being at all in a position to pass an informed verdict when it comes to their moral justification. I continue, however, to cite my thumb as evidence to the effect that there are evils we know not to lead to good or to prevent evil as great. You may mock my example. You may say, 'What is Davies's thumb pain compared with the agony endured in Auschwitz or Belsen or Dachau?' And it is, of course, nothing indeed. It is *less than nothing* by comparison. But I felt pain when I trapped my thumb, and even a single instance of pain (however slight) is relevant when it comes to the idea that a morally good God would not bring about any badness without a morally sufficient reason. The 'We Can't See All the Picture' Argument seems to be reasonably indicted by my thumb. Its defender may reply, 'Since you are not omniscient you cannot rule out the possibility that your wounding your thumb does play some role in a good scheme of things.'[29] Yet this seems a rather desperate move to make. True, I am not omniscient, so I may sometimes be wrong when it comes to what I think I know. Unless you want to embrace a position of full-blown scepticism, however, you will concede that there are things that people can know even though they are not omniscient. And I am suggesting that I have good reason to claim to know that my thumb accident effected no good and prevented no evil.[30] To be sure, from 'It seems to me that such and such is the case' it does not follow that such and such is the case. With that thought in mind someone might insist that we can never be sure that what we take to be evil lacks a compensating and justifying good. And such a person may well be right. So let us agree that viewed against the background of some scheme of things unknown to us at present, my thumb pain might somehow be morally justified on God's part. It still remains that so far as we can see (or as far as I can see), it appears not to be.[31] Suppose that someone says that the world was made in six twenty-four-hour days and that what people take to show otherwise (e.g. fossils) does not do so since, for all we know, this 'evidence' should be interpreted differently. We protest: 'But the evidence seems to support a conclusion at odds with the six-day-creation thesis.' The reply comes back: 'But there may be truths to which we have no access.' In a sense, it is hard to argue with that reply. *Of course*, and not just when we are thinking about theological matters, there may be truths to which we lack access, truths which, if we knew about them, would lead us to conclude that what seems to us to be so is not so. But it is surely not reasonable to work on that assumption if we do, indeed, seem to have good reason to believe that something or other is the case. And, so I am suggesting, we do have good reason to think that there are evils which result in no good or do not essentially contribute to some good outcome. And this fact is important if what we are interested in is the moral exoneration of God (or even the possibility of a moral exoneration of him). If there is a morally justifiable God, then perhaps it is the case that what we take to be evil leading to no good is nothing of the kind. Yet if there is no morally justifiable God, what seems to us to be evil leading to no good is what we might very well expect to find in the world in which we live. In this sense it counts against a morally justifiable God.[32]

Even if you reject that line of thinking, however, there is a second problem with the 'We Can't See All the Picture' position: it embraces an arguably objectionable consequentialism that tries to trump evil by focusing attention away from victims of suffering. In terms of the 'We Can't See All the Picture' Argument, the rape of a child, for example, may be something morally permitted by God because of various goods (though we might not be able to see how). Yet why should we countenance the rape of a child while acknowledging good which it allows or brings about? You might say that, though the benefits to *others* involved in the occurrence or permission of something that happens to someone might not justify its taking place, there can be benefits to *the victim* which do (morally) justify it. And this seems to be true. It is not good to have one's arm punctured by a needle, yet if this is done as an inoculation, the patient benefits from it. It is not good for a child to be painfully knocked across a room, though we shall think differently of this scenario if we come to realize that the child's parents pushed it to stop a pan of boiling fat from falling on it. I am sure that you can think up lots of comparable examples. Yet victims do not always thrive as a result of what happens to them. They sometimes perish painfully. They are finished off by the evil that afflicts them, and, though this evil might allow for certain goods or prevent certain evils, it still remains evil with an uncompensated victim. As I shall note in a moment, some authors would deny this by raising the possibility of post-mortem life for human beings – a life in which people can come to accept how their sufferings make some kind of sense. Even if we are attracted to this line of thinking, however, there remain instances of non-human suffering, suffering which, so far as I know, nobody seriously takes to be compensated for in a post-mortem life of the sufferers in question (cats, for example).

Being as happy as we could be

Many people, however, think that God (if he exists) would want to maximize human happiness and that God is bad or non-existent since he does not do so. In response to this line of thinking others have challenged the view that it is always morally good to maximize happiness. Here we come to the thesis numbered (5) at the start of this chapter, and I have to say that I take (5) to be a plausible thesis.

Someone who brings out its worth well is George N. Schlesinger.[33] He asks us to consider two scenarios. In the first we can keep a retarded child happy for life by not treating it in a way that will make it like other children who, like most of us, grow up to endure various miseries. In the second, we can, without their consent, plug people into a machine that will physically support them for the rest of their natural lives while also causing them to have very pleasurable experiences for as long as they are plugged into the machine. Should we morally blame people for treating the retarded child? Should we morally blame them for refusing to plug people into the happiness machine? Schlesinger (rightly, I think) notes that most people would reply 'No' to both questions. If that is the right response, however, it is wrong to suppose that being moral automatically means always maximizing happiness. As Schlesinger goes on to observe, someone might blame God morally for not giving us more opportunities for enjoyment than we have – for not, for example, giving us more senses by which to enjoy the presence of things around us. Yet, as Schlesinger also says, there seem to be no limits to what can be added to people by way of what we might call 'enjoyment-achieving mechanisms':

> One can easily conceive a super-Socrates who has a much higher intelligence and many more than five senses through which to enjoy the world, and who stands to Socrates as the latter stands to the pig. And there is the possibility of a super-super Socrates, and so on *ad infinitum*.[34]

If we condemn God for not producing a super-Socrates, what could he have produced that we can condemn him for not producing? On the assumption that God can only bring about what is logically possible, and on the supposition that there is no limit when it comes to possible enjoyment-achieving mechanisms, the answer is surely 'Nothing'. In that case, however, we have no special reason for condemning God morally for setting things up as they actually exist now. Suppose someone says that there is a universal ethical principle according to which, everything being equal, one should increase the degree of desirability of the state of someone by as much as possible. Agreeing with this person, we may conclude that God is to blame for not acting on it. Schlesinger's point, however, is that this principle is not something that God could act on, since it is demanding what is not logically possible. Or, in his words:

> No matter to what degree of desirability [of state] is increased, it is always logically possible to increase it further. A mortal's possibilities are physically limited, and hence, in his case there is a natural limit to the principle; but there is no limit to what God can do. It is therefore logically impossible for Him to fulfil the ethical principle . . . Just as it is logically impossible to name the highest integer, it is impossible to grant a creature a degree of desirability of state higher than which is inconceivable; thus it is logically impossible for God to fulfil what is required by the universal ethical principle, and therefore He cannot fulfil it, and so is not obliged to fulfil it.[35]

So there is a moral principle to which God cannot conform and with respect to which he cannot, therefore, be blamed. Schlesinger, however, takes this fact to mean that 'the problem of evil could be said to have vanished'.[36] And here I part company with him. For even if we accept his basic argument, there is plenty to blame God for if we are assuming that God is a moral agent. Moral agents do not, for example, permit the rape of children to occur. In so far as they can, they prevent this. God, however, clearly does not do so. Schlesinger might say that this fact does nothing to prove God to be badly behaved given God's omnipotence and the impossible demand that he should create a world in which things enjoy a state of being than which no greater can be conceived for them. Once again, however, moral agents do not, for example, permit the rape of children to occur, while God clearly does. Champions of means–ends theodicy such as Richard Swinburne will immediately say that God does so for morally justified reasons – e.g. so as to allow people to be virtuous, so as to preserve a world in which people have freedom of choice, and so on.[37] As I have argued, however, this line of thinking (especially given its often non-victim-oriented consequentialist character) does not count as a moral justification of God. It portrays him as one who is happy to countenance suffering in a way that few of us would. God may not be able to give us a certain level of happiness, but he can surely be morally condemned for planning what most of us would deem to be unjustifiable if planned by any human person. Defenders of the 'We Can't See All the Picture' Argument will have a response to this conclusion. I have already said, however, how I take that argument to fall short. Defenders of the Free Will Defence will also have a response to my conclusion here. I have already explained, however, how I take that defence to fall short.

The best possible world

Some, however, have suggested that our world is the best possible one. If that is true, then we should hardly raise our moral eyebrows at God for producing it (or permitting it). But is our world the best possible one? Common sense would seem to suggest that it is not. Consider once again the accident with my thumb. Would not the world have been just a little better if I had not trapped it in the door? If so, then ours is not the best possible world. For we can conceive of a world in which I avoided the pain I suffered when my thumb got whacked.

Or can we? To speak of conceiving of worlds is surely to engage in pretty odd talk. I can form an idea of what my bedroom would look like if my bed were removed from it. But what would I be trying to think of if I tried to think of a *world* in which my bed was not in my bedroom? As far as I can see, I would be trying to think of a non-existent world. For my bed *is* in my bedroom. And there *is* no world in which it is not. So there is literally nothing to think of when it comes to focusing on a world in which my bed is not in my bedroom. In this sense, there just is no such world, in which case it cannot be compared well or favourably with the real world. We can note particular ways in which the history of the real world might go, and we might intelligibly say that such and such an outcome would be better than another. But we would not be contrasting different worlds. We would be noting how the one real world might become better or worse.

Yet this does not mean that there is no sense to be made of the claim that I can conceive of a world in which I avoided the pain I suffered when my thumb got whacked. I know what it is like not to have a painful thumb. Or, if you do not like that way of putting it, I know what it is for it to be true that I suffer no pain in my thumb. So I can grasp how things are (or have been) without my suffering thumb. In this sense I can surely think of the actual world as being without my wounded thumb. In this sense I *can* conceive of a world in which I avoided the pain I suffered when my thumb got whacked. We actually do this kind of thing all the time – whenever we regret actions we have performed, for instance, or whenever we lament the fact that someone died because of a sickness they might have been spared had they not been in a certain place or not engaged in certain activities. It does not seem terribly hard to think of the actual world as containing less badness than it does (or did).

Some philosophers would say that this line of thinking just misses the point being made by the claim that our world is the best possible world. For, so they would note, to claim that ours is the best world possible is to argue about what *has* to be the case regardless of how we might be able to conceive of things being the case. Here they might go on to cite G. W. Leibniz (1646–1716) – probably the originator of the 'This is the best possible world' position, and certainly its most famous exponent. So perhaps I should now say something about Leibniz's defence of this position.

You can find it presented in his *Theodicy* (1710).[38] Here the argument runs as follows:

(1) God is omnipotent, omniscient and good.
(2) When choosing to create, God is presented with an infinity of possible worlds, only one of which he can bring into being.
(3) God does nothing without a sufficient reason.
(4) It is God's goodness that settles his choice when it comes to which possible world to create.
(5) Being perfectly good, God will only create the best possible world.
(6) If there is no best possible world, God would not create at all.
(7) But God has created.
(8) So there is a best possible world and our world is that world.[39]

An initial problem with this argument is that it does nothing to defend theism against people who think that evil casts doubt on God's existence. For it starts from the assumption that God exists. A defender of Leibniz might say, however, that his argument does well enough as a response to someone claiming that evil shows that there *could not* be a God. If the argument works, so one might suggest, then at least it shows us how evil in the world might be thought not to exclude the logical possibility of God's existence. And that, I think, is true. If the premises of Leibniz's argument are possibly true, and if the argument is not invalid, then it shows why we might be less than confident in concluding that, given evil, there could not possibly be a God. In recent years Alvin Plantinga has distinguished between a 'theodicy' and a 'defence'. If I understand him correctly, he takes a theodicy to be an attempt to explain just how God and evil fit together – as John Milton (1608–1674) said he was doing in *Paradise Lost* (1667), which aims 'to justify the ways of God to men'. Yet, says Plantinga, one might defend theists from the charge that they subscribe to inconsistent beliefs by noting possibilities which should prevent us from concluding that there actually is inconsistency in what theists believe.[40] Plantinga's point seems to be reasonable considered in the abstract, and one might therefore invoke it with an eye on Leibniz's best-possible-world argument.[41]

That argument, however, is committed to the view that 'the best possible world' is an expression designating something that is genuinely possible. Yet why should we suppose that it does so? There can be no greatest prime number, so why suppose that there can be a best possible world? After all, given any world one might think that one can conceive of, one can always think of one that contains an additional good member (an additional healthy cat, for instance). You might say that if there were just one more healthy cat in our world, then our world would be worse than some other conceivable world. But why on earth would one think this claim to be plausible? Leibniz might say 'Because of my argument'. But we can readily conceive of simple ways in which our world could be better than it is, ones which count as powerful rebuttals to Leibniz.

Aquinas makes this point (though not, of course, with reference to Leibniz). In the *Summa Theologiae* he asks whether God could make things better than he does. He concedes that there is a sense in which God cannot do this – that he cannot, for example, make something better than it is *essentially*. In Aquinas's view, goodness has a lot to do with nature. In his view, badness arises as things with particular natures flounder and suffer given what they naturally are. So he thinks that God cannot, for example, make a human being to be better than what it is by nature. The reason? Because this would mean not making a human being. Or, as Aquinas puts it: 'It is analogous to how God cannot make 4 to be more than 4, for then it would not be 4 but another number.'[42] God can make a human being, thinks Aquinas, but he cannot make one who is essentially better than what humans are essentially (an uncreated and uncreateable human being, for example). But Aquinas does not take this conclusion to entail that God cannot make things to be better than they are. For, he notes, some things are genuinely improvable. Also, he argues, God can make better things than there actually are – beings of a more exalted standing than people, for example. He writes:

> God cannot make something better than it is essentially, though he can make something that is better than it . . . Things can also have goodness which goes beyond their essence or nature – as a human being can come to be virtuous and wise. God can make things better than they are by giving them goodness like this. And to speak without reservation, God can make something better than anything he has made.[43]

I see no good reason to disagree with Aquinas here. One might reply that the smallest change in the way things are or will be could result in a world which is overall worse than the present one. But this view seems pretty hard to swallow. Nor does it seem to cohere with the notion of divine omnipotence. If ours is the best possible world, then (assuming that omnipotence does not extend to bringing about what is not logically possible) even omnipotence cannot produce a better one. If, however, we take 'God is omnipotent' to mean that God can make to be anything intrinsically able to be, then it seems to follow that ours is not the best possible world. A world with just one more saint (or even one more cat) would surely be better than our world (since it would contain a bit more that is good). And there could surely be just one more saint (or cat) in our world. You might reply that what God can bring about depends on what free creatures decide to do. You might then say that there is (or might be) no possible world in which free creatures do any better than they do in this one.[44] But that response presumes that the free choices of creatures are not and cannot be caused by God – a position I have already rejected.

The suffering God

Finally, so far as the present chapter goes, I come to the suggestion that evil provides no case for God to answer since he is also its victim – a suggestion to which, in Chapter 1, I linked the names of Jon Sobrino and Jürgen Moltmann. By now, however, you will realize why I think that this is a suggestion that ought to be rejected. I do so because I take it to confuse the distinction between creature and Creator. I reject it because I take it to be idolatrous. If what I have previously argued (in Chapters 2 and 3) is correct, there can be no question of God literally suffering. For God to suffer would be for him to be on the receiving end of the operation of something other than himself, and he can never be this if he is the Creator, the reason why there is something rather than nothing.[45]

Yet why do people like Moltmann and Sobrino take the line that they do? They certainly do not do so because they think that they have hit on a set of philosophical arguments showing that there is, in fact, a God who undergoes suffering (they appear not to be very interested in philosophical arguments). They do so for other reasons. To be more precise, they do so because they think that a suffering God is more admirable than one who does not suffer or who is incapable of suffering. They also do so (or, at least, Sobrino does so) because they think that God cannot be thought of as loving if he does not suffer and is not, therefore, a victim of evil. Yet these are not good reasons for concluding that God undergoes suffering or that it is desirable that he should do so.

To start with, why is a suffering X more admirable than an X which undergoes no suffering at all? Here you might wish to return to the principle 'Better Socrates dissatisfied than a pig satisfied'. You might say that there can be suffering individuals who are far more admirable than non-suffering ones. And I would not wish to quarrel with you here. I think that we should value a dissatisfied Socrates more than we should value a happy pig. Or again, I think that we should value someone dying in pain more than we should value a turnip or a desk-lamp. Yet this does not mean that suffering, as such, is something to be valued. Unless we are sadists, we do not, when we suffer, want others to do so as well. We want them to understand what is happening to us, and we want them, if possible, to do something about it. And if they end up suffering themselves, we are grieved. Suffering is a limitation, a restriction on one's freedom. There is therefore no reason for thinking better of God if he undergoes suffering and is not immune to it. *We* may be in the soup, so to speak; but we can recognize this as a mark of our impotence or finitude. It seems odd to suppose that a God who is also in the soup would be better than one who is not. Moltmann and Sobrino lay stress on God's suffering to indicate how wonderful he is. If what they say is true, however, God would seem to be something vulnerable and passive.

Then again, why should 'X loves' be thought to entail 'X suffers'? One may certainly show one's love by being prepared to suffer. Yet this does not mean that 'loving' and 'suffering' are synonymous. In our world, love often leads to suffering on the part of those who love. But they love *before* they suffer; they do not love *because* they suffer (even if they love *as* they suffer). Love and limitation do not have to go together. Sharing in actual pain is neither necessary nor sufficient for compassion. To love is surely to be drawn to what one takes to be good or desirable. So X can be said to love in so far as it wills what is good or desirable. X can do this, however, without being a victim of suffering, and God can be said to love if he wills what is good or desirable. Assuming that there are good and desirable things willed by God, we have sufficient reason to say that God loves (more on this later). We do not need to hold that God can only be said to love on the supposition that he suffers. We might, on the contrary, hold that God can only be truly thought of as unlimitedly loving on the supposition that he does not suffer. For suffering restricts agents and curbs their ability to bring about good.

It has been said that to deny that God suffers is to think of him as inert or indifferent or uninvolved with our world. Yet this is not so. To deny that X is F (e.g. able to suffer) is not the same as saying that X is G (e.g. inert or indifferent or uninvolved). To say, for example, that someone is not French is not say that he or she is Australian or Brazilian or Welsh. It is simply to say that there is something that the person in question is not. In the same way, there is no reason to suppose that anything positive is being said about God if it is said (as I argue it needs to be) that God is not capable of suffering. It is just bad logic to suppose that 'God does not suffer' entails 'God is inert, indifferent, or uninvolved'. 'God does not suffer' tells us what God is not, not what God is. Statements saying what something is not sometimes have positive implications to which we ought to subscribe. If a husband is told that the child his wife has successfully given birth to is not a boy, he might reasonably conclude that he has a daughter. With this thought in mind one might suggest that 'God does not suffer' implies that God is inert, indifferent, or uninvolved. Given what I have argued earlier, however, 'God does not suffer' does not imply this. If God is the Creator of all things, then he acts in all things. So he is not inert. If God wills things to exist, he can hardly be said to be indifferent or uninvolved when it comes to them. Indeed, if the account of God the Creator which I have given is correct, then God is more intimately involved with all creatures than any creature can be with another. Or, as Herbert McCabe observes: 'It makes perfect sense to say both that it is not in the nature of God to suffer and also that it is not in the nature of God to lack the most intimate possible involvement with the sufferings of his creatures.'[46] We can only be present to the sufferings of others as observers. We are not within them. My line of reasoning in this book, however, leads to the conclusion that God is no observer of us as we suffer. He is in us as making us to be. So he is with us in our suffering as nothing else is. He cannot, however, be this if he is also a victim of suffering.

Yet if God is creatively present in our suffering, should we not conclude that he causes this and is therefore bad? And if we agree that God causes the free actions of people, should we not conclude that God is the source of the evil that people do? I have been arguing that (apart from God) there is nothing real that is not God's doing. Yet there does seem to be an awful lot of badness around. Should we not therefore think of God as a cause of evil and therefore as bad? This is the question I aim to discuss in the next chapter.

Notes

1. For some of these positions I am able to cite authors who defend them. Others, however, are less easy to attach names to since they come (to me at least) in the form of ideas often floated, though with no quotable pro-

tagonists. Since (going by what people tell me) they are ideas which have weighed heavily with some individuals (maybe you), they are, I think, therefore worth discussing.

2. St Augustine sometimes offers aesthetic analogies when talking about evil, though he does not do so in order to offer a moral justification of God. See, for example, *Enchiridion*, III, 2. Is the line of thinking I am talking about now another example of a means and ends defence of God? I suppose that it might be taken to be so (along the lines: we could not have the good world we have if it were not for the presence of evil). As I understand it, however, the reasoning I am now concerned with chiefly wishes us to accept that, means and ends aside, the evil in the world contributes to its goodness and is, therefore, not something for which to blame God.

3. I recognize that this is a controversial thesis. I shall return to it in more detail later. For now I prefer to make a few points in a brief way.

4. P. T. Geach, *Logic Matters* (Basil Blackwell: Oxford, 1972), p. 305.

5. Romans 8:18.

6. I might say that if John says 'X is good' he means to say that he approves of X. And (on the supposition that John is not lying) I would surely be right to say this, since 'good' is a term of commendation and since (presumably) to commend is to express approval. But if John also intends to say that X is good in itself and regardless of whether or not he approves of it, he is committed to a position which is not compatible with the view that 'X is good' *only* means that X is approved of by someone.

7. P. T. Geach, 'Good and Evil', in Philippa Foot (ed.), *Theories of Ethics* (Oxford University Press: Oxford, 1967), p. 64. Geach's paper originally appeared in *Analysis* 17 (1956).

8. Ibid.

9. Herbert McCabe, *God Matters* (Geoffrey Chapman: London, 1987), p. 29.

10. Ibid.

11. He says: 'Mes frères, vous êtes dans le malheur, mes frères, vous l'avez mérité' ('Calamity has come upon you, my brethren and, my brethren, you deserved it'): Albert Camus, *La Peste* (Editions Gallimard: Paris, 1947), p. 110.

12. Those who say that it should be are arguing that one who commits an offence must pay something back which equals the badness of the offence – the paying back here being considered as a matter of pain to the offender.

13. Some have argued that punishment (e.g. being sent to jail) is justifiable on the assumption that it helps to make the punished offender better (repentant, better motivated, etc.). Others have argued that it is justifiable if it encourages others not to offend or makes them afraid to do so. Some, of course, have offered positions that embrace both of these conclusions.

14. Of course, if what I am asking the judge to force you to give me is something that might pose a threat to me or to others, things would be different.

15. I am assuming here that, for example, I can suffer more pain than my cat since I am something that can suffer in ways that my cat cannot. Like my cat, I can be physically damaged. Unlike my cat, however, I can mourn the loss of loved ones and be desolate because the one I love has rejected me.

16. As I noted in the Introduction, it has been said that non-human animals really do not experience pain, fear, anxiety, frustration and the like. Such a conclusion depends on the assumption that bodily behaviour does not give us grounds for ascribing pain, fear, anxiety, frustration, and the like to individual things. I cannot argue the case here, but someone who accepts this assumption might benefit hugely from, for example, the way in which Wittgenstein talks about how we come to ascribe things like pain to people. See Ludwig Wittgenstein, *Philosophical Investigations* (Basil Blackwell: Oxford, 1968), §§350ff. For a painless introduction to Wittgenstein on this matter see P. M. S. Hacker, *Wittgenstein* (Phoenix: London, 1997), pp. 39ff. As I said in the previous note, however, I do not wish to deny that there is suffering attributable to people which is not attributable to other animals.

17. I refrain from commenting on whether or not homosexual activity should be deemed 'sinful'. For an extended discussion of this question see Gareth Moore, *A Question of Truth: Christianity and Homosexuality* (Continuum: London and New York, 2003). Moore seems to me to talk a lot of sense, but the present book is not the place for me to get involved in the debate to which his book is a contribution.

18. Proverbs 3:33.

19. Job 9:21–23. 'He' here is, of course, God.

20. Jeremiah 12:1b.

21. Luke 13:2–3a. In the wake of the famous Lisbon earthquake (1755) Voltaire (1694–1778) made a similar comment. Obviously expecting the answer 'No', he asked whether God had selected the least virtuous of the Portuguese to die in the Lisbon disaster.

22. John 9:3.

23. Romans 5:12–14a.

24. I quote from Norman P. Tanner (ed.), *Decrees of the Ecumenical Councils*, vol. 2 (Sheed and Ward: London and Georgetown University Press: Washington, DC, 1990), p. 666.

25. According to Genesis Eve committed the first sin; Adam then did what she had done (Genesis 3:6).

26. In *Absolute Value* (George Allen and Unwin: London, 1970) Illtyd Trethowan refers to the view that 'the fall is not an historical event because Adam and Eve are not historical characters' (p. 148). As he goes on to say, 'it is a sufficient answer that sin must have started sometime'.

27. For a reasonable discussion of it see Christopher Kirwan, *Augustine* (Routledge: London and New York, 1989), ch. 7.

28. This is very much the line William Alston takes in 'The Inductive Argument from Evil', in Daniel Howard-Snyder (ed.), *The Evidential*

Argument from Evil (Indiana University Press: Bloomington, Ind. and Indianapolis, 1996), from which I quoted in Ch. 1.

29. Alvin Plantinga argues along these lines in 'Epistemic Probability and Evil', reprinted in Daniel Howard-Snyder (ed.), *The Evidential Argument from Evil* (Indiana University Press: Bloomington and Indianapolis, 1996).

30. I suppose you could say that it provided me with an example to use in the present chapter. If that example is a good coming out of evil, however, then perhaps you should agree with the point I am presently making.

31. In response to some of his critics, William Rowe makes this point in 'The Evidential Argument from Evil: A Second Look', in Howard-Snyder (ed.), *The Evidential Argument from Evil*.

32. If I understand him correctly, David O'Connor seems to be arguing along these lines in *God and Inscrutable Evil* (Rowan and Littlefield: Lanham, Md and Oxford, 1998), ch. 10.

33. George N. Schlesinger, *New Perspectives on Old-Time Religion* (Clarendon Press: Oxford, 1998), ch. 2.

34. Ibid., p. 55. Here, of course, Schlesinger has in mind the famous, and usually accepted, dictum, 'Better Socrates dissatisfied than a pig satisfied'.

35. Ibid. As he continues, Schlesinger replies to various published criticisms of this line of thinking. It seems to me that his replies meet the objections to which they are directed.

36. Ibid.

37. Schlesinger also defends this general position; see ibid., pp. 63–66.

38. See G. W. Leibniz, *Theodicy*, ed. W. Stark (Yale University Press: New Haven, 1952), part 1, 9ff., pp. 128f.

39. Leibniz's claim that ours is the best possible world is remorselessly satirized by Voltaire in *Candide* (1759). Voltaire's attack on Leibniz seems unfair, however. It supposes that Leibniz is refuted by what we observe to take place in the world. Yet Leibniz's argument is clearly not an empirical one. Leibniz also thought it unaffected by the fact that all sorts of horrors and atrocities take place. Given that his argument is not an empirical one, I believe he was right to think this.

40. See Alvin Plantinga, *The Nature of Necessity* (Clarendon Press: Oxford, 1974), ch. 9. A similar distinction is invoked by Peter van Inwagen in 'The Argument from Particular Horrendous Evils', *American Catholic Philosophical Quarterly* 74 (2000), pp. 66f.

41. There are distinct similarities between what Leibniz and Plantinga have to say about God and evil. Both make considerable use of the notion of possible worlds. Both argue in a somewhat *a priori* fashion. Both end up saying that it cannot be shown that our world is worse than any other God could have made.

42. Thomas Aquinas, *Summa Theologiae*, Ia.25.6 (my translation).

43. Ibid.

44. Alvin Plantinga argues along these lines. See *The Nature of Necessity*, ch. 9.
45. If someone claims that evil shows that there cannot be a God or that there probably is no God, then to say that God suffers deals with that claim effectively. It is obviously true that evil tells us nothing about God's certain or probable non-existence if God is a victim of evil. My point, of course, is that we have reason to deny that God is such a victim.
46. McCabe, *God Matters*, p. 46.

Seven

Evil, Causation and God

If God is the creative cause of everything other than himself, then does it not follow that he is the cause of evil? Does it also not follow that God wills evil as an end? If the right answer to these questions is 'Yes', then it would seem that theists have no business calling God good. For even if we are willing to agree that God's goodness cannot be that of a good moral agent acting dutifully or virtuously, it seems hard to see how the word 'good' could intelligibly be applied to an agent who directly wills evil as a goal in its own right. I shall be turning to the question 'What can we mean when calling God "good"?' in the next chapter. For now, though, I take it for granted (am simply prepared to accept) that God cannot be thought of as good if he deliberately causes evil as an end in itself – if, so to speak, he chooses to bring about evil for its own sake. The question, therefore, is: does he? In this chapter I shall be arguing that he does not.

Kinds of evil

As I have noted, philosophers have tended to distinguish between two kinds of evil. One involves pain and suffering inflicted on things by other things. The other consists in morally wrong behaviour. I am happy to accept this distinction, though a few initial points need to be made concerning it.

Sometimes people talk as though pain and suffering which is not the result of morally bad choices is an entirely 'natural' affair – something that can in no way be traced to human choices. Yet that is not entirely true. If I lie dying in an earthquake zone, then, of course, I am very much a victim of nature. I am being affected by what I cannot control. On the other hand, however, we know something about where earthquakes are likely to strike and can choose to avoid such places. So the suffering of someone in an earthquake need not be unrelated to human choices. You might rightly reply, of course, that some people have no choice when it comes to where they live. Yet this does not mean that choices (or a refusal to make certain choices) have not led them to being stuck in the situations in which they find themselves. People forced to live where earthquakes threaten are usually there because they cannot afford to be somewhere else – a situation which is not a natural one, unlike, say, being able to catch a cold. The financial situation of people is never unconnected with choices that they or (more usually) other people have made (or refused to make).

Then again, consider those who are suffering from lung cancer or heart disease because of their cigarette consumption. It would be ludicrous to deny that their situation lacks 'natural' causes. They are afflicted by physiological processes over which they have no direct control. Nor do they desire these processes to occur. However, if their illness is the result of their cigarette consumption, and assuming that they were previously free to smoke or not to smoke, then it is not unconnected with human decision-making. And, I suspect, human suffering is so connected when it comes to many cases of evil where one's first thought is *exclusively* to blame natural causes. I might endure agony as my aircraft plunges to the ground. But maybe I did not have to walk on the plane in the first place ('He died because he chose to fly' is a causal statement). I might become disabled in my bedroom because of carbon monoxide poisoning. But I might have been warned to install a carbon monoxide alarm and decided not to bother ('He suffered because he chose to ignore good advice' is a causal statement). I might contract AIDS from sleeping with someone who is HIV-positive. It is a virus that is affecting me, but maybe I could have chosen to take more care when it comes to my sex life ('He got sick because he did not take precautions' is a causal statement). I am not, of course, saying that, for example, those who perish in plane crashes, or those affected by chemical poisoning or AIDS, 'have only themselves to blame'. I am merely drawing attention to the fact that it is none too easy to draw a sharp line between evil that is due to natural causes and evil that is due (at least partly) to choices that people make or refuse to make.[1]

Another point that needs to be noted when it comes to the distinction between the kinds of evil mentioned above concerns the evil involved in moral evil – the point being that moral evil has nothing to do with the consequences of people's actions. In listening to people talk, the impression I have formed is that they often think otherwise. For many of them, someone's moral standing is to be determined with reference to the good or bad effects of what they choose to do. It seems to me, however, that '____ is morally bad' tells us something about an individual, not the consequences which that individual manages to effect. One might instinctively feel that Hitler's moral badness consists in the fact that he artfully accomplished acts of genocide. My view, however, is that it did not consist in this at all.

Suppose that I say that X is a bad telephone. In that case, I am telling you something about X – that it does not meet agreed expectations when it comes to what a telephone should be. I am not telling you anything about what X has effected (e.g. giving Smokey concussion because I knocked the telephone off my desk and onto his head). I am telling you that it falls short considered as the kind of thing that it is, and, as I have said, noting that something is bad seems always to be drawing attention to this kind of failure. As we generally use the word 'bad' a bad X is one that somehow fails to function well considered as what it is.

So now consider a bad person. It may seem odd to suggest that people, as people, have a function. It may seem natural to ask 'What are telephones for?' or 'What are trains for?' It is not, perhaps, in the same sense natural to ask what people are for.[2] Yet we do distinguish between morally good and bad people. So what are we up to when doing so? I take it that we are trying to describe people, trying to say what they actually are. Yet the consequences of their actions can hardly be part of what they actually are. What they actually are might enable them to effect certain changes in the world. These changes, however, are distinct from them. So if people are bad, that is not because they have managed to effect certain changes in the world. It is because of what they desire (their desires being very much part of what they are).

Suppose that you go for a walk down a country lane in winter with a strong wind blowing. The wind causes a branch of a tree to break. The branch crashes onto you and you end up dead.

Again, suppose that you go for a walk down a country lane in winter with a strong wind blowing. This time, however, I am lurking with a branch, I crash it onto you, and you end up dead.

When it comes to consequences, we have identical scenarios here: you dead by virtue of a branch hitting you. Morally speaking, however, we have totally different situations. In one, there is no moral evil. In the other, there is. And the difference lies in the fact that one scenario is intended by someone. It is intention to do wrong (or intention to refuse to aim for some good for which one should strive) that constitutes moral badness or evil. In this sense, moral badness lies only in individual agents and not in the effects of their actions. Of course, we may deem Y to be a worse person than Z because Y tried to bring about more badness than Z. But Y's badness is still not constituted by what Y actually brought about. After all, my attempts to murder thousands of people (in an act of terrorism, say) may be thwarted (e.g. by security guards), yet this does not render me any better than I would be had my efforts succeeded. Bad luck does not exonerate. By the same token, of course, it does not make for guilt. I might have the misfortune to hurt others unintentionally (their misfortune also), but it does not therefore automatically follow that I am morally to be censured. You might say that I can be to blame for not taking steps which would prevent me unwittingly contributing to the amount of evil in the world. And that might be so. Yet it surely does not have to be so. Without knowing about it, for instance, I might contract an infectious disease which I pass on to other people while doing what is normally expected of me in day-to-day life.

With all that said, however, I am happy to distinguish between naturally occurring evil and moral evil – or, as I prefer to call them, 'evil suffered' and 'evil done'.[3] I take *evil suffered* to be evil that afflicts individuals as non-rational things in the world eat away at them in various ways – badness that *happens to* people or to other animals (or even to things other than animals).[4] I take *evil done* to consist in freely conceiving to act badly and/or actually doing so.[5] This I take to be *self-inflicted* evil – badness that consists in moral failure. With respect to these two kinds of evil, my question now is 'What is God's causal relationship to them?'

Evil suffered

With respect to evil suffered, let me first pick up on what I argued in the last chapter – that badness is essentially negative, a lack of what ought to be present or an absence of what is desirable for something or other.

Evil suffered is real enough in the sense that people and other things are certainly afflicted by viruses, by cars that run over them, by knives that cut them, by hurricanes that wreck their homes, by floods that wash them away, and so on. But it does not make sense to say that evil is one of the things that exist. Many modern logicians tell us that to say that something exists is to say that a first-level predicable truly applies to something or other – that, for example, 'Cats exist' is true if '____ is a cat' is truly affirmable of some object or individual.[6] Yet 'badness' is not the name of any object or individual. So, going by the analysis just noted, it cannot be said to exist.

To be sure, we often make existence statements without talking about particular objects or individuals. We say, for example, that cats exist or that dinosaurs do not (as opposed to 'Smokey exists' or 'Dino does not' – these being statements about specific things). According to the above analysis, however, these statements ultimately take us back to talk about particular objects or individuals. Hence, 'Cats exist' turns out to mean 'Something or other is a cat', that '____ is a cat' is truly affirmable of something.

Such an analysis, however, does not allow us to single out badness as an object or individual, since badness is not an object or individual. It warrants us in saying that 'Badness exists' is true if something or other is bad. It does not license the conclusion that there is something (a particular individual or even a particular property) called badness, something that is thus and so. And even if we are not entirely happy with the analysis of existential claims to which I have just referred, we ought surely to be able to see that judging something to be bad is, quite generally, to declare that something desirable is missing. For how do we defend our claim that something or other is bad? We do so, and we *always* do so, by noting how it is lacking in some respect. We are lamenting an absence of being, the fact that what could and should be there is not there.

When it comes to evil suffered, therefore, we are dealing with what, though no illusion, does not, in a serious sense, exist. The evil in evil suffered is not an existent *entity*. It is no identifiable *substance* or *positive quality*. Evil suffered occurs as existing things fail to be as good as they could be. In that case, however, I immediately conclude that the evil in evil suffered cannot be caused by God. For God, as I have argued, is the cause of the being of all that is real apart from himself, and the evil in evil suffered is not something with being, not something actual, and, therefore, not something created by him. It cannot be thought of as a creature that God creates. Considered as amounting to the gap between what is there and what should be but is not, it is neither createable nor created. Considered as such, it cannot be attributed to God as an agent-cause, whose causality primarily extends to making things to be.

There are holes in walls, but holes have no independent existence. There are holes in walls only because there are walls with something missing. There are blind people. But blindness has no independent existence. There are blind people only because there are people who cannot see. In a similar way, evil suffered has no independent existence. It 'is there' only in the sense that something is missing. But what is *not there* cannot be thought of as made to be by the source of the being of things. It cannot be thought to be made to be by God. Following Aristotle, Aquinas distinguishes between the use of 'is' in sentences like 'John is blind' and 'John is' (i.e. exists). He takes the first use to signify that a predicate (i.e. '____ is blind') can be attached to the name 'John' so as to result in a true statement. He takes the second use to signify that 'John' is a genuine name (i.e. a word which labels something in the real world, something which has what Aquinas calls *esse*, or actual existence).[7] In the light of these considerations, Aquinas maintains that, since God is the source of there being what has *esse* (being/existence), God cannot be thought of as causing evil to be. For evil is not anything actual (whether a substance or a property). It is what we may talk of things as 'being' only in the sense that we may speak of people as 'being blind'. Evil is the unreality we acknowledge when we call things bad, sick, maimed, defective, thwarted, and so on. And here, so I suggest, Aquinas is right. Evil, including evil suffered, cannot intelligibly be thought of as something which God has made to be.

Yet evil suffered seems to be all around us. So just what account can we give of it with an eye on God's causality? My reply to this question is to say that evil suffered can only reasonably be regarded as 'due' to God because of goodness that he is producing. My claim is that when it comes to evil suffered all we have is the creative activity of God bringing about what is good – that God brings about everything that is good and does not directly bring about anything we might think of as evil suffered.

A point to bear in mind here is that though badness consists of defect or absence, it is still parasitic on goodness. You can, I think, have goodness without badness.[8] Badness, however, depends on there being goodness to start with. As I have suggested, to call something bad is to complain that it does not match up to expectations in some way. Yet something has to succeed in being a thing of a certain kind if it is to be deemed to be a bad example of its kind. I may assert that Mary is a bad singer, but my assertion makes no sense if Mary is not a singer at all. If I hand you a carrot and complain that it is a bad singer, you will make nothing of what I am saying. There cannot be bad singers unless there are singers to start with. So even the worst singer has to be good to some extent – has to have made it into the realm of singers. Someone who has not done this is not even a singer and cannot, therefore, be a bad one. A bad X has to succeed in being an X. In this sense, badness is parasitic on goodness.

Parasitic considered as what? Certainly not as a substance or positive quality, attribute or property inhering in anything. If what I have argued is correct, badness is parasitic on goodness only in the sense that there is no badness unless there is a gap between what something actually is (what something succeeds in being) and what it ought or needs to be but is not. There is badness because there are things which are not as good as they ought or need to be considered as the kinds of things they are. It that case, however, it seems that badness is not something *produced*, whether by God or by anything else. Of course, any old agent can bring it about that something is bad (i.e. failing, faulty, thwarted, defective, lacking). I can do that just by sitting on Smokey, setting fire to my apartment, or poking myself in the eye. To bring it about that something is bad, however, cannot be to bring it about that something new (whether a substance or a positive attribute) comes to be in the world. For the badness of what is bad is not anything actually existing. It consists of what is not there in something that is there. To be sure, we can truly predicate badness of things. We can say, quite generally, that X, Y, or Z are bad, and we might be right to do so. Or we can be more specific and say 'X is a bad glass of wine' or 'Y is a person suffering from an ailment' or 'Z is a bad philosopher'. To speak in this way, however, is always to draw attention to what is lacking. To draw attention to badness is to complain that what we want to be there is not. As I have argued, though, it is also to draw attention to what is there and somehow succeeds in being what it is considered as what it is.

So my argument is that badness exists in so far as things are good to a certain extent but lacking in one or more respects. When it comes to evil suffered, therefore, I obviously have to conclude (given what I have maintained earlier in this book) that God is causally responsible for the goodness to be found in things. If we think of God as making the 'difference' between there being something and nothing, if we think of God as an agent-cause bringing it about that everything (whether an individual or a positive attribute) exists, then whatever is good is caused to be by God. For to be good is to succeed in being in some way. This thought, however, does not force us to conclude that God is an agent-cause who brings badness or evil to be. For badness or evil lack existence in the way that individuals and positive attributes do not. God may be the Creator of all things, but he cannot create badness or evil. He can only create things which succeed in being good to some extent while also failing.

God, therefore, is not causally responsible for the existence of evil or badness, for, *in the sense I have tried to explain,* evil or badness does not exist. From this it seems to follow that God does not will evil suffered as an end in itself. He does not and cannot will it to exist as a creature. Yet he does seem to will it somehow. For there are lots of examples of evil suffered. Cats get sat on by absent-minded philosophers. Zebras are mauled by tigers. People become sick. Tidal waves devastate communities made up of thousands of people. So where does God come into all of this? My answer is 'Only as making what is good'.

You will, of course, realize that I am not saying that it is, without qualification, good for there to be evil suffered. I am not, for example, endorsing the position of Voltaire's Pangloss in *Candide*. Confronted by various evils, Pangloss continues to insist that this is the best of all possible worlds. That, however, is not what I am saying.[9] Nor am I siding with those who argue that a good God would be sure to lay on a lot of evil suffered.[10] My point is that there is goodness, but only to a certain degree, that God makes all that is good to be, and that God cannot be accused of creating evil. My claim is that, when it comes to evil suffered, evil is not created by (caused by) God. For God to create is for him to make it to be that something actually exists. The evil in evil suffered, I am saying, does not actually exist. It is what we can refer to only because we can identify individuals or attributes which actually exist and note ways in which they are failing or lacking when it comes to being. The badness in a diseased cat is nothing real in the cat. It is what we grieve about as we note how an actual cat fails to thrive in some way. Of course it is true that this animal might be failing because of something positive in it – a key it has swallowed, for instance. What worries us about such objects in cats (or whatever) is, however, not that they are there but that they diminish those cats (or whatever) in which they exist. If growing an extra hair caused people to become sick, we would regard the presence of an extra hair as bad. We do not do that, since an increase in hairs does not eat away at our well-being. A hair, for us, is just one more appendage. It harms us in no way. By the same token, cancer growths would not worry us (except perhaps aesthetically) if they did no harm to things in which they arise. Cancer growths are not intrinsically bad. We think of them as bad because they render certain things (especially ourselves) less than we want them to be. We think of them as bad because they bring it about that various things (especially ourselves) are failing to be what we would like them to be.

One may still ask, however, what it is that God is bringing about as evil suffered occurs. Yet my answer, once again, is 'nothing but good'. For, so it seems to me, every example of evil suffered is either an *instance* of goodness or something that is only there *because of* goodness. As I have suggested, even victims of evil suffered have also to be things which somehow succeed in being good. I cannot be a human being with a toothache if I am not (do not succeed in being) a human being, and so on. Yet my being a victim of evil suffered is always naturally explicable in terms of the flourishing of something other than me. So we have evil suffered when we have something which is good to a certain degree while thwarted by what is also good to a certain degree. We have evil suffered only when we have goodness curtailed by goodness. Or, to put it another way, there is always concomitant good when it comes to evil suffered, for evil suffered only occurs as something thrives at the expense of something else. It may be bad for a lamb to be eaten by a lion, yet, as Herbert McCabe coyly observes, 'the lion is being fulfilled, indeed he is being filled, precisely by what damages the lamb and renders it defective'.[11]

Another way of making this point is to say that evil suffered is always, in principle, *scientifically explicable*. Confronted by evil suffered we seek to understand what it is that by being good in its way renders something bad. We do not throw up our hands and say 'Oh, there is no natural explanation for this'. We look for causes, for things which are doing well considered as what they are, things the flourishing of which accounts for the badness suffered by other things. Once again, therefore, I say that God is only bringing goodness about when it comes to evil suffered.

You might reply that there is *more* evil suffered than there needs to be and that God is therefore to be blamed. William Rowe seems to be saying this. Remember his example of the fawn dying in a forest fire.[12] Rowe clearly thinks that the suffering of the fawn is suffering that need not be. In a sense, of course, he is right. It is not logically necessary that there be any fawns at all. But the actual suffering of an actual fawn is only more suffering than there need be (and is therefore, as Rowe likes to say, 'pointless') if it lacks natural causes, if it is scientifically inexplicable. Assuming that it is scientifically explicable, however, then it arises because something other than the fawn is flourishing at some level. Here, once again, I agree with McCabe:

It may be argued that God could have made a material world without *so much* sheer pain in it. But let us look at what is being said if we say this. Ordinarily if I have a headache the doctor will explain what brought it about – it was that fifth whiskey last night. It was the whiskey behaving like good whiskey – as whiskey may be expected to behave – which brought about my headache. There is no mystery about my headache. Similarly with my cancer or my influenza – always there is a natural explanation and always the explanation is in terms of some things, cells or germs or whatever doing what comes naturally, being good. Sometimes of course and rather more often than he admits, the doctor is baffled. But he puts this down to his own ignorance; he says: 'Well, eventually we may hope to find out what is causing this, what things are bringing it about simply by being their good selves, but for the moment we don't know'. What he does *not* say is this: there is no explanation in nature for this, it is an anti-miracle worked by a malignant God. But that is what he would *have* to say if he thought that there was more pain in the world than there need be. More suffering than there need be would be suffering that had no natural cause, that was not the obverse of some good, that was scientifically inexplicable . . . The pain and agony of the world is just what you would expect to find in a material world – no more and no less. If we think otherwise we do not just give up belief in a good God, we give up belief in the rational scientific intelligibility of the world.[13]

In reply to this line of argument you might say that it would be best for there to be no material world in which some things do well while others do badly.[14] However, and passing over the fact that most of us seem glad to be here, it remains that evil suffered cannot be cited in defence of the claim that God wills evil as an end in itself. When it comes to evil suffered, God is only making what, to various degrees, is good. He is intending and effecting nothing but that. You might say that God could have made a material world and prevented any sufferings in it by a series of miraculous interventions. However, and passing over the difficulties of knowing what such a world would be like (it certainly would not be anything like ours), it remains that actual evil suffered (evil suffered in the real world) cannot be thought of as directly willed by God as an end in itself.

Evil done

When it comes to evil done, however, we are clearly dealing with something significantly different from evil suffered. For, as far as I can see, in the case of evil done there *is* no concomitant good. When a lion attacks a lamb, something, at least, is doing well. Not so, however, when I fail morally speaking, or when (to use religious language) I sin. Here there is no flourishing to account for the evil that is present. There seems to be nothing but failure.

Here, once again, I want to draw attention to the fact that the evil of evil done lies only in those who act badly. Bad human choices can certainly result in evil suffered – as, for example, when I torture you. But the evil suffered here is in you, not in me, and the evil done is in me and not in you (though, of course, there can be evil suffered in me because of evil done by me – as, for example, when I lose a limb while trying to blow up a safe in a bank that I am robbing). Also, as I have noted, there can be evil done when there are no bad effects following from the actions of those who seek what is sinful or morally bad. When it comes to evil done the only victims are those who do evil (who successfully choose to bring about effects which they should not choose to bring about) or who plan evil (who, whether successful or not, are intent on bringing about effects which they should not choose to bring about). So we cannot relate God causally to evil done by saying that it occurs, since God is bringing about a good which goes with it, a good which accounts for it. Evil done is self-inflicted evil with no corresponding good.[15] Since bad intentions can lead to good results, it may well be, of course, that evil done might bring about what is good. I suspect that nobody denies that good can come from evil, including evil done. Such good, however, can only arise accidentally from evil done. It is not an accident that a lion's feeding on a lamb leads to a diminishment in the lamb and an improvement in the lion. Here there is a non-contingent causal connection between goodness and badness. Given that a lion is feeding on a lamb, you expect the lamb to be in a bad way (because of what you know about lions and lambs). Unless you take miracles to be the norm, there are no surprises here. We might well be surprised, though, to learn that my murdering you brought about what is good. Let us suppose that you are a vicious dictator who engages in acts of genocide. I murder you and your people become liberated (forgive the simplicity of this example). Here there seems to be good which arises from evil done, but it is good which arises only accidentally, because of the work of all sorts of causes other than me. It does not follow from what I do, as the demise of a lamb follows from the gnawing of a lion.

So evil done is in itself a dead loss. There is no flourishing in it, no intrinsic gain, no good at all. How, then, should we think of God's causal role when it comes to it? I have already argued that God is what makes everything to be. So I seem to be committed to the conclusion that when Fred goes in for evil done God is the cause of all that is real in Fred. And this is a conclusion which I do, indeed, accept. I do not, however, think that this conclusion commits me to the view that evil done is God's doing. In Aquinas's language, what it commits me to is the view that God causes the 'act of sin' but does not cause sin itself.

By 'God's doing' I mean 'something creatively produced by God'. A slinky, grey cat prowling around a flower bed is God's doing since God is present to it as making it to be as it prowls around. Yet the evil in evil done cannot, in this sense, be God's doing. We have evil done when someone fails to act well (whether by commission or omission). If I rob you, I act unjustly, so I fail by commission (by deliberately acting so as to bring about a situation that I ought not to bring about).

When I say nothing when noting that you are about to damage yourself, I do not do what I should do, so I fail by omission. Whether I fail by commission or omission, however, the fact remains that I fail. Goodness I should be displaying is just not being displayed by me. Of course it may be true that evil done might involve the presence of much that could, all things being equal, be thought of as good. Someone adept at genocide, for example, has to exhibit skills that, in some contexts, we would love to see exercised – artful planning, for example, or an ability to organize people. It remains, however, that evil done, like evil suffered (and like evil as such), is an absence of what ought to be there, an absence of what is due, fitting, appropriate, obligatory, and so on. So it is not something that, strictly speaking, exists. It is no thing, entity, or substance. It is no positive quality or attribute. Its being consists of a failure to be. In that case, however, it cannot be thought of as being (creatively) made to be by God. Just as God cannot cause the existence of the evil in evil suffered, so he cannot cause the existence of the evil in evil done.

So where does it come from? At one level, of course, it does not come from anything since 'it' is not really an it. The evil of evil done is not an entity or positive attribute of any kind. It is not, for example, something that Aristotle could have fitted into his account in the *Categories* of ways in which things are.[16] Yet we are not always talking nonsense when we say that so and so has acted badly or is morally evil. It can surely be true that Fred, or whoever, is morally deficient. So perhaps we need to distinguish between existential assertions that tell us what really exists and those which, without doing this, are nevertheless true. And, I think, we can sensibly do so. As I have already noted, there are true existential statements which are not asserting that some individual, substance, property or quality is actually there in the real world. 'Blindness exists' is an example. To endorse this statement is not to suggest that we shall anywhere find an object or property called 'Blindness'. It is to say that something or other fails to see, and it is logically different from, say, 'The Trojan Horse still exists'. Is there blindness? Obviously there is, for we can truly say that, for example, some people are blind. To be blind, however, is nothing other than not being able to see, to be deprived of a way of being. So blindness is nothing real in itself and, in this sense, is not an 'it'. It can be said to have causes, but not ones making it to be as an independent entity or positive property.[17]

Similarly, evil done can be said to have causes, but not ones making it to be as an independent entity or positive property. In that case, however, the evil of evil done cannot be causally traced to God. As I have argued, God makes things to be as opposed to there being nothing. So he cannot be thought of as making the evil of evil done. He cannot be thought of as creating it. This, however, does not mean that the evil of evil done (the fact that we can truly say that people have acted badly) is causally inexplicable. Indeed, it seems to me, evil done is always (in principle) causally explicable.

Suppose that I rob you and that I do so freely. Now why did I choose to rob you? Passing over the suggestion that this is a question we need never raise, most of us would here be looking for a motive. We might, for example, feel satisfied if told that I was just about to be evicted from my home and saw your money as a way of keeping me in it. So my robbing you admits of causal explanation. I robbed you *because* I wanted to stay in my home and saw your money as a way for me to do so. Or again, suppose that John rapes Mary. Assuming that he chose to do so, we would make sense of a statement along the lines 'John raped Mary because he was infatuated with her and wanted nothing more than to have sex with her'. In both of these cases, and, I think, in all quotable instances of evil done, we have agents who act with an eye on what they want. And knowing what they want helps us to understand why their acts happened.

A point to bear in mind here is that we cannot make sense of people choosing to do what they do if we do not take them to be choosing what they think a good thing to do. Of course people often choose to do what is bad, but never as wanting what they take to be bad. As I argued earlier, if people are acting voluntarily, it always makes sense to ask them 'With a view to what are you doing that?' And voluntary behaviour is action geared to what the actor is attracted to (even if only as constrained by circumstances from which the actor would rather escape). To act voluntarily is to pursue one's desires. So desires can explain evil done. It makes perfect sense, for instance, to say that Fred killed Bill because he wanted to inherit his money. Fred's desire for wealth explains his decision to commit murder. It is a causal factor when it comes to Bill's demise.[18]

Yet it does not follow from this that evil done can be thought to be something produced by God. Causally explicable it may be, but not causally explicable as created by God. For it is essentially negative –

it amounts to the absence of a good that should be there. We have evil
done when agents choose or settle for goods for which they ought not
to settle given their circumstances. These goods, indeed, may be
genuine goods considered in the abstract. It is, for example, and in
the abstract, good to have money, for money can be used to preserve
one's health, nurture one's family, or aid the poor. But, as I assume
you agree, it is not good to obtain money by acting unjustly – e.g. by
murdering someone. To do so is to value personal and material well-
being over a life of virtue. And, I am saying, evil done consists precisely in a kind of wrong valuing. It occurs as a good that should be
sought is not sought. And what is not done by us cannot be thought
of as done by (as produced by) God.

If what I have previously been arguing is correct, however, then
God can hardly be causally *uninvolved* when it comes to those who
choose to do what is bad or morally wrong. Indeed, he must be
causally present when it comes to all that they do. Their doing, in fact,
has also, in some sense, to be his doing – his as their Creator making
all that is real in them to be. Yet it does not follow from this that God
causes the evil in evil done. Here, as I briefly indicated above, I find
Aquinas to have something useful to say. 'Does God Cause Sin?', he
asks.[19] His answer is 'No', and he defends this conclusion along the
lines that I have done. He says, for example, that 'sin as we properly
speak of it in moral matters, and as it has the nature of moral wrong,
comes about because the will by tending toward an improper end
fails to attain its proper end'.[20] Yet Aquinas goes on to ask, 'Do Acts of
Sin Come from God?', and his answer to this question is 'Yes'.[21] I think
that his reasons for this answer are good ones, though I do not take
them to conflict with his claim that God does not cause sin. So let me
now follow him a little as he develops his case.

He begins by noting that those who think that God does not cause
sin (the evil in evil done) have sometimes concluded that God cannot,
therefore, cause acts of sin. Aquinas has previously agreed that God
cannot be thought to cause the evil of sin, since this is an absence of
being and since for God to cause is for God to make something to be.
Aquinas, however, finds it impossible to believe that when, for
example, I shoot you by pulling the trigger on a gun, my pulling the
trigger of the gun lacks being. 'Acts of sin', he observes, 'are evidently
beings and classified in the category of being. And so we need to say
that the acts are from God.'[22] Aquinas thinks that these acts are from

God, since he takes God to be the creative source of all that is real. In his words:

> Since God is by his essence being, for his essence is his existing, everything existing in whatever way derives from himself. For there is nothing else that can be its own existing; rather we call everything else a being by some participation. And everything we call such a thing by participation derives from what is such by essence. For example, everything on fire derives from what is fire by essence . . . And so we need to say that the acts [sc. acts of sin] are from God.[23]

Aquinas's use of the word 'participation' here presumably derives from Neo-Platonic authors with whom he was acquainted.[24] We need not let that faze us at this point, however, for it is clear what Aquinas is saying in the passage just quoted. He is insisting that, since everything other than God only exists because God makes it to be, acts of sin, being perfectly real, are made to be by God.

Among the things that exist, of course, are those that undergo change. And with this thought in mind Aquinas offers a further reason for saying that acts of sin come from God. In his view (one which he has to hold given his commitment to the claim that all reality other than God owes its being to God), all real creaturely change derives from God. According to Aquinas, when X really changes from being actually F so as to become actually G (when, for example, my hot, buttered toast becomes cold, soggy sludge), something which was not comes into being and does so because of God considered as the source of the being of everything. Now the coming to be of an act of sin is the coming to be of what previously was not. So Aquinas traces it to God. He writes:

> Every movement of secondary causes needs to be caused by the first mover . . . But God is the first mover regarding all movements . . . So, since acts of sin are movements of free choice, we need to say that such acts as acts come from God.[25]

Given what I have argued above, I obviously accept this line of thinking. I think that we have to say that acts of sin (or, if you like, morally reprehensible acts) are caused to exist by God. If this were not so, they would simply not be there to be noted and discussed. A failure to act cannot, however, have an agent-cause (something that brings it about as something positive – as, for example, parent cats bring about kittens, or as chefs produce meals). And the badness in evil done is just a failure in action. So even if God causes the act of sin (even if God makes me to be as shooting you), he cannot be seriously thought of as causing the badness of evil done. All he is causing is what is actually there (and the evil in evil done is not). Or, as Aquinas observes:

> Sin can be called a being and an action only in the sense that something is missing. And this missing element comes from a created cause, i.e., the free will in its departure from order to the First Agent who is God. Accordingly, this defect is not ascribed to God as its cause, but to the free will, just as the limp in a cripple comes from his deformity and not from his power to move even though this power enables him to limp. Hence God is the cause of the act of sinning but not the cause of sin for he does not bring about the defect.[26]

According to Aquinas, sin arises because we do not choose to act as we should. We cannot do this, he thinks, without actually doing something, and God accounts for what we actually do. But God cannot account for (directly cause) the badness of what we do. This is not something that he can be thought of as creating. And here, again, I agree with Aquinas. My failure to do what I ought, though possibly taking the form of many nasty deeds (all of them, perhaps, capturable on video), is a failure, an absence, a non-being. So it is not created by God. It is not due to God that any moral failure is due to me. God does not make absences, non-beings, failures. You might, of course, say that since God is the author of all that is real and positive in the world, God is, by extension, the author of all of its privations, including that of sin. You might say that, even if it is true that evil is a privation, it does not follow that God is not the author of evils, since what is positively willed by God is a sufficient condition for some evil to obtain. And I agree that there would be no evil if it were not for God. The question to focus on, however, is what is God's *causal* role when it comes to evil. The phrase 'sufficient condition' is a somewhat vague one. A sufficient condition, I suppose, is what is *enough* for some outcome to ensue. In that case, though, it seems wrong to describe God as a sufficient condition of anything. Of course, he is *enough* to ensure some result. Yet he is that even if he does not choose to create at all. So how are we to think of him on the supposition that he has ensured results? My argument is that for God to ensure results is simply for God to create (to make to be what can be singled out as a genuine substance or positive property). And, I am saying, privations are not createable things. So God does not make them to be even if he makes a world in which they can be noted as being the privations they are. If he is the 'author' of privations, he is so only as making to be that which is not a privation, and not as willing (creating) evil as an end in itself.

Evil done and God's responsibility to prevent it

Yet might not God have made me better than I am? Might he not have ensured that I never did anything wrong? As we have seen, some thinkers hold that God could not have done this. They maintain that, since I enjoy human freedom, how good I am is up to me. God, they think, cannot cause me to be better than I am. If God is to leave me with my freedom, he has to permit me to sin if I choose to. Given what I have already argued concerning God and human freedom, however, you will realize why I deny all this. Without disbelieving in the reality of human freedom I, like Aquinas, see no reason why God could not have made me to be better than I am when it comes to the choices I make – no reason why God could not have brought it about that I (and all other people) always choose well and never exhibit evil done. In that case, however, should we not deem God to be causally accountable for evil done in so far as he is guilty *by neglect* – guilty for not having seen to it that people never choose to do what is bad?

My reply to this question basically takes me back to what I was saying in Chapter 4. To say that God is guilty by neglect is to say that there is something he ought to have done but has not – it is to hold him morally accountable. But it is a mistake to think of God as morally accountable. One might say that just as the captain of a ship has a duty to make sure that his vessel does not run aground, so God has a duty to ensure that his free creatures commit no sin. The analogy, however, does not hold. The captain of a ship is part of a world in which individuals can be held accountable given their place in it. God, on the other hand, is no such individual. It is a sea captain's job to keep his vessel afloat, but how can we suppose that it is God's job to keep us from acting wrongly? To do so would involve conceiving of God as a particular kind of thing subject to duties and obligations, and I have already tried to explain why we should not think of God in that way. Of course we can agree that God would be bad if he willed the evil of evil done directly and as an end in itself. As I have been arguing, however, God cannot be thought of as doing this. When it comes to evil done we are confronted by an absence of goodness and only that. You might insist that when it comes to evil done there is an absence that ought not to be there. We would surely be mistaken, however, if we expressed this thought by saying that God ought to have made more goodness than he has. To say that would effectively be to say that God is under an obligation to create – for as goods in the world come about they only do so as made to be (as created) by God. What, however, could justify the claim that God is under an obligation to create? That claim certainly does not square with traditional talk about God. This views God's act of creating as gratuitous. In any case, though, how can we make sense of the notion that God is obliged to create? Because there is a law stating that any decent God would create? That suggestion is hardly to be taken seriously.

There is a tradition of thought according to which goodness naturally pours itself forth. Hence, for example, Aquinas writes:

> The communication of being and goodness arises from goodness. This is evident from the very nature and definition of the good. By nature, the good of each thing is its act and perfection. Now each thing acts in so far as it is in act, and in acting it diffuses being and goodness to other things.[27]

For Aquinas, goodness consists in desirable existence. He also thinks that anything acting is somehow good and also brings goodness about. So he is happy with the conclusion that goodness can be thought of as naturally leading to goodness. But he does not take this to imply that the goodness of God is such that it has to result in the existence of any creature. We can see, he thinks, that goodness naturally leads to goodness among creatures (that, for example, medicines sometimes heal). Yet, so he also thinks, God's goodness (which is nothing different from God) is not something which has to produce or act as an agent-cause (even if it is true that God never acts except as willing what is good). For one thing, says Aquinas, God gains no good (is not himself improved) by creating; he does not need creatures in order to be the goodness that he is.[28]

Is Aquinas right here? It seems to me that he is. As I have argued, we need to think of God as unchangeable. So there can be no question of the emergence of creatures improving God or adding to his goodness. Nor can we think that God's goodness would not be what it is without the existence of creatures. The contrary must surely be the case. There would be no creaturely goodness without God being God to start with and independently of it. Or, as Aquinas says:

> The will is not directed to what is for the sake of an end if the end can be without it. For, on the basis of his intention to heal, a doctor does not necessarily have to give to a sick person the medicine without which the sick person can nevertheless be healed. Since, then, the divine goodness can be without other things, and, indeed, is in no way increased by other things, it is under no necessity to will other things from the fact of willing its own goodness.[29]

If Aquinas is right here, as I think he is, then God's goodness does not entail the existence of any creaturely goodness and we cannot conclude from 'goodness naturally pours itself out' (assuming that we accept this dictum) that God could never fail to produce a world or that he could never fail to produce a world containing more good than ours has exhibited, now exhibits, or will exhibit. We can speak of there being a necessity in created things given certain suppositions concerning God. If God immutably wills to create, for example, then the existence of created things is assured. Again, given that God has created such and such, then there is no question of the such and such in question not existing. And if God is to make things of certain kinds, then he is constrained when it comes to what he produces and there is necessity when it comes to what they are (God cannot, for instance, given what cats are, make a non-mammalian cat; so any cats made by God are necessarily mammals). The suppositions here, however, are nothing but suppositions. They tell us what has to be when it comes to created things *given* that God has created. They do not tell us that God has to create or that he has to make more good than there is.

Goodness and being

At this point it is worth noting that we can reasonably regard God's creating and the coming about of good as two sides of one and the same coin – that for God to create just is for him to bring about what is good. For something is good only in so far as it exists and succeeds in being in some way, and what God brings about is, and is only, that things exist. Yes, we can say that God brings it about that things, for example, undergo change. But to undergo change is to be in some way. Yes, we can say that God has made a world in which evil suffered occurs. But we cannot mean by this that God is creating something bad. We have to mean that he is making certain things to be good, things which bring it about that other things are diminished when it comes to their good ways of being. We can also say that God has made a world in which evil done is rampant – but not as creating the evil in evil done. When it comes to what is actually there, evil done is nothing but a matter of success or goodness – the thriving of those who turn away from what is truly good. Here, of course, I am not taking 'thriving' to mean 'the having of what is really good for them'. I am simply drawing attention to the fact that freely to do what is morally bad is also, paradoxically, to be good (to be a success) in certain ways. In referring to this fact above I used the example of genocide, but one can draw attention to what, considered independently of context, is good when it comes to *any* instance of evil done. All things being equal, it is not good for men to succeed in beating up women. They cannot do so, however, without being able, agile, strong, active, and so on. All things being equal, it is not good for people to bring it about that other people become drug-dependent. They cannot do so, however, without living, breathing, using their intelligence, and so on.

In that case, however, what can it mean to speak of God as being good? I have already tried to resist the suggestion that God is morally good. Yet might we be able to develop a reasoned case for calling God good without ending up saying that he is well behaved? And what of the famous claim that God is good because he is loving? How should we think of God's love when it comes to the topic of God and evil? I turn to all these questions in the next chapter, in which I also want to ask how we should think of God as acting for reasons. Confronted by evil, people often say '*Why* has God done or allowed that?' Before seeking to reply to these people, we might, as I shall soon be suggesting, pause to ask what the sense of the question is and whether it is answerable even in principle.

Notes

1. I might add that what are sometimes cited as naturally occurring evils are not, in themselves, necessarily evil. We might spontaneously speak of the evil of an earthquake in which thousands of people died. But earthquakes themselves are hardly evil. They are simply naturally occurring events. We describe them as evils in so far as they affect things of different kinds (principally ourselves and other animals, though sometimes also natural phenomena, such as scenic landscapes we value). Here I agree, though would add to (with an eye, for example, on non-human animals and scenic landscapes), what Nicholas Wolterstorff says as he writes: 'When we speak of hurricanes, floods, and the like as evils, what we really have in mind is their effects on the human beings in the region. Strictly speaking, it's those effects that are the evils.' See Nicholas Wolterstorff, 'Identifying Good and Evil', in Predrag Cicovacki (ed.), *Destined for Evil? The Twentieth Century Responses* (University of Rochester Press: Rochester, NY, 2005), p. 48.
2. Of course, this does not mean that people are not, in fact, for something (e.g., for enjoying union with God).
3. Following Herbert McCabe, I am here echoing the distinction Aquinas makes between what he calls *malum poenae* and *malum culpae*. For Aquinas, see, for example, *Summa Theologiae*, Ia.48.5 and *De Malo*, 1.4. For McCabe, see Herbert McCabe, *God Matters* (Geoffrey Chapman: London, 1987), ch. 3. *Malum poenae* and *malum culpae* literally mean 'evil of punishment' and 'evil of fault'.
4. A meteor devastating an island uninhabited by people or animals would be damaging it (though I suppose that there is no such island on our planet, at any rate). So I take non-animate things to be potential victims of evil suffered.
5. I am assuming here that a refusal to act can also be thought of as an action. The assumption seems a reasonable one since one can only refuse to act by choosing to do something else (even something as static as sitting in a chair with one's arms folded).
6. For a classic defence of this position, see, once again, C. J. F. Williams, *What is Existence?* (Clarendon Press: Oxford, 1981). A first-level predicable is one that can be sensibly applied to an object or individual rather than to a concept. Thus '____ is feline' can be sensibly predicated of my cat at first level while '____ is numerous' cannot. It makes sense to say that, for example, 'Cats are numerous', but this statement cannot be read as describing any particular cat. Rather, it seems to be telling us something about how to make use of the word 'cat' while trying to speak truly.

Note that I take a predicable to be an expression which might be used as part of a proposition to say something about something. I take a predicate to be an expression which is actually so used.

7. See Thomas Aquinas, *De Ente et Essentia*, 1, *Commentary on Aristotle's 'Metaphysics'*, bk 5, *lectio* 9, *Summa Theologiae*, Ia.3.4 ad 2 and Ia.48.2 ad 2.

8. I touched on this point in Ch. 6. I shall have more to say about it in Ch. 8.

9. See Ch. 6 above.

10. See Ch. 5 above.

11. McCabe, *God Matters*, p. 31.

12. See Ch. 1 above.

13. McCabe, *God Matters*, pp. 32f. One may, of course, wish to challenge belief in what McCabe calls 'the rational scientific intelligibility of the world'. Or one may want to say that examples of evil suffered really are anti-miracles worked by a malignant God. Few people, however, would embrace either of these positions – ones which, in any case, I cannot engage with in this book.

14. However, if by this you mean that it would be best for there to be no created order at all, then I have to say that I do not understand what you might mean. We evaluate situations in a created world in terms of good and bad. So we can intelligibly say, for example, 'The best thing to do in these circumstances is ____' or 'It would be best to put the flowers there rather than here'. There can be no way, however, of making a comparative evaluation when it comes to there being nothing and there being a created order, since there is no intelligible contrast to be made here. Nothing (there being nothing created) is not different from anything.

15. As Nicholas Wolterstorff says: 'When I act in a morally wrong way, I impair the excellence of my life; I impair my flourishing . . . Moral evil, in its very nature, is impairment evil in the life of the person who perpetrated the moral evil.' See Wolterstorff, 'Identifying Good and Evil', pp. 48f.

16. For a reliable translation of Aristotle's *Categories* see *Aristotle's Categories and* De Interpretatione, tr. J. L. Ackrill (Oxford: Clarendon Press, 1963).

17. For more on this see C. F. J. Martin, *Thomas Aquinas: God and Explanations* (Edinburgh University Press: Edinburgh, 1997), ch. 5.

18. Marcus G. Singer argues that one can want what is bad because of its badness, and he takes malevolence to be 'the doing or willing of what is wrong because it is wrong'. See Marcus G. Singer, 'The Concept of Evil', *Philosophy* 79 (2004), p. 205. 'It is not self-contradictory', says Singer earlier in the same paper, 'to say that I want to attain something, but do not regard my attaining it as good' (p. 203). I think, however, that Singer is wrong here. To want something is to be drawn to it, to find it attractive in some way. Since, like Aristotle, I take the most basic meaning of 'good' to be 'attractive', I suggest that it is indeed contradictory to say that someone wants what he or she takes not to be good (at least under some

description). Prudence and desire can be in conflict, so we may yearn for what we know to be bad for us and may even go on to act so as to obtain it (we may, for example, finally eat that fatty meal that the doctor has been warning us against). It is, however, simplistic to say, as Singer does, that 'It is, clearly, just false that everyone conceives of everything they want as good' (p. 202). Or, more precisely, it is simplistic to say this if it is thought to mean or entail that in making the choices we make we are not aiming at something we view as somehow good, something we want, something we desire. Milton's Satan says 'Evil be thou my good' (*Paradise Lost*, bk 4). But we cannot take this line as indicating that one can choose what one takes to be bad. Even in the context of *Paradise Lost* it is clear that Satan is attracted to the goals he seeks in his action. In the line just quoted, he is using 'evil' parasitically – i.e. he is using it as his enemies, including God, do.

19. Aquinas, *De Malo*, III.1. I quote here and below from Thomas Aquinas, *On Evil*, tr. Richard Regan, ed. Brian Davies (Oxford University Press: Oxford and New York, 2003).

20. Aquinas, *De Malo*, III.1; *On Evil*, p. 143. One might ask whether God causes sin by sinning himself. I have not gone into that question since few people, if any, would say that it makes sense to speak of God sinning. In *De Malo*, III.1, however, Aquinas raises and deals with the question. His position (surely a reasonable one if one thinks that God is perfectly good) is that God cannot sin, since to sin would involve God in acting against his nature. God's will, says Aquinas, 'by nature adheres to, and cannot defect from, the supreme good, just as the natural appetites of things cannot fail to seek their natural good' (*On Evil*, pp. 143f.). Anselm takes a similar line in *Proslogion*, 7. I shall be returning to the topic of God's goodness in the next chapter.

21. Aquinas, *De Malo*, III.2.

22. Ibid., *On Evil*, p. 147.

23. Ibid.

24. Proclus (*c.* AD 410–485), for example. The influence of Proclus is undeniable in Aquinas's *Super Librum de Causis Expositio*. For an English edition of this see Thomas Aquinas, *Commentary on the Book of Causes*, tr. Vincent A. Guagliardo, Charles R. Hess and Richard C. Taylor (Catholic University of America Press: Washington, DC, 1996).

25. Aquinas, *De Malo*, III.2; *On Evil*, p. 147.

26. Aquinas, *Summa Theologiae*, IaIIae.79.2. I quote from vol. 25 of the Blackfriars edition of the *Summa Theologiae* (Eyre & Spottiswoode: London and McGraw-Hill: New York, 1969).

27. Aquinas, *Summa Contra Gentiles*, I.37. I quote from Anton C. Pegis's translation of *Summa Contra Gentiles*, bk 1 (University of Notre Dame Press: Notre Dame, Ind. and London, 1975), p. 152.

28. Cf. Aquinas, *Summa Contra Gentiles*, I.81.

29. Ibid.

Eight

Goodness, Love
and Reasons

As I have noted, discussions of God and evil (recent ones, anyway) more often than not work on the assumption that to say that God is good is to say that he is morally good, that he does what he ought to do, or that he acts in accordance with standards of goodness to which he needs to conform. In their attempts to exonerate or excoriate God, these discussions naturally then go on to defend or attack God in ways in which we morally defend or attack each other. In doing so, they forget about or ignore ways in which God must be different from creatures, including human beings.

Yet might not those who argue this way reply that they are only working from the normal meaning of 'good'? Might they not defend themselves by asking what it could mean to call God good without wishing to say that he is morally good? Paul Helm is someone who argues that God has to be thought of as morally good.[1] Commenting on a previous work of mine in which I argue for the opposite position, Helm says that though what I have to say 'may seem to be a neat side-stepping of the problem' (sc. of evil) it is open to two objections.[2] So let me begin this chapter by commenting on the way in which Helm develops this thought.

Goodness and being

To begin with Helm asks 'What sort of goodness might God have that is not *moral* goodness?', and continues,

> What is the concept of non-moral goodness? We speak sometimes of good knives and good motorcars, but here we are using 'good'

in a purely functional or instrumental sense; good *as a knife*. But such a sense is hardly relevant here; we can make little sense of the idea that God is good as God.[3]

I presume that 'God is good as God' in what Helm says here really means 'God is good as *a* God', and if so, I entirely agree that we can make little sense of the idea that God is a good God. For if there is only one God, and if there cannot be two Gods (conclusions I defended in Chapter 3 above), then God does not belong to a class of Gods with members to which he can intelligibly be compared, whether favourably or otherwise.[4] Yet, it seems to me, Helm moves too quickly when saying that the expressions 'good knife' and 'good motorcar' employ the word 'good' in 'a purely functional or instrumental sense'. He seems to mean that 'good' in 'good knife' and 'good motorcar' has a special (functional) sense, one which must differ from its use in, for example, 'good moral agent' or 'good God'. Yet such, I think, is not the case.

Are we punning when we apply the word 'good' to things as diverse as knives, motorcars, people, and God? I mean, are we to suppose that 'good' as applied to these various things is to be thought of as used equivocally?[5] Is there nothing in common between, say, a good knife and a good person? I see no reason to think so. Of course, as we justify our claims that various things are good we will invoke descriptions which vary enormously. Good knives are things that can cut bread into slices while good motorcars are hard to get into the kitchen. Good motorcars help us to travel long distances while good knives would make for an uncomfortable ride. These facts, however, do not imply that there is no common meaning when it comes to 'good' as it is used to talk about different things, even things as different as knives and people.

Once again, it is important to remember that 'good' is generally what Peter Geach calls a logically attributive adjective.[6] Picking up on Geach's point, Bernard Williams notes that such an adjective 'is logically glued to the substantive it qualifies'.[7] In other words, and leaving God aside, we are seriously in the dark when told that such and such is good if we do not know what kind of thing the such and such in question is. In Geach's words, 'there is no such thing as being just good or bad, there is only being a good or bad so-and-so'.[8] Or, as Williams says:

> The attributiveness of 'good' demands a more intimate connection with its substantive than is demanded in the case of a merely comparative adjective like 'large'. Since 'good' in this sort of construction is intimately connected with the substantive that it qualifies, the meaning of a phrase of the form 'a good x' has to be taken as a whole; and its meaning is partly determined by what takes the place of 'x'.

We cannot infer from this, however, that 'good' is used equivocally when things of different kinds are said to be good. For, as I suggested earlier on, it makes sense to say that all good things, whatever they are, succeed in being in some way. 'Good' may not signify a single empirical property had by all good things. And it seems implausible to say that it signifies a single non-empirical property.[9] But in saying that something is good we are always noting ways in which it manages to meet up to expectations that we have. We are always drawing attention to what is, and should be, there. Or, as we might say, there is a serious connection between goodness and being.

One can see this by thinking in very simple terms. For something to be good is for it to be in a certain way. For something to be bad is for it to fail to be in some way. So goodness and being go together in that badness lacks being while goodness amounts to having it. I am not, of course, suggesting that 'good' and 'being' are synonyms, or that being is some kind of stuff that some things might have while others lack it. I am, however, saying that nothing is good unless it is actually thus and so – positively describable as having actual rather than negative attributes. John may be blind. But his blindness is no reality in him. He is blind only because he cannot see. His blindness is nothing actual in him (like his having a thumb). The fact that he does not see is just that: the fact that he *does not see*. His blindness is no substance with any attributes and, considered as such, it simply does not exist even though it is true to say that John is blind. To say that something is good, however, is precisely to draw attention to what is actually present in things, not to what they fail to have. It is to draw attention to what exists as opposed to what does not exist – as

Aquinas classically argues in texts such as *Summa Theologiae*, Ia.5.1. Here we read:

> Goodness and being are really the same. They differ only concep-
> tually. The goodness of something consists in its being desirable.
> Hence Aristotle's dictum that 'good is what everything desires'. But
> desirability evidently follows upon perfection, for things always
> desire their perfection. And the perfection of a thing depends on
> the extent to which it has achieved actuality. So, something is obvi-
> ously good inasmuch as it is a being . . . So, good clearly does not
> really differ from being, though the word 'good' expresses a notion
> of desirability not expressed by the word 'being'.[10]

Indeed, and as Aquinas goes on to say, there is a difference in meaning
between '*X* is good' and '*X* exists'. Yet it still remains that to be good
is to exist somehow and that to exist somehow is to be good – for to
exist somehow is to succeed in being in some way. Or, as Aquinas
again observes:

> Every being, considered as such, is good. For every being, consid-
> ered as such, is actual and therefore in some way perfect (all actu-
> ality being a sort of perfection). Now . . . anything perfect is
> desirable and good. So, every being, considered as such, is good.[11]

Of course, Aquinas is not here saying that everything is good without
qualification. All he is saying, and here he seems to me right, is that to
be is to succeed in some way and, in this sense, to be good. A sick cat
has at least to succeed in being a cat. And so on.

Contrary to what Helm seems to think, therefore, we do not have
to think of goodness as either moral or purely functional. 'It is hard',
says Helm, 'to grasp the idea of a goodness which is neither a moral
nor a functional goodness.'[12] On the contrary, it is relatively easy to
conceive of goodness as what you have when things, whatever they
are, achieve a degree of perfection. Certainly there is functional
goodness. This is largely a matter of convention in the sense that,
when it comes to artefacts anyway, functional goodness is merely a
product of our purposes (I mean that *we decide* what makes a knife
or a motorcar or a DVD player to be a good one).[13] Functional
goodness, like moral goodness, is, however, goodness. And, if I am

right, there is non-functional and non-moral goodness – the goodness had by anything which succeeds in being in some way. If I am right, it also seems that moral and functional goodness are simply examples of the goodness which is present in anything which succeeds in being. A morally good person is one who displays (actually has) the virtues we look for in human beings. A good knife or motorcar is one which exhibits (actually has) features that we look for in such things. Even when it comes to moral and functional goodness we are dealing with existence as opposed to non-existence.

Helm might still say, however, that God's goodness *must* be moral goodness – which brings me to his second objection to my line of thinking on God and evil. This is how he expresses it:

> If God is worshipful as good (because of his goodness), then that goodness must bear some fairly close relationship to the goodness which, from time to time, we ascribe to human actions and which is ascribed supremely to Christ. Scripture warns us against creating a God in our own image, consequently we must always allow for the real possibility that our ideas about God are mistaken and in need of revision. Nevertheless, even allowing for this, the goodness of God must bear some positive relation to the sorts of human actions we regard as good. Otherwise, why ascribe *goodness* to God?[14]

As I stressed in Chapter 4, however, I am not denying that God *in fact* does what we praise people for doing. What sorts of human actions do we regard as good? Examples might include helping people in need, freeing slaves, making people to be physically fit, and declaring the truth. Yet nothing I have said in this book implies that God does not do all of these things. The opposite is true, for I have been insisting on the fact that God brings about all that comes to pass in the universe (which certainly includes the helping of people in need, the freeing of slaves, the making of people to be physically fit). Nor do I wish to deny that God states what is true (e.g. by means of his prophets or through writings inspired by him). My point is that it would be wrong to say (as is often said in discussions of God and evil) that God does all these things as one who is obliged to, or as one who should be deemed morally bad if he does not do them. In reply to me at this point Helm might insist on there being 'some fairly close relationship' between God's goodness and the goodness of morally good human beings. But how close is close? If someone should say that God is good because, like morally good people, he manages to conform to moral standards to which people should conform, then, for reasons I have already laboured, I think that such a person would be wrong on both philosophical and biblical grounds. Yet I do not want to say that there is no connection between what we are doing when calling people good and what we are doing when calling God good. So let me now try to explain why there is. In other words, let me now try to answer Helm's question, 'Why ascribe *goodness* to God?'

The goodness of God

(a) Perfection and God

One reason for doing so lies in the traditional teaching that God is perfect.[15] I take it that to call something perfect is to imply that it is good (though not vice versa). If we have reason to call God perfect, therefore, we have reason for calling him good. And it seems to me that, even apart from the fact that talk of God being perfect is traditional, we have reason to say that God is perfect – though it is reason which does not entail moral excellence on God's part.

I have been arguing that we shall not understand 'X is good' unless we know what X is. The same is true when it comes to 'X is perfect'. What perfection amounts to in something of one kind (e.g. a perfect wife) may be descriptively very different from what it amounts to in something of another kind (e.g. a perfect horse). But it does not follow from this that we are wholly at sea when trying to give some general account of what perfection is. For, though perfect things may not all share the same attributes or properties, they are all alike in one respect. For, as with all good things, they are succeeding in some respect. Or, rather, they are all as good as it is possible to be considering the sort of thing they are. A perfect X is an X which cannot be improved upon as an X. A perfect X is a wholly realized X, one which cannot have anything added to it to make it better.[16]

This notion of 'not being improvable' is one we can employ when talking about God. For if God is the source of the being of everything, then God is no inhabitant of the world. And if God is no inhabitant of the world, then, as I argued in Chapter 3, God is not something changing or changeable, for he is no inhabitant of space and time. From this it follows that there can be no gap between what God is and what God might become, from which it follows, in turn, that the notion of God improving (or, for that matter, getting worse) can have no place in thinking about divinity. If God exists, therefore, then God is unchangeably all that it takes to be God. And from this I conclude that God can be said to be perfect and, therefore, good.

Here I agree with what Aquinas says when he turns to the topic of God's perfection. Aquinas thinks that perfection is the opposite of imperfection. He also thinks that imperfection is present when something which is potentially perfect (i.e. able to be perfect, though not actually perfect) is actually imperfect. For Aquinas, something imperfect fails because it is not what it could and needs (or ought) to be, because, in Aquinas's language, it lacks a certain sort of actuality. And, since he takes God to be wholly actual, Aquinas therefore concludes that God can be thought of as perfect:

> The first origin of all activity must be the most actual, and therefore the most perfect, of all things. For we call things perfect when they have achieved actuality (a perfect thing being that in which nothing required by its particular mode of perfection fails to exist) ... So, because we call things that are made 'perfect' when they are drawn from mere potentiality into actuality, we extend the word to refer to anything not lacking in actuality, whether made or not.[17]

Aquinas is saying that God must be perfect since he is in no way potential – since there is nothing which he could be but is not. Since God, for Aquinas, has no potentiality, he cannot be modified and therefore cannot be either improved or made worse. There is with him no 'could be thus and so but is not'. For God to be, therefore, is for God to be as divine as it takes divinity to be. It is for God to be fully God and, therefore, perfectly God. Since I find Aquinas's reasoning sound at this point, I suggest that God is perfect and therefore good. This suggestion, please note, makes no claim to understand what the perfection of God amounts to. It is another piece of negative theology, a reminder of what God *cannot* be (in this case, imperfect and, therefore, not good). All the same, it is enough to give sense to the claim that God is good, and it does so without asserting that God is morally good like good human moral agents. Some philosophers have argued that God's perfection actually requires him to be morally good. Taking their stand on the notion that God is maximally perfect, and advocating what they call 'perfect being theology', they suggest that, since anything maximally perfect would be morally good, it follows that God is morally good.[18] Yet it is far from obvious that anything maximally perfect would be morally good.[19] A perfect human being would, of course, be someone impeccably moral. But we can refer to something greater than human beings, for we can talk about God, who, if what I have been arguing has any merit, should not be thought of as a moral agent able to be morally good or morally bad as people can be thought of as being. In any case, and as I have just been maintaining, belief in God's perfection can be defended as a piece of negative theology rather than a description of God.

(b) God as maker of creaturely goodness

Another reason for saying that God is good arises from the fact that, being the Creator, he is the maker of all creaturely goodness. Notice, however, that in saying this I am not supporting a line of thinking some-times advanced – that God is good just because he makes good things. That line of thinking is a common one, but it does not serve to show that God in and of himself is good. For it does not establish that God is *essentially* good – i.e. good whether or not he creates. If the claim is that God is essentially good, then, assuming that God does not have to create, his goodness cannot be constituted by what he has brought about creatively. And the fact that God makes good things no more shows that he is essentially good than the fact that he makes wooden things shows that he is essentially wooden. As Aquinas observes: 'God is just as much the cause of bodies as he is of goodness in things. So, if "God is good" means no more than that God is the cause of goodness in things, why not say "God is a body" since he is the cause of bodies?'[20]

Yet Aquinas does think it right to reason to God's goodness with an eye on God as the cause of the goodness he makes to be. For, he argues, the goodness of created things must reflect what God is essentially. Or, in Aquinas's own words:

> We should especially associate goodness with God. For something is good in so far as it is desirable. But everything desires its perfection, and an effect's perfection and form consists in resembling its efficient cause (since every efficient cause produces an effect like itself). So an efficient cause is desirable and may be called good because what is desired from it is that the effect share its

goodness by resembling it. Clearly then, since God is the first efficient cause of everything, goodness and desirability belong to him. That is why Dionysius ascribes goodness to God as to the first efficient cause, saying that we call God good 'as the source of all subsistence'.[21]

This is a difficult passage, however, so let me try to unpack it a little.

In saying that 'something is good insofar as it is desirable' Aquinas, echoing Aristotle, means that 'good' can be thought of as equivalent to 'attractive'. In the *Nicomachean Ethics*, Aristotle says that goodness is 'that at which all things aim'.[22] According to Aristotle, goodness is what attracts or is desired. Aristotle, of course, is perfectly aware that people might be drawn to what is bad for them and for others. So he does not assume that what I actually desire on a given occasion is actually good for me or for others. Yet, he holds, we can make nothing of the suggestion that something is good without introducing the notions of attractiveness or desirability. And that is what Aquinas thinks. He would maintain, for example, that a *good* bicycle is one you would be *attracted by* if you wanted one for *cycling* (as distinct from, say, an object to photograph or help you to kill someone). And, with this thought in mind, Aquinas wants to say that God is good since God is attractive.

But how is God attractive? In the above quotation from Aquinas, his answer lies in the following words: 'everything desires its perfection, and an effect's perfection and form consists in resembling its efficient cause (since every efficient cause produces an effect like itself). So an efficient cause is desirable and may be called good because what is desired from it is that the effect share its goodness by resembling it. Clearly then, since God is the first efficient cause of everything, goodness and desirability belong to him'. Here Aquinas's argument seems to be:

(1) All things seek their good (that which attracts).
(2) All things seeking their good are effects of God (things made to be by God).
(3) Effects are somehow like their causes.
(4) Therefore, the goodness which creatures are drawn to is like God, who can therefore be thought of as attractive (or good) like the goodness to which creatures are attracted.

But, here again, we have some puzzling notions which need explanation. The most baffling, perhaps, is the suggestion that effects are like their causes, which seems evidently false. A stew, for example, does not look at all like a human cook. A car crash does not look like the factors that brought it about.

In trying to understand Aquinas at this point, however, it is important to recognize that he is not asserting that effects always *look like* their (agent-)causes (though he thinks that they sometimes do since, for example, children often physically resemble their parents). Rather, his thesis is that causes (in the sense of agents in the world which bring about changes in the world) explain their effects and do so precisely because of what they are. For him, we have an explanation of some development in the world when we reach the point of saying, 'Oh, I see. Of course that explains it.' And we have this, Aquinas thinks, when we see how a cause is *expressing its nature in* its effect.

Suppose that John is staggering around. We ask 'How come?' Then we learn that he has been drinking a lot of whisky, and we say, 'Oh, I see. Of course that explains it.' But what do we 'see'?

One might be tempted to say something like 'We see that it is not surprising that John should be staggering since people who drink whisky often do that.' One might say that what 'seeing' means here is that we note that what is now occurring has happened a large number of times before.

But if one occurrence is puzzling (if, for example, John's staggering is puzzling), why should a thousand such occurrences be less puzzling? That drinking whisky is followed (or regularly followed) by staggering does not *explain* what has happened. It simply reports what we have become used to observing. Someone offering only such a report would be in the position of what Aristotle calls the man of 'experience' as distinct from the 'wise' men who do see why the drinking is connected with the staggering.[23]

Until quite recent times, nobody did see the connection. To see it you need a chemical account of alcohol and an account of the effect of this substance on the brain (molecular biology is relevant here), and of the effect of these events in the brain on the movements of our legs. Only when you have developed this kind of understanding to give an account of what is happening with the staggering drunk can you be said to *see why* he is staggering. And what you would at last see is why it has to be the case that the drunk is staggering. To see, in this sense, is to have what Aquinas would have called *scientia*. And when he says that causes are *like their effects* he simply means that seeing why the effects spring from their causes is seeing how the nature of the cause explains the effect and renders its effect necessary, and therefore unsurprising. He means that though, when drunk, I cannot be described as looking like alcohol, I am, when drunk, certainly showing forth what alcohol is. In this sense, so he thinks, I resemble alcohol. For him, the drunken man is, when properly understood, alcohol *in action*, alcohol expressing its nature in something – something which is, therefore, 'like' alcohol.

Hence, Aquinas argues, creatures which aim at their good can be thought of as expressing what God is in himself. We cannot, he thinks, have a *scientia* (knowledge) which allows us to say something like 'Now we can see why God has produced these particular effects'. Aquinas does not suppose that God is something with respect to which we can develop a science which explains why God has the effects which he has. For him, any such thing would be a creature. But, trying to say something about the source of the being of all things, Aquinas finds it natural or appropriate (or, at least, not inappropriate) to suggest that since effects in nature show forth the nature of their causes, we can think of God as being shown forth in his effects.[24] And since the goodness which creatures seek is something created by God, it can, thinks Aquinas, be thought of as being like what God is. Aquinas does not mean that God's goodness depends on his having created. Nor does he mean that we have any picture or image of God's goodness. But, he thinks, we have grounds for calling God good since, whether or not God created, he would still be whatever he is as shown forth by the created world. And, since Aquinas thinks that the created world gives us grounds for calling God good as being 'like' that to which all creatures are attracted (i.e. goodness), he thinks we have grounds for calling God 'good'.

And Aquinas, I think, is right. In the sense implied by him, effects do 'resemble' their causes. If you pour exactly one mole of sulphuric acid on one mole of zinc metal, the zinc will always fizz, and disappear, and give off an inflammable gas, and the sulphuric acid will lose its corrosive power.[25] But why? Because:

$$Zn_{(s)} + H_2SO_{4(aq)} \rightarrow ZnSO_{4(aq)} + H_{2(g)}$$

Here you see (in a literal sense) that what is on the right side of the →
is the same as the elements on the left side. In this sense, the products
of the reaction resemble the reactants. So you can now say 'Yes, I see,
of course'. Effects really do reflect what their causes are. What
Aquinas calls the likeness of an effect to its cause is precisely what we
are seeking as we look for scientific explanations. And since all
effects are ultimately God's effects, and since these include creatures
who are attracted to what is good, God can be called 'good' as the
source of all that is attractive. He can be called this even on the (traditional Christian) assumption that a created world is in no way necessary to God (that God might never have created a world at all). For,
we may say, in calling God good with an eye on his creation, we are
alluding to what God is in himself, whether or not he creates – we are
saying that the reality of the created order gives us a reason to say
what God essentially is. Jane and John might at first decide never to
have children. But, having changed their minds, the children they
actually produce reflect what they are even if they had chosen never
to procreate. By the same token, so we may argue, the actual world
reflects what God is apart from creation. You cannot give what you
have not got, and God, so we may say, is what the goodness aimed at
(and often achieved) by creatures is. He is attractive and, therefore,
good (since 'good' can be equated with 'attractive' or 'desired'). This
is not, of course, to say that we have any understanding of what God's
goodness amounts to. But it is to say, as I argued above with respect
to 'God is perfect', that we have reason for calling God good – another
reason which does not amount to the suggestion that God is a morally
good individual, like a morally good human being. My argument does
not rule out seeing human moral goodness as a reflection of God, for
what I am saying is that human moral goodness reflects God and
shows us something of what God is. So I have no problem in agreeing
that human moral goodness reflects what God is. But that is not the
same as saying that the goodness of God is, quite simply, moral
goodness (a matter of being well behaved).

The love of God

So, I have argued, we can defend the claim that God is good without
supposing that God is morally good. And we can do so in a way that
respects the difference between God and all creatures, a way that

does not presume God to be one of a kind, an agent among agents, a member of any environment. As I have noted, Rowan Williams, writing on the topic of God and evil, has said: 'God is never going to be an element, a square centimetre, in any picture, not because God's agency is incalculably greater but because it simply cannot be fitted into the same space.'[26] I have been saying as much throughout this book. Contrary to what authors like Paul Helm suggest, however, this does not leave me having to conclude that God is not good. Can I, however, speak of God as *loving*? Those who worry about God and evil sometimes say that evil shows that God is not loving. Are they right, or can we make a case for actually ascribing love to God?

As I have noted, the Bible only infrequently says that God is good. But it often says that he loves.[27] The question, of course (my question at the moment anyway), is whether or not there is any non-biblical reason for speaking of God as loving, and one might be intuitively inclined to say that there cannot be. For love, as we often refer to it, is an emotion, and we have philosophical grounds for denying that God undergoes emotions.

To have an emotion is to be acted on (moved) by something else. Yet God, considered as the Maker of all things (considered as the source of the existence of everything other than himself) cannot be acted on by anything. The action of everything other than God must derive from him, while what is true of him cannot be an effect of anything created. It makes as much sense to ascribe emotions to God as it does to attribute physical properties to him.[28] Many people, of course, do like to think that God undergoes emotions. Perhaps they think that he would be deficient as a person if he did not. All I can say at this point by way of reply to this idea is that, though emotionless people seem decidedly lacking, a God who experiences emotion cannot be the source of the being of everything other than himself. An emotion is an *effect*, yet there cannot be effects in that which accounts for the existence of everything other than itself. This, of course, does not mean that one cannot attribute emotions to God figuratively – just as it does not mean that one cannot figuratively speak of him as having an eye or a wing. We need to remember, however, that we shall not then be noting what is really or literally true when it comes to God.

Another problem with ascribing love to God springs from what seems to be required for there to be love in at least *one* sense of 'love'.

For think of mature, adult love. Have we reason to ascribe this to God? You may say that we do – meaning that as, for example, spouses give themselves in love to each other, God gives himself in love to at least some of his creatures. Yet it is hard to make sense of this suggestion. For the love now in question presupposes equality between lover and beloved. It does not mean, for example, that they have to weigh the same, to be equally intelligent, or to have identical incomes. But it does mean that mature, adult love only exists as people can, so to speak, see themselves in each other. It depends on them being able to value each other as they do themselves. It involves a mutual giving and sharing. Yet it seems ludicrous to suppose that God can love creatures in this sense. For creatures are not God's equal. They are totally dependent on him and vastly different from him. To speak of God 'giving himself in love' to a creature is like speaking of me as 'giving myself in love' to a cat or a spider. I may be kind to my cat (or my spider). I might even be fond of it. What I cannot seriously be thought of as doing, however, is loving it as mature adults can love each other. By the same token, we cannot seriously think of God loving creatures as mature adults can love each other.[29] As Herbert McCabe observes:

> It is evident that whatever relationship there may be between God and creatures it cannot be one of love. The relationship here is just as unequal as it is possible to be. There may be many other relationships; we can think of God as caring for his creatures and doing good for them, beginning with the primal good of bringing them into existence and sustaining them in existence. We can think of God as source of all the value that is in them. We can think of God as rewarding them or ignoring their offences. We can think of him on the model of a kindly caring master instead of a frightening despotic master, but what we cannot do is think of him as giving himself in love to a creature . . . There cannot be a relationship of *love* between creator and creature. Not that *adult* love between equals that we just occasionally achieve ourselves . . . If we take God seriously and creation seriously then, in the end, the creature is something like a slave – at least in the sense that the master/slave relationship is exclusive of adult love.[30]

Yet it does not follow from this that we cannot ascribe love to God. For one thing, we can say that if God does good to people (and other things), then he can be thought of as loving them. We can then note that since, as Creator, God clearly does bring about what is good for people (and other things), he can be thought of as loving. One might object to this line of thinking by saying that God clearly does not make all things to be equally good, and the objection seems sound since not all things are equally good (people in hospital are, for example, less healthy than those who are competing in the Olympics). On the other hand, however, it remains true that God *does* will good for creatures (he does so by creating all the good that creatures display) and can therefore be said to love them. You might say that 'doing good to X' is not equivalent to 'loving X'. Yet we have a perfectly familiar sense of 'love' in which it means just that. I doubt that anyone would have a problem with the suggestion that Peter and Amy are loving parents because they look after their children and provide for them, because they bring about what is good for them. They might, of course, and for all sorts of reasons, end up doing nothing to help other children. This fact, however, need not lead us to conclude that Peter and Amy are not loving parents. Nor does it preclude us attributing love to God. Here again I agree with Aquinas. As he puts it:

> God loves all existing things. For everything that exists is, as such, good, because the very existing of each thing is a certain good, as are each of its perfections. Now . . . God's will is the cause of all things and . . . everything therefore has to be willed by God in so far as it has reality or any goodness at all. So, God wills some good to every existing thing. Since loving is the same as willing good to something, God clearly loves everything. Yet he does not love things as we do. For since our will is not the cause of things being good, but responds to that goodness as to its objective, our love in willing good for something is not the cause of that goodness. Instead, its goodness (real or imagined) evokes the love by which we will for the thing both that it retains the goodness it has and that it gains goodness which it lacks, and we act so as to bring this about. But God's love pours out and creates the goodness of things.[31]

Notice, however, that this will not give us the conclusion that God loves *by nature*. Aquinas is here arguing that, given that God has created, we have reason to speak of him as loving things. But what if we suppose that God might never have created? What if we suppose that there might have been nothing but God? Then we have no grounds for supposing that God has to love other things and therefore loves by nature or essentially. As Aquinas also notes, however, there is a case to be made for supposing that there is love in God even if there is nothing but God. For why not say that God must love the supreme good that he himself is?

In considering this question, first ask what is going on when something is loved. The answer, surely, is that the thing, whatever it may be, is recognized as good and, therefore, as somehow attractive. But to see something as good or attractive is to be drawn to it, to want it. So there is love when there is a being drawn to a perceived good. Of course, we might take something painful to be good for us, and one might wonder how we could be said to love it. Nasty-tasting medicine which we know to be good for us is hardly something we love. Yet to focus on that thought is to think of love in largely emotional terms, to think of its paradigm as being what Romeo had for Juliet. Doubtless Romeo never felt about nasty-tasting medicine as he felt for Juliet. If he took it because he thought it to be good for him, however, he was most certainly drawn to it, and it always remains true that, even if we dislike something under one description (e.g. how it tastes), our taking it to be good is to be drawn to it, to want it, and, in this sense, to love it. It is not that we *first* take something to be good and are *then* drawn to it. Seeing something as good just *is* to be drawn to it. To recognize something as good just *is* to be attracted to it, and, therefore, to love it.

So knowing what is good means loving it. The two notions are inseparable. But now consider the case of God. If God is indeed essentially good, and if God knows what he is, then it would seem to follow that he cannot but love himself and is therefore essentially loving apart from being loving as willing goodness in creatures.

The obvious objection to this conclusion is that it seems to make God incredibly narcissistic. It inevitably brings to mind a picture of God gazing at himself and finding himself irresistible. Such a picture, however, obviously has to be misleading. Not misleading, however, is the thought that when goodness knows itself for what it is, it rests in itself as an object of love. And that is a thought which seems forced on us if we take God to be the goodness that he is (just as, not being distinguishable from his nature, he is whatever else he is) and if we take him to comprise a knowledge of what he is. If there is knowledge in God (if 'God knows' is true) and if God knows what he is, then he essentially loves the goodness that he is just as he loves the goodness of anything there might happen to be apart from himself.

Shall we say, however, that God knows the goodness that he is? A truly adequate answer to that question requires more space than I can devote to it in this book. Perhaps, though, I can briefly make a few points with an eye on it.

To start with, in discussions of God and evil it seems generally taken for granted that God (whether or not he exists) can be thought of as omniscient. Rightly or wrongly, his not being so, or it being inconceivable that he should be so, is rarely treated as a serious option in these discussions. If we go with tradition here, therefore, we might allow that God, if he exists, knows himself and, therefore, loves what he knows.

Second, it seems *prima facie* hard to understand how anything can, and without being forced to, produce a world containing goodness (including the goodness of beings with awareness) without possessing knowledge in some sense. For the freely chosen pursuit of what is good seems to imply both intellect and will on the part of the chooser. If that is so, however, and given that God makes goodness to be as one who wills it, it seems natural to say that there is knowledge in God and that this comprises knowledge of what is good. Given that this is so, it seems to follow that, being good, God knows himself as such and, therefore, loves himself as such – loves the goodness from which all creaturely goodness derives.

Third, if God is indeed wholly simple, God's actually knowing cannot be different from God. I can exist without actually knowing anything at all (indeed, I did so once). If, though, 'all that is in God is God', and assuming that there is knowledge in God, then there can be no real distinction between God and his knowledge (his actually knowing). This knowledge (this actually knowing on his part) cannot be thought of as something produced in God by any outside source – meaning that we would be hard-pressed to think of it as knowledge of what is not God, knowledge which God achieves as something other than himself has an effect on him. In that case, however, there can be no real distinction between what God knows and God himself – meaning that, if there is knowledge in God, we have reason to speak of it along the model of self-knowledge.

Once again, therefore, I suggest that it makes sense to speak of God as being essentially loving. On the basis of created things, we can speak of God as loving since he wills or desires what is good for others. But we can also say that God, knowing the good that he is, has to be drawn to it and, therefore, has to love it.

Such a conclusion, however, might seem not especially worthy of note when it comes to God and evil. Someone might say: 'OK. Suppose I concede that God wills good for certain creatures. Suppose I also agree that God wills good to all creatures simply by making them to exist. Suppose I even accept that love belongs to God by nature (that God, if you like, is love) since he cannot but be drawn to and is not distinguishable from the goodness that he eternally is. This still leaves us with problems when it comes to the relationship between God and evil (whether 'evil done' or 'evil suffered'). For there is a whole lot of evil around. *Why*, therefore, does God allow this to be the case? *Why* does he favour some people more than others? *Why* did he not make a world containing no evil at all? *Why* is he not producing more good than he does?'

People often raise questions like these. They ask why God allows evil at all. They ask why good people perish while bad people thrive. One way of dealing with such questions is to argue along some of the ways I have already argued. One may suggest, for example, that some evil exists as a necessary concomitant to goods of various kinds. Or one might note that God produces nothing but what is good. Such responses, however, might be rejected on the ground that they do not engage with the questions to which they are offered as responses. These questions, so those who pose them might stress, are looking for God's *motives*, his *reasons* for allowing things to be as they are. *Why*, they might ask, is God acting or not acting as he does?

What are we to say to someone who presses this line of enquiry? It seems a perfectly fair one to pursue when it comes to people. Why did David abandon his family? Why did Margaret give a million dollars to Christopher? These are not silly questions to raise. People act, or fail to act, for reasons, and we might legitimately wonder what these reasons are. Indeed, our assessment of people may very much hinge on knowing what reasons they had for doing what they did or for refraining from doing what they did not do. So why not ask about God's reasons when it comes to good and evil in the world? Why not even say that evil should be viewed as telling against God's goodness or existence if his reasons here cannot be laid out for inspection?

God's reasons

Perhaps we should consider such questions by first asking what it is to act (or not act) for reasons. I take it that in order to do so we have to start with what is going on when people act (or do not act) for reasons. So what is going on here? It surely has something to do with how people would answer the question 'Why did you do/not do that?'

Charlie turns over in bed while asleep. We wake him up and ask 'Why did you do that? Why did you not stay where you were?' Charlie would now have grounds for being annoyed. Why? Because his rolling over in bed admits of no answer that he can give to the question 'Why did you do that?' Why not? Because Charlie had no aim in mind in rolling over. He was not intending anything. There might be a physiological answer to the question 'Why did Charlie roll over in bed?' Perhaps he rolled over because of a muscle spasm. But such an explanation does not tell us about any motive on Charlie's part. In this sense it does not tell us why he rolled over. It tells us nothing about Charlie's reasons. Ascertaining his reasons for doing or not doing something depends on getting him to tell us about some goal for which he was consciously striving.

Having awoken from a disturbed night's sleep, Charlie now goes to his bathroom and brushes his teeth. Still obnoxiously present to him, we ask 'Why are you doing that?' He replies, 'Because I want to stop my teeth from decaying.'

We follow him into his kitchen and watch him tuck into a bowl of bran. 'Why are you doing that?', we ask. He says, 'Because I want to make my bowels work, and please keep out of my bathroom.'

Having waited a while, however, we note that Charlie is making a phone call. He is telling someone to fix it that Fred gets killed. Resisting the temptation to run away, we ask him 'Why did you do that?' He snarls, 'Because I want the bastard wasted. He is a threat to me.'

Now we seem to have a sense of Charlie as someone acting for reasons. He does so because he wants something – either something that he has or something that he lacks. Let us suppose that his teeth are in fine shape and that he knows that. So he brushes them to keep things as they are with him. And he eats bran to bring about a presently non-existing state of affairs. Either way, Charlie is acting for reasons and doing so because he wants something or other. And that seems always to be going on when people act for reasons, when they can tell us why they did such and such so as to explicate their motives. In our case, reasons for acting invariably coincide with wants.

Of course, we might try to think of someone more altruistic than Charlie. He seems pretty much obsessed with what is going on with his body. What, though, of Katy, who leaves a well-paying job to devote herself to looking after poor people in Calcutta (she is a fan of Mother Teresa, the founder of the Sisters of Charity)? 'Why did you do that?' we might ask her. She might be envisaged as replying along these lines: 'Because I want to help people more than I want to earn money.' Is Katy so very different from Charlie, however? Obviously she is, since she seems to care for others. Like Charlie, however, her acting for reasons is a matter of pursuing her wants. Katy, happily, wants to help people. Charlie, alas, wants someone to be murdered. But the reasons for what both of them do lie in what they want. More specifically, they lie in *needs* that they have (or think that they have), needs that would remain unsatisfied if they did not act in certain ways.

Does it make sense, however, to suppose that God has needs that would remain unsatisfied if he did not act in certain ways? I do not see that it does. If God is the source of all that exists (the reason why there is something rather than nothing), then he cannot have a need that would be met by how things go in the created order. For how things go there will be his doing, not something he waits on or desires to help him on his way. And if God is unchangeable, then nothing he does can satisfy a need that he has, for a need something has can only be satisfied on the assumption that the thing in question is mutable.

For these reasons, therefore, I think that we should back away from the suggestion that God acts for reasons as people do. One might say that God does such and such *in order that* something or other might come about. One might say, for example, that God has made people to enjoy communion with him, or that God has made clouds so that they might water the Earth. At this point in the discussion, however, we are well and truly moving away from what we are usually doing when ascribing to people reasons for their actions or non-actions. Maybe it is true that God has made people to enjoy communion with him. But this does not mean that God is thereby aiming to grasp at something he needs. All it means is that God makes people with a certain (possible) destiny. Maybe it is true that God has made clouds so as to water the Earth. But this too does not mean that he is thereby aiming to grasp at something he needs. All it means is that God makes clouds which, as it happens, water the Earth given how he has made things to be.

One way of putting all this is to deny that God engages in practical reasoning. Philosophers have traditionally distinguished between theoretical reasoning and practical reasoning. Theoretical reasoning takes place as we reflect on what we might call basic matters of truth – as, for example, when we note that if Smokey is a cat, and if all cats have hearts, then Smokey has a heart. Practical reasoning, by contrast, has to do with getting what we want. Suppose I aim to get to Paris in the quickest time possible. I might reflect thus: 'A plane will get me to Paris quicker than anything else. So I should hop on a plane.'[32] Now it is with respect to practical reasoning that talk about reasons for acting is naturally at home. Why did Davies rush to the airport? Because he wanted to get to Paris as quickly as possible. Why did Mary not prevent John from falling? Because she wanted him to endure pain. Yet it seems to make little sense to think of God as engaging in practical reasoning. When we engage in such reasoning we are trying to figure out how best to ensure that what we want (and therefore, to start with, lack and take ourselves to need) comes about. But God lacks nothing. As I have argued, there is no gap between what he is and could be but is not.

You might say that God lacks the company of creatures and would be improved or benefited by having it. But that would involve thinking of creatures as able to change or modify God for the better, while, as I have argued, the truth must be that all that is good in creatures derives from what is first in God and then in them. For people, company is certainly a good thing, something that helps them.[33] So it is not hard to understand why we seek out others or why we seek to reproduce ourselves. It is simply absurd, however, to suppose that the Maker of all things, the source of the being of everything other than itself, the reason why there is something rather than nothing, is essentially in a state which could be helped by the existence of creatures. Such a supposition would be a classic example of a failure to distinguish between God and what he produces.

In any case, how can we entertain the notion of God figuring out what it would be best for him to do? If there is no goodness lacking to him, then there is no way of acting which he needs to reflect on while working out how to achieve what he wants. And if he transcends the world of change, he cannot reach conclusions by means of argument or a process of reasoning. You might say that one can see at a glance what should be done in a given set of circumstances, and you would be right to say that. Our use of practical reasoning need not involve us in laboriously identifying premises and reasoning to a conclusion over time. It might do so, and it often does so; but it need not. If we are sufficiently smart we could, perhaps, be able to recognize in a flash what needs to be done given how things are. Yet there is always (logically speaking, anyway) a process when it comes to human practical reasoning. First we identify a goal, then we recognize how best to achieve it, then we act. Going through such a process, however, seems impossible when it comes to what is wholly and entirely perfect in itself and without possibility of change.

I am therefore highly suspicious of the suggestion that God acts for reasons in any intelligible sense that we can attach to the expression 'act for a reason'. Of course, one might certainly say that God has arranged (or willed) that X should come to pass because of Y. One might say, for example, that God has arranged (willed) that plants grow because they are watered. One might go on to add that a reason for there being water is the growing of plants. But this is not a reason we can ascribe to God as we ascribe reasons to people for what they do. To say that water is a reason for the growing of plants is to say that water helps plants to grow, not that God has a reason for seeing to it that there is any water or that there are any plants. You might reply that God *must* have a reason for creating, for otherwise there would be nothing created. Once again, however, we come back to what I have been saying above. If 'having a reason' means anything like what it means when it comes to people having reasons for acting, the notion seems inapplicable when talking about what can be ascribed to God. The truth of 'God wills X so that Y might come about' does not leave us with a God acting for reasons. It leaves us with a God who, in fact, brings Y about by virtue of X.[34]

So I fear that there is no intelligible answer to questions like 'Why did God do this to me?' or 'Why did God make the world as it is?' Such questions, I think, just ought not to be asked if they are requests for reasons that God has. They resemble questions like 'Why is my cat not humble?' or 'Why are you not your own father?' Questions like these, though grammatically well formed, lack sense because they are not taking account of what certain things are or could not be. Cats are not capable of being humble, so asking why my cat is not humble is to raise a bogus question. People cannot father themselves, so asking why I am not my own father is also to raise a bogus question. In a similar way, we are raising bogus questions if, looking for God's reasons, we seek explanations of the sort that we gain as people account for themselves and for what they do or do not do. It is not that God has reasons of which we are ignorant. My point is that God is not something we should think of as having reasons for acting or not acting in the first place. As I have said, talk about reasons for acting is at home when we are thinking of people. To apply it to God is to take it into a context where it ceases to mean anything like what it does as usually employed – though I shall be qualifying this judgement a little in the next chapter.

Notes

1. Paul Helm, *The Providence of God* (Inter-Varsity Press: Leicester, 1993), pp. 166–68.
2. Ibid., p. 167.
3. Ibid.
4. If Helm's 'God is good as God' does not mean what I take it to, then I do not understand what it could mean. I suppose it could mean that, considered in himself, God is good. Yet I do not think that Helm would want to say that God is not, in himself, good.
5. I take a word to be used univocally when used to talk about different things if it means exactly the same in each occurrence. So I take 'horse' to be used univocally in 'Arkle is a horse' and 'Dobbin is a horse'. I take a word to be used equivocally about different things if its meaning in each occurrence is entirely different. So I take 'bank' to be used equivocally in 'We ran our boat into the bank of the river' and 'I keep my money in an offshore bank'.
6. See Ch. 6 above.
7. Bernard Williams, *Morality: An Introduction to Ethics* (Cambridge University Press: Cambridge, 1972), p. 54.
8. Peter Geach, 'Good and Evil', repr. In Philippa Foot (ed.), *Theories of Ethics* (Oxford University Press: Oxford, 1967), p. 65.
9. G. E. Moore (1873–1958) famously says that goodness is a 'non-natural property'. See G. E. Moore, *Principia Ethica* (Cambridge University Press: Cambridge, 1903). I take Moore's view to have been well criticized by Geach in 'Good and Evil'. For a comparable critique of Moore on goodness as a non-natural property, see Williams, *Morality*, pp. 52ff.
10. Thomas Aquinas, *Summa Theologiae*, Ia.5.1 (my translation).

11. Ibid., Ia.5.3 (my translation).

12. Helm, *The Providence of God*, p. 167.

13. My point here is just that artefacts we produce are good only in terms of what we want them to be. DVD players, for instance, are machines designed to work in a way that people who dreamed them up took to be desirable. So their goodness is, so to speak, man-made (i.e. it depends on what their makers were intending). In this sense, it is a matter of convention.

14. Helm, *The Providence of God*, p. 167.

15. That God is perfect is a biblical teaching: see e.g. Matthew 5:48. God's perfection is explicitly taught by the First Vatican Council; see its *Dogmatic Constitution on the Catholic Faith*, Ch. 1.

16. Here, of course, I am not saying that a perfect X is the best possible X. My point is that we can think of something as perfect if it lacks nothing required for its integrity or well-being considered as whatever it is.

17. Aquinas, *Summa Theologiae*, Ia.4.1 (my translation).

18. See, for example, Thomas V. Morris, *Our Idea of God* (University of Notre Dame Press: Notre Dame, Ind. and London, 1991), pp. 35ff.

19. Does the notion of maximal perfection (or of a maximally perfect being) have any serious positive content in and of itself? I am inclined to say that it does not, since what counts as a perfection can vary from thing to thing. You might say that something is maximally perfect if it can in no way be improved upon. This thought does not help, however, when it comes to generating an account of what maximal perfection (or a maximally perfect being) concretely includes.

20. Aquinas, *Summa Theologiae*, Ia13.2 (my translation).

21. Ibid., Ia.6.1 (my translation). The reference to Dionysius is to *The Divine Names*, 4. For an English edition of the Dionysius text see *Pseudo-Dionysius: The Complete Works*, tr. Colm Luibheid (Paulist Press: Mahwah, NY, 1987).

22. Aristotle, *Nicomachean Ethics*, I.1, 1094a3.

23. See Aristotle, *Metaphysics*, I.1.

24. For a fairly detailed exposition of Aquinas on this principle see John F. Wippel, 'Thomas Aquinas on Our Knowledge of God and the Axiom that Every Agent Produces Something Like Itself', *American Catholic Philosophical Quarterly* 74 (2000).

25. This is the language of Aristotle's man of 'experience'.

26. Rowan Williams, 'Redeeming Sorrows', in D. Z. Phillips (ed.), *Religion and Morality* (St Martin's Press: New York, 1996), p. 147.

27. See for example, Deuteronomy 7:13; Psalm 109:5; Proverbs 8:17; Isaiah 63:9; Hosea 11:4; John 14:23; 1 John 4:16.

28. Orthodox Christian belief holds that what can be said of Christ can be said of God. So in terms of classical Christology it makes sense to say that if Christ weighed 140 lbs, then God weighed 140 lbs. I am not at this point quarrelling with that way of talking (I shall return to it later). Notice, however, that classical Christology does not teach that if Christ weighed

140 lbs, then the divine nature did. Here I am simply concerned with what can be said of the divine nature.

29. Mature adults can, of course, love their children. But the love of parents for children is surely different from the love that parents can have for each other. Parents can love their children by being fond of them, being willing to protect them at all costs, and so on. They cannot, however, love them as equals to whom they give themselves in love as they do to each other. Of course, a father might feel for and act with his daughter as someone else might feel for and act with his wife. We would not, however (or so I assume), think of him as genuinely exhibiting what I am now calling mature adult love.

30. Herbert McCabe, *God Matters* (Geoffrey Chapman: London, 1987), pp. 17f.

31. Aquinas, *Summa Theologiae*, Ia.120.2 (my translation).

32. I am not implying, of course, that practical reasoning is unconcerned with truth. The point, however, is that its purpose is to enable us to decide what should be done.

33. Religious hermits might shun human company. But they are exceptions to a fairly general rule. In any case, they would probably say that, in their solitude, they are seeking company: the company of God.

34. Cf. Williams, 'Redeeming Sorrows': 'We might say that God "decides" to create, if we like, but we'd better be aware that, while we have no other obvious way of saying that no one and nothing "made" God create, we cannot attempt to understand this "decision" as if it were a decision comparable to the ones we make at particular moments, faced with a range of options' (pp. 143f.).

Nine

God, Evil and Goodness

In a famous paper first published in 1955, and subsequently reprinted dozens of times, Antony Flew raises what many would take to be the problem of evil in its classic form.[1] He focuses on the proposition 'God loves us as a father loves his children' and wonders how seriously it can be taken given what we encounter in the world. We see, for example, children dying of cancer. Their earthly fathers are driven frantic in their efforts to help, but God seems unconcerned. Flew notes how religious believers have tended to qualify God's love by saying things like 'God's love is not a merely human love' or 'It is an inscrutable love'. Yet Flew's final thought is that saying things like these may lead to what he calls a 'death by a thousand qualifications' – that they might leave 'God loves us as a father loves his children' empty of content or failing to assert anything. 'To assert that such and such is the case', Flew observes, 'is necessarily equivalent to denying that such and such is not the case.' He continues:

> Suppose then that we are in doubt as to what someone who gives vent to an utterance is asserting, or suppose that, more radically, we are sceptical as to whether he is really asserting anything at all, one way of trying to understand (or perhaps it will be to expose) his utterance is to attempt to find what he would regard as counting against, or as being incompatible with, its truth. For if the utterance is indeed an assertion, it will necessarily be equivalent to a denial of the negation of that assertion. And anything which would count against the assertion, or which would induce the speaker to withdraw it and to admit that it had been mistaken, must be part of (or the whole of) the meaning of the negation of that assertion. And to know the meaning of the negation of an

assertion is as near as makes no matter to know the meaning of that assertion. And if there is nothing which a putative assertion denies then there is nothing which it asserts either: and so it is not really an assertion.[2]

Applying all of this to ways in which believers qualify 'God loves us as a father loves his children', Flew then presses the question, 'What would have to happen not merely (morally and wrongly) to tempt but also (logically and rightly) to entitle us to say "God does not love us" or even "God does not exist"?' Flew himself has no answer to this question, and, he seems to imply, neither do those who believe in God's love. At the conclusion of Flew's paper, the suggestion appears to be that, since those who believe in God's love and God's existence are not prepared to allow anything to count against them, to assert their reality is actually to fail to say anything significant.

Now one's first reaction to Flew here might be to say that he is moving far too quickly and should rather be engaging with the topic of God and evil by, for example, carefully evaluating theodicies such as those I referred to earlier, or by examining the concept of God in considerable detail. And that reaction may well be justified. Yet there is a disarming simplicity in Flew's paper, one which leaves me feeling that he has quickly put his finger on a problem. If we insist that God loves us, or that he exists at all, we cannot indefinitely qualify the meaning of the terms we use when doing so. Not just anything can count as love, and that such and such exists is not compatible with any and every state of affairs. Flew's choice of theological statement is also rather telling. Very few religious believers say such things as 'This is the best of all possible worlds' (Leibniz) or 'We need to be created at an epistemic distance from God' (Hick and Swinburne). But many of them say that God is our Father and that he loves us – an assertion which just does, at first blush, seem strikingly falsified by what happens to many people, including children dying of cancer. As Flew says, their earthly parents display love for them by doing all that they can to relieve them of their misfortune. Yet the Father of us all often does nothing to make them well – even though, if he is omnipotent and omniscient, he could presumably cure them in an instant. Thoughts like this are what have kept the problem of evil alive for centuries, and Flew presents them crisply and pointedly.[3]

The reality of God and the problem of evil

Yet I do not agree with the implication of Flew's paper – that to say that God loves us, or that God exists, is to say what is falsified by what we find to occur in the world (is to say, in short, that evil counts decisively against God's existence).

For one thing, what happens in the world can hardly show that there is no God, since, if God exists and is, indeed, the Maker of all things (as I have argued), then anything that happens in the world has to depend on him and can hardly count as disproving his existence.[4] A necessary condition for something being the case cannot be unreal if the something in question is the case. God has traditionally been thought of as needed for the world to be at all (and at any time), so the way the world is (at any time) cannot count against his existence if God is indeed needed for the world to be at all (and at any time). To be sure, 'If there is a God, then he is the cause of all happenings' does not mean that there can be no happenings which show that there is no God. My argument, though, is that there is a God to be conceived of as accounting for all happenings, none of which, therefore, can be deemed to count against his existence.

Then again, and as I have argued, we have positive reason for saying not only that God exists (as accounting for there being something rather than nothing) but that goodness, perfection and love can be ascribed to him literally. I take it for granted that 'father' in 'God loves us as a father loves his children' can only be understood metaphorically. Not so, however, with 'good', 'perfect' and 'loving' as applied to God for the reasons that I applied them earlier. The answer to what is implied by Flew, therefore, is that we simply do have grounds for thinking of God as existing and as loving. To be sure, I have not given any reason to suppose that God loves everything equally, for, in so far as love towards a creature can be ascribed to God on the basis of goodness effected in the creature by God, it seems obvious that God does not love all creatures equally. Some have more goodness than others. It remains the case, though, that love of creatures (and love of perfect goodness) can truly be ascribed to God.

There is therefore much to be said in favour of what I have called the 'We Know that God Exists' line of thinking. To know that p is true is to know that p is possibly true, and also to know that it is not certainly false. My claim is that 'God exists, is perfect, is good and is loving' is a philosophically defensible proposition, one which deserves to be described as one that is known to be true. Philosophers, of course, have differed in their accounts of what it is to know something, and this is not the place for me to try to engage with all that they have said on the matter. Yet it seems reasonable to claim that when we embrace a conclusion, seeing that it follows from premises that we are justified in taking to be true, we can speak of ourselves as knowing the conclusion to be true. My claim is that 'God exists, is perfect, is good and is loving' follows from premises that we ought to be able to recognize as true (or ought to concede to be true), so it seems reasonable for me to say that the proposition is one we can or do know to be true. One might, of course, be justified in accepting premises which are, in fact, false.[5] Yet all philosophical arguments stand under the threat of that possibility except, perhaps, ones which move from necessarily true premises to necessarily true conclusions. Unless you want to say that no philosophical arguments can or do give us knowledge (and abstracting from those that use only premises that are necessarily true), then you ought to agree that we can or do know that God exists and that he is perfect, good and loving – assuming, of course, that you agree with what I have argued on this matter.

Yet there are different ways in which one might seek to employ the 'We Know that God Exists' approach with an eye on the topic of God and evil. One might, for example, simply take it as an adequate reply to those who think that evil shows that there is not or cannot be a God who is morally good. From what I argued in Chapters 4 and 8, however, you will realize that this is not an option open to me. In my view, we have reason for rejecting the claim that God is a moral agent. I take goodness in God not to be a matter of God being well behaved. In commending the 'We Know that God Exists' Argument, therefore, all that I am doing is noting how, on certain understandings of 'God', 'perfect', 'good' and 'loving', we are entitled to say that evil does not show that God possibly or certainly does not exist. If what I have been suggesting in this book is correct, however, that still leaves the 'We Know that God Exists' Argument in pretty good shape as a debating tool in discussions of God and evil.

Understanding God

Yet just how far does this argument take us when it comes to what we might call 'making sense' of God and evil? Let me begin to reply to this question by first saying why I think that it does not take us very far.

Suppose that you can correctly trace a certain instance of evil to me. You might then come to wonder just how perfect, good, or loving I am. You might, however, end up happy with me as you come to see that the evil that can be traced to me is something I could not have prevented without allowing a greater one. Or you might come to see it as something I was morally justified in bringing about (or bound to bring about) in order to achieve a certain good. In other words, you might come to understand what my perfection, goodness and love amount to – and on this basis you might absolve or even praise me. If what I have been arguing in this book is correct, however, we lack a comparable understanding of God's perfection, goodness and love. If God is the Creator of all things, then he is no member of the world and we cannot get our minds around him as we can when it comes to what is in the world. If there is no distinction in God between the individual that he is and the nature that he has, then we cannot understand him to be an individual – in the sense of 'individual' according to which an individual is one of whom there could always be more of the same kind. If God is perfect since he lacks nothing appropriate or necessary when it comes to the existence of the divine nature, then we know what it means to call God perfect, but we do not know what that perfection amounts to, since it is nothing other than God, who, as source of the existence of everything other than himself, is no object of scientific investigation – is not a thing of a sort that we can fathom as we can fathom things within the universe. If God is good, since he contains in himself the goodness of all created things, which therefore reflect what he is, then we know what it means to call him good. But we have no picture of that goodness. If the goodness of every created thing is a reflection of what God is, there can be no such picture since the goodness of every created thing does not amount to anything we can sensibly think of as a picture. I spoke in Chapter 3 about 'the oddness of God', and that oddness is surely pretty striking. At any rate, it seems to preclude us (in this life anyway) having anything that we could seriously call an understanding of God, and, if that is so, then knowing that God exists, or that he is perfect, loving and good, is not to understand what exactly he is. Knowledge of God it may be (and, I have argued, it is). But it cannot be an understanding of what God is in and of himself – not in the sense that you can have an understanding of what I am in and of myself. The differences there must be (and which I have tried to spell out) between God and creatures seem to make such an understanding on our part impossible.

Notice that I am not here merely trying vaguely to say that God is mysterious. All sorts of things can seem mysterious to people, and for all sorts of reasons. So to call God a mystery need not, by itself, amount to anything like a clear thesis. My point, however, is that, if I am right in what I think that we have to say about God, these are precise reasons why we lack an understanding of what he is. At the risk of repeating myself, my basic argument here is as follows:

(1) Normally, we understand what something (some actually existing thing) is in so far as we are able to single it out against the background of other things in the world (whether the thing be one of many of the same kind or the one and only instance of its kind).

(2) God is not an item in the universe.

(3) God is not an instance of a kind.

(4) God is not even the one and only instance of a kind, since such an instance is something the nature and existence of which can be distinguished from each other, while nature and existence in God are not distinguishable from each other. Given the existence of God the Creator, we have to say that whatever God's nature is cannot be distinguished from God himself: that, if you like, God is his nature (or that everything in God is God).

(5) So God is not something we can understand as we normally understand what something is.

Now, as I have argued, we can make true statements about something without understanding what it is that (what reality it is that) makes those statements true. So I take nothing in (1)–(5) above to show that we cannot make true statements about God – e.g., that God exists, that God is perfect, that God is good, or that God is loving. But I do take (1)–(5) to show that we are seriously in the dark when it comes to what it is for God to exist, or to be perfect, or to be good, or to be loving. There are reasons for saying that God exists. There are also reasons for calling him perfect, good and loving. Yet these reasons do not give us an understanding of what God is. In the sense that I can know what it is for a human being to exist, I cannot know what it is for God to exist. In the sense that I can know what it is for a circle to be a perfect one, I cannot know what it is for God to be perfect. In the sense that I can know what it is for a strawberry to be good, I cannot know what it is for God to be good. In the sense that I can know what it is for Fred to be loving, I cannot know what it is for God to be loving.

For these reasons, therefore, I take it that the 'We Know that God Exists' Argument yields limited results. At any rate, it certainly does nothing to explain how evil and God fit together. As we have seen, there are thinkers who hold that they can offer explanations here. In particular, there are those who try to tell us why God is morally justified in allowing evils of various kinds. As we have also seen, however, there are reasons for resisting their approach. If God is not a moral agent, and if his goodness is not human moral goodness, then there can be no *explanation* of evils in terms of ways in which God is morally justified for allowing X, Y, or Z. You cannot explain why cats yawn by noting that they are made of coal. By the same token, you cannot explain why God is morally justified in allowing for evil, since God is not something morally justifiable or morally unjustifiable (just as cats are not made out of coal).

One might say that evil would be explicable if we knew God's reasons for permitting it or for doing what brings it about. As I argued in the previous chapter, however, it is exceedingly hard to make sense of the phrase 'reasons that God has'. We may certainly say that God, by willing, aims at what is good, implying that he aims at it because it is good. But such aiming on God's part has to be vastly different from what we have in mind when we ascribe reasons for acting to people. It cannot be that God does what he does after having reflected on what to do. It cannot be that God does what he does because he needs something. And so on. Aquinas says that God wills the good of creatures 'on account of himself' (*propter se*).[6] From this you might conclude that Aquinas is suggesting that we can ascribe a reason to God's willing of good for creatures. Yet that is not what he is doing at all (not if 'ascribing a reason to' means what it commonly does as we speak about people). His view is that in making creatures to be, God is making them to share (as creatures) in the goodness that he has by nature. In this sense, thinks Aquinas, God creates *propter se* – with an eye (so to speak) on his own goodness as something communicable, something in which creatures can share. This thought of Aquinas would, however, be badly misconstrued if interpreted as ascribing reasons, in the normal sense, to God. Aquinas actually denies that God is rational (has reasons). Rational agents, he holds, are agents who think and judge and (sometimes) act on the basis of their thinking and judging. But Aquinas does not think of God as thinking (as a user of language who has thoughts on that basis). Nor does he conceive of God as going through any kind of reflective process (he takes God to be changeless and timeless). Aquinas certainly thinks that there is understanding in God – that God knows. But he does not take God's knowledge to be the result of any thinking (whether reasonable or otherwise). Thinking things (and, therefore, rational things), for Aquinas, are always essentially creaturely – a view which, you will now realize, I thoroughly endorse.

God, goodness, and evil

Yet I do wish to suggest that evil does not show that there is no God or that God's existence is unlikely. This conclusion is not based on any attempt to justify God's behaviour (or lack of it) at the bar of morality. It is not grounded in a theodicy of any kind. It follows, I argue, from what we need to say about God in himself. It follows from the reality and from the nature of God as we can try to express that given that he is the Creator, the Maker of all things other than himself. Theodicy, I have suggested, typically goes astray at the outset in so far as it construes God's agency as that of a moral agent modelled on human moral agency. As I have also suggested, in some of its forms theodicy goes astray by simply not offering a cogent moral defence of anything.

Where does all this leave us, however, when it comes to saying something positive concerning God and evil? If I am right, evil does not render God's existence impossible or unlikely. To say only that, however, is not to give any particular answer to the question 'How do God and evil fit together?' I argued in Chapter 7 that God does not cause evil directly and that all that God creates is good. But this conclusion is, in a sense, also negative. I mean that, rather than telling us how actually to think about evil within God's scheme of things, it basically only notes that evil cannot be something for which, in a certain sense, God is causally responsible. And one might wonder whether there is more to be said than that. Can we, for instance, acknowledge the reality and gravity of evil and, without presenting a theodicy, still end up plausibly holding that evil as we encounter it is something we can actually value or deem to cohere with the goodness of God? Can we, so to speak, offer a cogent *theology* of God and evil, one which has something to say about how they relate to each other?

It has been suggested that we can if we postulate a certain possible scenario for people following their deaths. Someone taking this line is Marilyn McCord Adams, who develops it at length in *Horrendous Evils and the Goodness of God.*[7] According to Adams, horrendous evils are 'evils the participation in which (that is, the doing or suffering of which) constitutes prima facie reason to doubt whether the participant's life could (given their inclusion in it) be a great good to him/her on the whole'.[8] What makes such evils so pernicious, says Adams, 'is their life-ruining potential, their power prima facie to degrade the individual by devouring the possibility of positive personal meaning in one swift gulp . . . horrors afflict persons insofar as they are actual or potential meaning-makers'.[9] Some would try to theorize about what Adams calls horrendous evils by indulging in theodicy, by telling us how God is morally justified in permitting them. Adams, however, seems generally unimpressed with theodicy. She believes that when thinking of God's goodness we need to say something that speaks to the actual suffering of particular victims. '[F]or God to be *good to* a created person,' says Adams, 'God must guarantee him/her a life that is a great good *to him/her* on the whole and one in which any participation in horrors is defeated within the context of his/her own life . . . [F]or a person's life to be a great good to him/her on the whole, it is not enough that his/her life be objectively full of positive meaning or that these meanings be appreciated by others; s/he must recognize and appropriate meanings sufficient to render it worth living.'[10] To respond to this need Adams suggests ways in which we might think of God so as to view our sufferings as compensated for or trumped. In particular, she argues that the notion that everyone ends up in union with God would allow us (even as victims of horrendous evils) to rejoice in our lives and in God's goodness.

I have considerable sympathy with Adams's approach here. Rightly eschewing theodicy, rightly turning her back on attempts to show that

God is basically well behaved, she wants, as I do, to turn discussion of God and evil in a different direction from the one it has lately taken. If I understand her correctly, her response to authors like Mackie (critical of theism) and Swinburne (apologetically defensive of theism with an eye on God's moral integrity) is to say: a plague on both your houses. And that is my position. Yet I do not see how noting the fact that God might do great good to people after their deaths helps very much as we note the evils that exist. For one thing, I am sceptical of the claim that people (or that all people) after death will, in fact, and regardless of their circumstances, be able to conclude (or be right in concluding) that the evils they have experienced have been trumped in some way.[11] Joy can make sadness seem to pale. But not always. More importantly, though, I do not see how Adams has seriously helped us to understand why we can, here and now, think of God as good in spite of evil. Her chief focus is on what people might come to think in a glorious life to come. This focus, however, and whatever its merits may be, turns attention away from the less than glorious world in which we currently find ourselves. If we (as we are here and now) want credibly to claim that God is indeed good, then, it seems to me, we need to be able to point to what we can draw attention to when it comes to the here and now. Suppose that someone accepts (a) that God exists and (b) that God is good, though not morally good. Suppose also that this person still asks how it can be said that God is good. What reply can we offer?

To start with, of course, we can say that it is no mean thing to have recognized that God is good. We may not be able to understand what God is, but to know that we have reason to ascribe goodness to him is to have achieved something of importance. I have argued that God is good since he is what is reflected by all creaturely goodness. It cannot be that 'reflected' here means 'looks like'. It means 'reflected as an agent-cause can be reflected in effects of it which might be very different from it'. Yet to know that creaturely goodness reflects God like this is at least to know that what we value in creatures cannot be less than what is in God (or what God is). It is to know that the goodness of creatures derives from something the nature of which calls it into being and empowers it.

A second point we might make is that we are saying quite a lot about God's goodness when noting, as I have, that God creates nothing but what is good. I said above that this thesis can be viewed as a somewhat negative one – as noting that God does not, in a certain sense, cause evil. Yet it is also a pretty positive thesis. For it tells us that there are no created goods which are not God's doing. And that thought allows us to wax positively eloquent when it comes to God's goodness (though poets might be able to do this better than most of us, and certainly better than I can). It allows us to point to any created good and to say 'God is at work there; he is making it to be'. And if God makes things to be by virtue of will (i.e. not because anything in or apart from himself is forcing him to do so), then created goods are nothing less than freely given gifts from God. We approve of people with largesse, people willing to impart what they have to others. All the more, therefore, might we approve of a God who creates all that is good, whose gift of what is good extends to everything good in the created order, whose gift of what is good extends, so I have argued, to every creature merely in so far as it exists.

One might, of course, reply that lots of things are not as good as they could be. And this seems obviously true. My cat Smokey was sick when I was writing Chapter 3 of this book. I take it that he was, there-fore, not as good then as he could then have been. This evident truth, however, does not take away from the fact that there is a great deal of created goodness, all of it deriving from God (and with nothing forcing him to produce it). A lack of created goodness is not a sign of God's goodness (i.e. it gives us no reason to think of God as good). But the presence of created goodness gives us reason to think of God as good, and the fact that there is so much created goodness gives us reason to think of God's goodness as exceptional. Here, once again, I am not saying that God's being good depends on what he produces. My point is that if people accept that God is good for reasons of the kind that I presented in Chapter 8, and if they continue to wonder or worry about God's goodness, then we offer a decent reply to them if we draw their attention to the enormousness of the goodness that exists in creation. One might, perhaps, assent to the conclusion that all that is good comes from God. One might, however, still need to be reminded of *how much* good comes from God. We are talking here about the existence of absolutely everything created. We are also talking about all the multiple instances in which created goodness is present to a high degree.

One way of reiterating this last point is to observe that God is supremely involved with or present to his creatures. Theological critics of the view that God is unchangeable sometimes say that this view renders him distant or aloof from what he is supposed to have made. If what I have been arguing is correct, however, God cannot be this at all. For on my account it follows that God is totally present to all of his creatures – more present to them than any creature can be to any other. Of course, if God were just the number-one person living along-side creatures as a member of the universe, this could not be so. Not being bodily, he would, at best, be present to creatures only as knowing or observing them somehow. Certainly, he would be outside or apart from them. If we focus on the notion of God as making everything to be for as long as it exists, however, a different picture emerges.

Here it helps to ask in what sense God can be thought of as being everywhere.

That God is everywhere is a familiar theological teaching (some-times referred to as the doctrine of divine ubiquity). But how can God be everywhere? If God is incorporeal, he cannot possibly be anywhere dimensively.[12] I can be somewhere, since my body can be somewhere. Yet if God is not a body, he cannot be in a place by phys-ically occupying a place. For the same reason, of course, it follows that God cannot be everywhere dimensively.

Yet we can, I think, make sense of God being somewhere if we focus on the fact that he is the creator of places. We normally say that some-thing is somewhere because we think of it as a physical object, or a col-lection of physical objects, that can be physically related to other physical objects. There are no such 'things' as places. These only exist because physical objects exist in relation to each other. Bodies make places 'to be' in so far as they are materially related to other bodies. As Creator, however, God makes *all* bodies to be. So he also makes places to be, and he does so by being creatively present to the bodies that make for places. Since, as I argued in Chapter 3, the being of the world is just what God's doing amounts to (on the principle that the action of an agent lies in the patient), this means that the existence of places is God as active and that God can therefore indeed be said to be in all places, or to be everywhere. And if God is not something composed of parts (see Chapter 3 again), it subsequently follows that for God to be somewhere is for him to be *entirely* there. In other words, given what I take to be a proper reading of the notion that God is the Creator, we can say that the whole of God, not just a bit of him, is actively present in all that exists.

Now we cannot say that of anything else. People and other things can be involved with what is around them – but not as being present to things in the way that God must be. He can never be outside his creatures. He has to be within all of them, making them to be themselves – a fact which might well be fitted into the equation when it comes to the topic of God, goodness and evil. Indeed there are things which lack goodness. But even these are full of God's creative presence. Or, so one might say, they, like everything else in the universe, are objects of God's compassion.

I take compassion to be a feeling (or a feeling-with) and I certainly do not want to ascribe feelings to God. He cannot have compassion for creatures as someone who is affected by what happens to them. People with compassion, however, are (impossibly of course) seeking to be at one with the object or objects of their compassion. As Herbert McCabe observes: 'We speak of "*sym*pathy" or "*com*passion" just because we want to say that it is *almost* as though we were not outside the other, but living her or his life, experiencing her or his suffering. A component of pity is frustration at having, in the end, to remain outside.'[13] Yet the Creator cannot in this way ever be outside his creatures. Or, as McCabe goes on to say:

> If the creator is the reason for everything that is, there can be no actual being which does not have the creator as its centre holding it in being. In our compassion we, in our feeble way, are seeking to be what God is all the time: united with and within the life of our friend. We can say in the psalm 'The Lord is compassion' but a sign that this is metaphorical language is that we can also say that the Lord has no need of compassion; he has something more wonderful, he has his creative act in which he is 'closer to the sufferer than she is to herself'.[14]

We cannot attribute compassion to God as we can to human beings. To do so would be to ride roughshod over the differences there must be between creatures and their Creator. We can, however, note that God is never distant from or uninvolved in what goes on as creatures continue to be – a fact which we might reasonably rejoice in, and one which can surely be fairly pressed when talking to people who, when reflecting on evil, feel that God must be distant or uninvolved. To people like this one can reasonably say that God is never absent from victims of evil. He is always entirely present to them. Victims of evil, in so far as they are capable of thinking at all, might find this thought unconsoling since it offers no *explanation* of what is happening to them, and in so far as it does it still offers little, considered just as a thought, to remedy their situation. It remains the case, however, that the thought is relevant when it comes to the topic of God and evil. Someone who thinks that God is wholly there in all that comes to pass has a quite different view from someone who holds that evil disproves God's existence or renders it improbable. Such a person also has a quite different view from someone who holds that evil leaves something out of the hands of a God who is good.

The goodness that exists

Yet people who believe in the existence and goodness of God might still ask whether anything can be said so as to let us see that evils of various kinds make sense in what we might call 'human terms'. I mean that, assuming that they have read and agreed with what I have written above, they might say something like this to me: 'You argue that there is, indeed, a God to whom goodness can be ascribed. Yet you stress the fact that God is not a human agent acting for reasons we can understand. You note that God makes a vast deal of goodness and you tell us that he is present in all things, including those that are victims of evil. Can you not, however, say something which can reasonably allow us to think of specific evils as serving good purposes, ones which we can value here and now?' The question is a very fair one. So let me now try to answer it.

You will realize, of course, that I cannot do so by attempting to offer a theodicy in the manner of people such as Swinburne or Hick. Given what I have already argued, I obviously cannot point to examples of evil and say that God is morally justified for allowing them for reasons *X*, *Y*, or *Z*. Having put theodicy behind me, however, I think that I can note various ways in which our world contains evils that *in fact* contribute to the existence of what is good, and which sometimes even do so as necessary conditions. I think that I can do so to start with by referring back to some lines of thinking noted in previous chapters.

As we have seen, the following arguments have been adduced in defence of God's goodness given the reality of evil:

(1) Evil often allows us to improve ourselves or to do great good to others.

(2) Naturally occurring evils allow us to recognize what we can do to help people or to improve things in general.

These are not theses which help when it comes to defending God's moral goodness, but they are respectable enough if viewed as merely drawing attention to the fact that good often does, as a matter of fact, come out of evil. Evil sometimes crushes people, but sometimes it also seems to prompt them (even if only in small and inadequate ways) to acts of kindness, tenderness, love and charity (good things, presumably).[15] Naturally occurring evils wreak great havoc. As Swinburne suggests, however, they can teach us what to do in order to help, albeit also to harm:[16]

> We (i.e. humans in general) learn that eating toadstools causes stomach pain by seeing people eat toadstools and then suffer pain . . . These observations open up a range of possible actions, good and bad, which would not otherwise be available . . . We know that rabies causes a terrible death. With this knowledge we have the possibility of preventing such death . . . Only with the knowledge of the effects of rabies are such possibilities open to us. That knowledge is provided by observations of various people suffering subsequently to being bitten by dogs and other animals with rabies in various circumstances. Or, again, how are humans to have the opportunity to stop future generations contracting asbestosis, except through knowledge of what causes asbestosis? We can choose to obtain that knowledge through laborious study of records which show that persons in contact with blue asbestos many years ago have died from asbestosis thirty years later.[17]

Swinburne wishes to press these remarks so as to conclude that God is morally justified in allowing for certain evils, and I have no wish to follow him down that road. Yet, taken on their own, the remarks seem perfectly reasonable. They illustrate how we can be thought of as able to do good because of the occurrence of evil, how good can come from evil. We may lament the fact that goodness (e.g. the goodness of those who care for the poor or the sick) presupposes what is bad. I think, though, that we cannot seriously deny that there is a great deal of goodness which, in fact, presupposes what is bad. Evil, indeed, does give rise to good.

In fact, it gives rise to a *vast* amount of good. It has sometimes been said that we should speak not of 'the problem of evil' but of 'the problem of good'. The idea here seems to be that we should be more struck by goodness than by evil and should therefore conclude that, rather than be worried about evil, we need to account for the goodness that exists. You will realize that I sympathize with this idea. I do not, however, want to press it now. Instead, I simply draw your attention to the fact that a huge amount of good comes from what can be thought of as bad. Thus, for example: the good of justice pursued arises from offences against justice; the good of nurturing and caring for others arises from situations in which people need to be nurtured and cared for; the good of health arises as people and animals feed on things which perish for them to do so; our recognition of our mortality often leads us to do good in the time available to us; the good of forgiveness often arises from the fact that there are people in need of it; the good of discovery constantly comes about as ignorance gives way to knowledge; and the goodness of generosity is continually in evidence as people respond to those in need. In noting such facts I am not for a moment saying that evil is good or that good results justify bad beginnings. I am merely observing that, *in fact*, evil gives rise to a great deal of good and that the world that God has made is one in which this happens. God's world contains a great deal of good, enough, so one might think, to warrant us in being cautious to conclude that God is not himself good.

Someone sensitive to this fact is Eleonore Stump. In a discussion of Aquinas's commentary on the book of Job, she notes (evidently with a fair degree of appreciation) how Aquinas is able to think about God and evil by noting the beneficial effects of what we would commonly take to be misfortunes.[18] Not doubting God's existence, Aquinas does not take the sufferings of Job to cast doubt on God's existence; but he does note how they, and comparable sufferings, can be thought of as beneficial. Such sufferings, he says, can lead us to acquire virtues of various kinds. He suggests that they can often be viewed as a kind of medication that leads to greater health. As Stump observes, we do not commonly think in such terms. We instinctively tend to recoil from pain and suffering. Yet, she adds, we might pause to consider how suffering can improve the sufferer. She is not remotely suggesting, of course, that we should seek suffering for its own sake, or that we should not seek to prevent it in so far as we can. Her point, emphasized also by Aquinas, is simply that evil can indeed lead to good.

Admittedly, though, Stump is thinking of goodness here in a way that many would not. Linking arms with Aquinas, she is not assuming that goodness should be automatically equated with things such as health, wealth, or bodily comfort. Without denying that these can be good, she is prepared to think of there being greater goods than these, goods which people might gain precisely by being deprived of them. In particular, she is thinking in Christian terms and is, therefore, prepared to entertain the thought that ultimate human happiness lies in union with God, a union which, for some people, might actually come to pass because of pain and suffering. As she writes: 'What Aquinas's interpretation of Job and general account of evil show us, whether we are inclined to accept or reject them, is that our approach to the problem of evil is a consequence of our attitude toward much larger issues, such as the nature of human happiness and the goal of human life.'[19] Given his Christian beliefs Aquinas was able to view at least some human suffering as medicinal – as able to result in, for example, trust in God, humility, patience and forgiveness. These are certainly not desirable on everyone's count. If they are desirable, however, then one might begin to see why it might be right for Aquinas, like Stump, to be prepared to view evil as something that can lead to good. Trust in God seems to presuppose adversity which gives rise to doubt. You can only be humbled in the light of things going as you would not like, to begin with. To be patient is to resign oneself to things not going as one wants them to go. Forgiveness is impossible if someone has not done something wrong. Of course, I am not saying at this point that God is justified in allowing for certain evils because they are a necessary means to some goods or other (I am not indulging in what I have called a means–ends theodicy). My point is that it just is the case that what we take to be bad can and does sometimes lead to what is good (or to what can intelligibly be thought of as good), and that it can do so as part of God's governing of his created order – a governing which might therefore be thought of as good (or, at least, not that of one who is not good).

God, evil, and Christianity

In this book I have not presumed the truth of any specifically Christian teaching. I have said why I think that we are rationally justified in asserting God's existence. At a purely philosophical level I have also tried to say, and with an eye on evil, what belief in God ought to be thought of as implying when it comes to an account of what God is (or is not) and what God does (or does not do). I have not, however, sought to approach the topic of God and evil by starting with theological conclusions. Stump's treatment of Aquinas's commentary on Job does, however, prompt the question, 'Can those coming from the Christian tradition, and appealing *only* to that, have something to say which might lead us think of God as good?' As I bring the present book to a close, I should like briefly to address this query.

To start with, perhaps I should say how I distinguish between philosophy and Christian theology.[20] To some extent, the distinction is hard to draw, since many philosophers argue for Christian conclusions and since many Christian theologians employ philosophical reasoning as they elaborate their positions. A traditional view, however, is that Christian theology is primarily concerned to reflect on teachings which cannot be demonstrated or otherwise shown to be true by purely rational reflection, by what philosophers in general take their business to be. According to this view, there are fundamental truths which have to be accepted in faith: revealed truths. Exponents of this position often think it important to apply philosophical reasoning to revealed truths (so as, for example, to consider whether or not they are logically consistent).[21] They also typically think that there are some reasons for accepting the truths in question.[22] They do not, however, suppose that truths of faith are ones to which philosophers can attain simply by practising their trade. And if we take 'truths of faith' to signify the teaching of texts like the Nicene Creed, then I think they are right. For example, I see no way of proving (or even of showing it probable) that God is Father, Son and Spirit (the doctrine of the Trinity). We can, I have argued, claim to know that God exists because of what he has made. Because of the created order, we can reasonably claim that *something* is divine. According to the doctrine of the Trinity, however, creation is the work of all the divine persons and therefore attests to them only in so far as they are divine, not in so far as they are numerable.[23] As Aquinas puts it:

The creative power of God is shared by the whole Trinity; hence it goes with the unity of nature, not with the distinction of persons. Therefore, through natural reason we can know what has to do with the unity of nature, but not with the distinction of persons.[24]

So I do not want to claim that all distinctively Christian teaching is provable. This is not to say, however, that philosophers cannot draw on it or even presuppose it as they go about their business. All of our reasoning (whether good, bad, or indifferent) is based on premises that we cannot prove, premises for which we cannot argue, premises from which we start. Someone thinking about God and evil might therefore justly claim that Christian premises might be legitimately invoked in face of the claim that 'reason' shows us that God is not good, or not loving. You might say that there are reasons for supposing that Christian thinking is inherently self-contradictory or that it can be shown to be misguided on some other count; and, if that is your position, my reply at the moment is 'You may be right'. But let us suppose that you are wrong. On that supposition, might it not be thought that Christian beliefs (completely ignored by many who have written on God and evil) give us grounds for thinking of God as good or as loving – grounds rarely appealed to in contemporary philosophical discussions of the problem of evil? I think that the answer to this question is 'Yes'.[25]

For one thing, Christian teaching warrants those who accept it in thinking that God is loving in something like the sense of 'loving' that we have in mind when we are concerned with love between equals. I argued in the previous chapter that we cannot sensibly think of God as *giving himself in love* to a creature, that what we take to be mature adult love presupposes a sameness in the lovers (as, for example, the love of people for cats, or even the love of parents for their children, does not) – a sameness that simply does not exist when it comes to God and creatures. According to the doctrine of the Trinity, however, God, so to speak, has an equal since the life of God is the life of three who are each divine. Contrary to those who think that belief in God is first and foremost belief that there is a single person (without a body) called God, the doctrine of the Trinity teaches that there is relationship in God, to be thought of as a relationship between equals who love each other. In terms of the doctrine of the Trinity, love between the divine persons constitutes what God is essentially (not, for example, what he is on the condition that he chooses to create). So the doctrine of the Trinity licenses those who accept it in believing that, as the New Testament says, 'God is love' – the sense of which seems to be, not that God loves in that he does good to creatures, but that love is in God eternally and by virtue of what it is to be God (what God is by nature).[26] I take it as obvious that the doctrine of the Trinity does not proclaim God to be three distinct centres of consciousness, or something like that. The doctrine is not asking us to think of God as three invisible people. But it does proclaim (puzzling though it might seem to say so) that there is at least one and another in God, that each of the three divine persons is an other to each of the other two.[27] It therefore gives those who believe in the doctrine of the Trinity reason for saying that God is essentially loving. You might say that we cannot understand what the Trinity is and therefore have little way of conceiving what it is for God, as triune, to be essentially loving. I do not, however, wish to suggest otherwise. It is sometimes said that we know what we are talking about as we refer to God but that our reason breaks down when it comes to the doctrine of the Trinity. I think that this view has to be wrong since, as I have already argued, our reason has seriously broken down in so far as we try to conceive of God at all. So I am not suggesting that Christians have a picture of the Trinity which allows them to stand back and say, 'Oh, of course, God is essentially loving after all.' My point is just that if the doctrine of the Trinity is true, then love has to be present in God by virtue of what God is.

One might respond to this thought by observing that love between the persons of the Trinity has little relevance to human beings, especially those who wonder what it might mean to say that God is good to us or even that he loves us. Let us suppose that the life of God is one of an eternal and loving union between the Father, the Son and the Holy Spirit. Does this fact, if indeed it is a fact, tell us anything about ourselves as we stumble along in a world full of evil?

Well, it certainly does if what Christians say about the Trinity is correct. Standard Christian reflection on the doctrine of the Trinity has not confined itself just to asserting that God is essentially Father, Son and Spirit. Christians have also traditionally spoken about how the Trinity is active in the world, especially how it is active when it comes to human beings, and in doing so they have regularly stressed how God, as Trinity, can be thought of as good or loving in spite of the evils that exist.

Classical Trinitarian thinking, of course, only emerged well after the New Testament period (around the fourth century AD) and as an attempt to summarize, or to draw out the implications of, some of the things said in the New Testament. There, for example, we find Jesus being spoken of as God's son and as God's equal.[28] There we find it said that there is a 'Spirit of truth' who proceeds from the Father and who will be sent to believers from the Father by Jesus.[29] There we also find Christians being told to baptize people 'in the name of the Father and of the Son and of the Holy Spirit'.[30] The New Testament never presents an explicit confession of faith in the Trinity of the kind that we find offered by the Council of Nicaea or the so-called Creed of Athanasius.[31] It does, however, contain texts which are naturally interpretable along classical Trinitarian lines, and the development of the doctrine of the Trinity took these into account so as to speak about what we might call the Trinity as *active in history* (the 'economic Trinity' as it sometimes called).[32] My point now is simply that if what theologians have said about the economic Trinity (while defending its reality) is true, then the doctrine of the Trinity has relevance to discussions of God and evil.[33]

To start with, classical Trinitarian thinking, in so far as it concentrates on history, holds that God the Son became a human being and, in his human nature, underwent pain and death. Now in holding to this teaching, classical Trinitarian thinking means that, in Christ, God literally suffered and died. In terms of classical Trinitarian thinking, therefore, God and evil are not opposed to each other in a sense which would mean that evil renders God's existence dubious in some way. If you begin with the classical notion of the Trinity you could never think it reasonable to make the move from 'There is evil' to 'Therefore there cannot be a God, or there probably is no God'. For the classical notion of the Trinity, with its insistence on the Incarnation of God the Son, our understanding of what God is (such as it is) already involves us acknowledging the reality of evil (in the form of the suffering and death of Christ).

You might say that exponents of the classical notion of the Trinity cannot be right to think in these terms since God cannot literally suffer. Yet though we might deny (and in my view rightly) that the divine nature can undergo suffering, it is not obvious that we contradict ourselves when saying that a divine subject (i.e. the second person of the Trinity) suffered as a human being. At any rate, the best-known defenders of the classical notion of the Trinity hold that we do not contradict ourselves when saying this.

Take, for example, Aquinas. Rejecting the view that propositions link names to assert identity by means of the verb 'to be', he argues that propositions single out subjects and predicate something of them.[34] He goes on to maintain that in propositions about Christ we are talking about a particular subject using a range of predicates some of which are applicable to Christ, in so far as he is human, and others of which are applicable to him in so far as he is divine – predicates applicable to Christ (the Son of God, the second person of the Trinity) in so far as he is a single subject with two distinct natures. As God, says Aquinas, Christ can truly be said to be incorporeal and immutable. As man, however, so Aquinas also maintains, Christ can truly be said to be bodily and changeable. According to Aquinas, if it makes sense to predicate *F* of a human being, it makes sense to predicate *F* of Christ, and if it makes sense to predicate *F* of God, then it makes equal sense to predicate *F* of Christ. For Aquinas, in virtue of Christ's human nature we speak of him as we would speak of any other human being. In virtue of his divine nature, we can also say more enigmatic and mysterious things. As Aquinas well recognizes, of course, human nature and the divine nature are radically different. But he does not therefore conclude that we contradict ourselves when asserting that Christ is both human and divine. For Aquinas, the name 'Christ' singles out a subject and has no descriptive force, and he goes on to maintain that to say that Christ is human and that Christ is God is simply to say of a single subject that different ways of talking about it can be true since the subject in question has, not one, but two distinct natures.[35]

Is Aquinas talking sense here? This is not the place to embark on a detailed discussion of that question. All that I wish to stress now is that (a) to accept classical Trinitarian thinking is to be committed to the position that when Christ suffered, then God literally suffered (Christ being a subject both human and divine), and (b) to accept classical Trinitarian thinking is to view evil as something in which God is truly involved as its victim, as something with respect to which he is not *other than us* but *one of us*. Since, as I have argued, we are seriously ignorant when it comes to God's nature (the divine nature ascribed to Christ in classical Trinitarian thinking), neither (a) nor (b) provides us with any understanding of what it is for there to be one who, though God, suffers as human (as exponents of classical Trinitarian thinking seem regularly to accept). They do, however, draw attention to a way of thinking about God which, if right, allows us to think of evil as not refuting his existence and as being something in which he is not so distant from us as those who reflect on evil often like to make him out to be.

Does classical Trinitarian thinking give us any reason to think of God as good, however? Does it say anything to suggest that God is desirable, loving, or just plain worth bothering with? I think that it does, given its claims about the Incarnation.[36] I am no theologian, so you shall have to forgive me if what I am about to say appears to be theologically inept. It seems to me, however, relevant when it comes to the topic of God and evil.

The point to focus on, I think, is that for classical Trinitarians Christ is literally divine. He is what God looks like when projected into the created order.[37] My use of 'projected' here is, of course, metaphorical. But the image is helpful when thinking about classical Trinitarian thinking, for God incarnate could not be anything other than a human being giving us an image of what God is from eternity. The Son of God made man just has to be the best picture we could ever have when it comes to a picture of the strictly non-picturable source of all things. Indeed, one might say, the life and death of the Son of God made man is nothing but the life of the Trinity told, as it were, in a story.

The Gospels, which record the life and death of Christ, give us a story, one which classical Trinitarians take to be a story about God. In eternity, of course, God has no life-history and therefore no story to be recorded. In time though, and if you believe that Christ was truly God (and not just a very holy man), God *does* have a life-history and a story to be told – the story of Christ, which according to classical Trinitarian thinking is also the story of the Trinity (Christ being all that God is).

So how does the story go? It begins by telling us about the birth of a male child in poverty. It goes on to report that as an adult he embraced and healed the sick, the demented, the deprived and the oppressed, that he looked for peace, that he abhorred revenge, that he told people to be wary of judging others and to forgive each other, that he despised hypocrisy, that he was warm and free and spontaneous with people, that he taught that there are better things than money, that he disparaged self-deception, that he sought to build bridges between people of different nationalities and religions, that he embraced the innocent and told others to do the same, that he castigated those who cause people to suffer unjustly, that he welcomed sinners or wrongdoers while encouraging them to change their ways, that he urged people to help and look after each other, and that he told them to focus on what he stood for rather than on himself.[38] The story of Christ, as the Gospels record it, ends with him being put to death (while forgiving those who killed him) at the behest of those who clearly did not like what he said and did – which he called doing the will of his father in heaven.[39]

This story is, of course, an intriguing one. More importantly, however, its centrepiece is hardly something easily to be written off as bad or as not good. If, as defenders of the doctrine of the Trinity hold, God is what Christ looks like (in so far as God can be said to look like anything), then I think that many people (though clearly not all) would find God attractive, desirable, and, therefore, good. To be sure, I am not saying that classical Trinitarianism is true, nor am I making any attempt to argue in its favour. It does seem, however, that its picture of God, involving reference to the words and actions of Christ as depicted in the Gospels, is a picture of what can be recognized as good.[40] Considered as such it surely, therefore, merits attention when it comes to the charge that God cannot be thought of as good – attention which it conspicuously lacks in recent treatments of God and evil, most of which still seem to proceed as though discussions of this topic should carry on with no reference to uniquely Christian thinking.

You might reply, of course, that there is no reason to bring Christian thinking into discussions of God and evil. You might say that such discussions should stick with what people take God to be. Yet that seems an odd line of thought to embrace. For in Christian thinking God *is* what Christians take God to be, and they take God to be more than what, for example, non-theists like J. L. Mackie and William Rowe, or theodicists such as Richard Swinburne and John Hick, typically take him to be as they embark on their various attempts to refute or defend belief in him.

In short, if we move beyond the confines of purely philosophical theism (or theism as commonly understood by philosophers who ignore much that Christians have had to say about God), one can begin to see a case for denying that belief in God (or, more specifically, belief in God's goodness) is refuted or seriously called into question just because of the evil that exists. One might, of course, see no such case if one thinks of God only as being a person with a moral case to answer (a person with respect to which even Christ might be thought right to hold him accountable). In this book, however, I have tried to explain why one should not think of God in those terms.

I have also spoken against various kinds of theodicies while suggesting that evil cannot be viewed as something created by God. And I have argued that evil does not show God's existence to be impossible or improbable. As you will now realize, however, I do not claim to be able to *explain* why evil exists on the scale it does or why it exists at all. On my account, God could have made a world containing nothing but good. He clearly has not. Does this make him bad? I have argued against the conclusion that it does. But that argument does not amount to any kind of explanation concerning the role of evil in God's created order.

In my view, there can be no such explanation. Trying to plot God's reasons for producing what he does or for not producing something that he does not seems, as I have argued, to proceed from an erroneous premise – that God can be thought of as acting for reasons as we do. The most we can say, I think, is what I have been trying to suggest in this book. We are right to suppose that God exists; we have a philosophical case to make for thinking of God as good and loving; we have no reason to think that God causes evil as an end in itself; if we believe in God we can hardly doubt that he creates an enormous amount of goodness; in so far as we sympathize with classical Christian thinking about the Trinity and the Incarnation, we have grounds for taking God to be loving and good. If those conclusions are true, however, then we are not, perhaps, entirely in the dark when it comes to the reality of God and the problem of evil.

Notes

1. Antony Flew, 'Theology and Falsification', in Antony Flew and Alasdair MacIntyre (eds), *New Essays in Philosophical Theology* (SCM Press: London, 1955).
2. Ibid., p. 98.
3. It is worth noting, however, that it is not, at any rate, biblical teaching that God loves us as a father loves his children – not if 'us' means all of us. The

Bible never says that God loves all people equally. Indeed, it often asserts the opposite (e.g. Romans 9:13). In chapter 14 of John's Gospel Jesus speaks of his father loving those who have loved him (John 14:20–23). John, however, is here clearly not viewing God the father's love as universal, as love to all people. I John 3:1 reads, 'See what love the Father has given us, that we should be called children of God'. Here, though, the fatherly love of God seems to be confined to those he has called to be followers of Christ. Note that the passages to which I have just referred are the *only* biblical ones in which the notion of God as father is conjoined with the notion of God as loving.

4. Some people say that science can disprove belief in God. Science, however, is an account of the way the world is. And if God accounts for there being any world at all, it is clearly ludicrous to suggest that science can disprove the existence of God.

5. Conceivably, given evidence to hand, one might be more reasonable than not to assert what is actually false – as, for example, when a jury wrongly convicts someone against whom the available evidence seems overwhelmingly incriminating.

6. See Thomas Aquinas, *Summa Contra Gentiles*, I.73.

7. Marilyn McCord Adams, *Horrendous Evils and the Goodness of God* (Cornell University Press: Ithaca, NY and London, 1999).

8. Ibid., p. 26.

9. Ibid., pp. 27f.

10. Ibid., p. 156.

11. At this point I leave aside the question 'Is it intelligible to think of people as surviving their death?' Many, of course, would say that it is not. D. Z. Phillips adopts this position in *The Problem of Evil and the Problem of God* (SCM Press: London, 2004). See esp. pp. 81–90.

12. Here, once again, I am abstracting from the orthodox doctrine of the Incarnation, according to which God was indeed once in a place (on the principle that if Christ was once somewhere, and if Christ was God, then God was once somewhere). Notice, however, that the orthodox doctrine of the Incarnation does not teach that the divine nature was ever in any place. It holds that God was in a place, since Christ (a human being and, considered as such, a creature) was in a place. And it certainly does not entail that God is everywhere by being everywhere dimensively.

13. Herbert McCabe, *God Matters* (Geoffrey Chapman: London, 1987), p. 44.

14. Ibid., pp. 44f.

15. I am loosely distinguishing here between love and charity, i.e. between doing good for another because one likes them (this being love) and doing good for another because one wishes them well regardless of one's feelings towards them (this being charity). I am not concerned here, however, to press any serious and general distinction between love and charity.

16. See Richard Swinburne, *Providence and the Problem of Evil* (Clarendon Press: Oxford, 1998), ch. 10.

17. Ibid., p. 186.
18. Eleonore Stump, 'Aquinas and the Sufferings of Job', in Eleonore Stump (ed.), *Reasoned Faith: Essays in Philosophical Theology in Honor of Norman Kretzmann* (Cornell University Press: Ithaca, NY and London, 1993).
19. Ibid., p. 356.
20. There are, of course, non-Christian theologians and non-Christian theological traditions. I am, alas, not competent to bring these into the present discussion.
21. Aquinas is an example of someone who deals philosophically with what he takes to be unprovable truths. According to him, we cannot, for example, demonstrate the truth of the doctrines of the Trinity or the Incarnation, but we can ask whether these doctrines fall foul of (can be refuted in the light of) logical truths or some other philosophical principles. See *Summa Theologiae*, Ia.1.8.
22. We often find it said, for example, that though revealed truths cannot be demonstrated, those who accept them do not do so entirely without reason. Aquinas, again, is a classical exponent of this position. See *Summa Contra Gentiles*, I.6.
23. Some medieval thinkers tried to argue that reason forces us to conclude that the doctrine of the Trinity is true. A notable example is Richard of St Victor (d. 1173); see his *De Trinitate*, 3.11. In recent years, Richard Swinburne has defended the same conclusion; see his 'Could There Be More Than One God?', *Faith and Philosophy* 5 (1988).
24. Aquinas, *Summa Theologiae*, Ia.32.1. I quote from vol. 6 of the Blackfriars edition of the *Summa Theologiae* (Eyre and Spottiswoode: London and McGraw-Hill: New York, 1965).
25. What counts as Christian belief? One answer might be 'Any belief that someone takes to be Christian'. But people evidently have very different ideas when it comes to what counts as Christian. I do not here wish to get myself entangled in a discussion of what does and does not count as Christian belief. Instead, I aim to proceed by focusing on New Testament texts and on Church councils up to and including Nicaea. So, for example, I am assuming the orthodox interpretation of the doctrine of the Incarnation and the doctrine of the Trinity (according to which Christ was literally divine and according to which there is a real distinction of persons within the Trinity). There are Christian theologians (theologians who describe themselves as Christian) who think that this orthodox interpretation needs to be revised (i.e. rejected). This is not the place for me to seek to argue with them. Nor do I need to, since my present purpose is only to consider what might be said about God, goodness and love on the *supposition* that what the New Testament or councils such as Nicaea tell us is true.
26. Cf. C. H. Dodd, *The Johannine Epistles* (Harper: New York, 1946), p. 107.
27. For a philosophically sophisticated discussion of the doctrine of the Trinity, see C. J. F. Williams, 'Neither Confounding the Persons nor

Dividing the Substance', in Alan G. Padgett (ed.), *Reason and the Christian Religion* (Clarendon Press: Oxford, 1994).

28. John 1:1–18 is a crucial text here.
29. John 15:26.
30. Matthew 28:19.
31. The Athanasian Creed, no longer believed to have been composed by St Athanasius (*c.* 296–373), is commonly dated by scholars to between 381 and 428.
32. In the context of Trinitarian theology a distinction is commonly made between the 'immanent trinity' and the 'economic Trinity'. Those who draw this distinction are not, of course, suggesting that there are two kinds of Trinity, as there might, for example, be two kinds of cheese. Their idea is that (a) we can seek to say what God, as Trinity, is in himself from eternity (and on the supposition that God might never have created anything), and (b) we can seek to note what the Trinity actually does in the created order, and what it therefore reveals of itself as, so to speak, going out of itself and acting in what is not divine.
33. Theologians, as might be expected, have disagreed with each other when it comes to what should be said concerning the Trinity. All of them know what was said about the Trinity by the Council of Nicaea and by authors like Augustine of Hippo and Thomas Aquinas (this is what I have in mind when I use the phrase 'classical Trinitarian thinking'). As I have noted, some of them have argued that classical Trinitarian thinking needs to be abandoned or, in some way, revised, and in this book I cannot engage with, or document, their reasons for thinking along these lines. For the moment, I content myself only with trying to note how classical Trinitarian thinking has a bearing on the topic of God and evil.
34. The 'two-name' theory of predication is one that Aquinas was arguably right to reject. As Peter Geach writes: 'Anyone who is tempted by it may try his hand at explaining in terms of it how we can fit together the three terms "David", "father", and "Solomon" (which on this theory are three *names*) to form the true proposition "David is the father of Solomon"': Peter Geach, *God and the Soul* (Routledge & Kegan Paul: London, 1969), p. 43.
35. For more on Aquinas on what we might call the logic of the Incarnation, see my *Aquinas* (Continuum: London and New York, 2002), ch. 17. See also Herbert McCabe, *God Still Matters* (Continuum: London and New York, 2002), ch. 10, and Thomas G. Weinandy, *Does God Change?* (St Bede's Publications: Still River, Mass., 1985), ch. 3.
36. Exponents of what I am calling classical Trinitarian thinking often say that goodness or love can be ascribed to God quite apart from anything suggested by what belief in the Incarnation might be taken to involve or imply. From what I have already said, you will realize that I agree with them. Now, however, I am concerned with what might be thought of God simply on the basis of the Incarnation considered as the coming to be of a particular human being who can truly be said to be both human and divine.

The Reality of God and the Problem of Evil

37. For what seems to me a helpful development of this image see McCabe, *God Matters*, pp. 48f.
38. I shall not here insert references to chapters and verses in the New Testament, since it seems to me obvious that even a casual reader of the Gospels will quickly be able to see that what I am reporting reflects the depiction of Christ as given in them.
39. Cf. Matthew 7:21;12:50; John 5:19–24; 6:38; 8:28; 12:44–50; 14:31.
40. There are biblical scholars who doubt that the Gospels give us anything remotely reliable as a history of Jesus. I am not concerned here to enter into a discussion of the merits of their view. For now, all I am drawing attention to is what emerges if one works within the framework of classical Trinitarianism and if one presumes, as Christians have for centuries, that the Gospels give us a reasonably faithful account of the sayings and doings of Christ. For an account of recent work on 'the historical Jesus' see Mark Allen Powell, *Jesus as a Figure in History* (Westminster John Knox Press: Louisville, Ky, 1998). As well as noting the conclusions of people who have been sceptical when it comes to the historical value of the Gospels, Powell copiously documents the arguments of those adopting a different position.

Appendix:
Is God Morally Indifferent?

It has been suggested to me that the account I provide in the previous pages is one that makes God out to be a morally indifferent being. It has also been suggested to me that my discussion effectively concedes to atheists all that they want us to believe: that the universe is run by causes which are morally blind, indifferent to suffering, well-being and justice. Careful readers of my text will, I hope, see that these suggestions are unfounded. Yet perhaps it might help to clarify my position if I here directly and briefly respond to them.

In one sense, of course, I *do* take God to be morally indifferent. For I do not think of God as a centre of consciousness (a Cartesian 'I') co-existing temporally with other things and (like any good human being) anxious to do the right thing in terms of standards to which he/she *ought to conform*. Nor do I think of God as literally being a passionately committed and morally commendable combatant in a fight against evil in all its varieties. As the source of all created goodness, and as good without qualification, God is not temporal (and, therefore, not literally anxious about anything). Nor can he be subject to standards of behaviour rightly to be thought of as morally binding on him. And since passions are only had by temporal things acted on by other such things, God, I maintain, is not literally passionately committed to anything. Nor is he literally involved in any fight. He is the Maker of all things in heaven and earth. Fighters exist in a context where they have to try to prevail over individuals who are in some serious sense their peers. To think of God as a fighter in this sense, however, is to take him to be part of what he makes. It is to think of him in wholly unbiblical and unacceptably anthropomorphic terms, and not as what accounts for there being any world of individuals at all.

To say all of that, however, is not to *describe* God. In the previous paragraph I have only been noting what *cannot* be truly affirmed of God. And what I have been saying certainly does not amount to the suggestion that God is (positively) morally indifferent in the sense we have in mind when we condemn people for being so. A morally indifferent person, so I presume most of us would agree, is someone on the planet Earth who lives a life with no regard to ethics. Such a person is a bad human being with little understanding of, or interest in, how people need to behave in order to live well together. As Aristotle would have said, such a person is someone who is just not concerned with being happy as a member of society. With this sense of 'morally indifferent' in mind, however, it is clearly ludicrous to suggest that God is morally indifferent, and I am not suggesting this. God is not a human being who needs to learn how to behave and how to respect those who teach him how to do so. He cannot be morally indifferent as people are.

Could it be that he is morally indifferent because his will is not fixed on what is good? Not in terms of my account as presented in this book. As I have argued, God should be thought of as willing all creaturely goodness: willing it as freely creating it. I agree, of course, that there are good things or situations which God has not made to be (e.g. my being healthier than I presently am). God's not creating certain imagined goods, however, cannot reasonably be taken as a sign of his moral indifference – not, at any rate, if we concede (as I have suggested that we should) that God stands under no obligations or commands to be thought of as binding on him. The Creator of all things (should there be one) cannot, it seems to me, be sensibly thought of as culpable for not creating specified imagined goods (just as he could not be sensibly thought of as culpable for not creating any goods at all).

You might reply that, given my account of God, it would seem that the moral values we live by reflect nothing of God's concerns and that God is, therefore, indeed morally indifferent. Yet I am not denying that the moral values we live by reflect God's concerns. As I said in Chapter 4, we may take what it is morally good for human beings to do to be constituted by God's will as making people to be what they are. Let us suppose that it is morally right for Mary or John to act in such and such a way. On my understanding, this can only be so if God has made a world in which this is so (and without anything making him do so). So, on my understanding, God is that which enables us to make true moral judgements concerning people. He positively (and freely) calls into being the world in which we have moral values by which to live. In that case, however, it would seem odd to suggest that he must be morally indifferent. That which freely calls into being the world in which we make moral distinctions can hardly be thought of as positively indifferent when it comes to morality, or as being positively unconcerned with the moral values by which we live.

It might be said that such a thing would be morally indifferent if it did not behave as people ought to behave. But to argue along those lines would be like suggesting that an opera singer is scientifically indifferent since she does not break off from her arias to give us a lecture on quantum physics. In the sense that people can be said to be morally indifferent, God cannot be so described. Morally indifferent people take their moral obligations lightly, or have little concern to cultivate virtues such as temperance, fortitude, courage, and so on. Yet, I have suggested, God is not subject to moral obligations and has no need of human virtues. The same, of course, could be said about a tennis ball, which may prompt someone to think that God, on my account, is morally indifferent in the sense that a tennis ball is. Yet, of course, I am not saying that God is something lifeless, inert, or sub-moral (like a tennis ball). Nor am I denying that God wills what is good (indeed, I have argued that God does this). I am merely suggesting that we go badly astray if we think of God as an invisible person anxious to do what it is right for him to do (what any decent God ought to do, so one might say). I am resisting attempts to construe God's goodness as being like (visible) human moral goodness. I deny that God can be sensibly thought of as either guilty or exonerable by human standards (to be evaluated as we evaluate human beings). As I have noted, many authors have suggested that we need to think of God (should there be one) as something to be graded by standards that we use when assessing the worth of our fellows. With this notion in place, some have gone on to say that the world provides no evidence of there being a God, or that the world as we find it shows that there is no God, or that evil can be thought of as compatible with God's existence, or that it cannot be proved that evil disproves God's existence. In my view, however, people embracing these lines of thought have made a big mistake at the outset: they are assuming that God is something to be evaluated by standards that we use when assessing the worth of our fellows. They are thinking of God too anthropomorphically.

Once again, to say this is not to suggest that God has nothing to do with morality or with values we hold dear. On my account, God is what freely gives us all that we deem to be good. And, as the cause of there being anything other than himself, he establishes (and freely continues to establish) the conditions which enable us to make moral judgements about people. He is, one might say, the ultimate source or foundation of moral thinking. So he is not morally indifferent. At the same time, though, he is not a person acting as we expect our fellows to act. Nor is he subject to the moral constraints by which we judge them. You might reply that for me to argue in this way is for me to depart from the very point of theistic religion. As I have argued in this book, however, my line of thinking is what needs to be pressed if we are seriously concerned with *theism* as opposed to idolatry. Much of my argument has been philosophical in character, and a respondent might claim that it conflicts with what we ought to be saying about God for non-philosophical reasons – because of what we read in the Bible. I am unconvinced, however, that what I am saying *does* conflict with biblical teaching taken as a whole. As I argued in Chapter 4, for example, my claim that God is not a moral agent seems to cohere more with biblical understandings of God than does the view that God is subject to duties or obligations, or the view that he is to be rated with reference to some standard outside him to which he needs to conform.

You might think that it follows from what I am saying that God is not on the side of right and is morally indifferent for that reason. Yet I am not denying that God is on the side of right. On my account, God wills what is good, since he causes what is good (including what is right). On my account, as freely creating us to make good ethical judgements about people (as making us to exist when making such judgements), God cannot seriously be thought of as not being on the side of right. The same would seem to be true if God commands us to act in various good ways, and I do not deny that he does.

You might reply that God is morally indifferent if he cannot be thought of as being what we take a morally good human being to be – e.g. someone actively engaged in a struggle against injustice and suffering. To echo something I said above, however, the notion of God being involved in a struggle seems bizarre if God is indeed the Maker of all things. Given that our world is made to be by God, then, in an obvious sense, God is not, without qualification, against injustice and suffering. For these are perfectly real and would not be there if not for God. Yet it also makes sense to say that God is against injustice: given my account, he is against it as creating a world in which for us to act unjustly is bad (and, therefore, not in accord with what is perfectly good, as God is). And we may (as I argued in Chapter 7) take God to be against suffering as not willing it as an end in itself, as bringing it about only in so far as he brings about goodness.

As I have been arguing in this book, we make a big mistake at the outset if we get hooked on the notion that God, if he exists, is morally good as people are morally good. Discussions of the problem of evil often make that mistake, and the mistake is one well worth exposing for the error that it is, without implying that God is morally indifferent.

Bibliography

Adams, Marilyn McCord, *Horrendous Evils and the Goodness of God* (Cornell University Press: Ithaca, NY and London, 1999).

Adams, Marilyn McCord, and Adams, Robert Merrihew (eds), *The Problem of Evil* (Oxford University Press: Oxford, 1990).

Adams, Robert M., *The Virtue of Faith and Other Essays in Philosophical Theology* (Oxford University Press: New York and Oxford, 1987).

Ahern, M. B., *The Problem of Evil* (Routledge & Kegan Paul: London, 1971).

Anscombe, G. E. M., 'Times, Beginnings and Causes', *Proceedings of the British Academy* 60 (1974).

—— '"Whatever Has a Beginning of Existence Must Have a Cause": Hume's Argument Exposed', *Analysis* 34 (1974).

Anscombe, G. E. M., and Geach, P. T., *Three Philosophers* (Basil Blackwell: Oxford, 1961).

Aquinas, Thomas, *Commentary on Aristotle's 'De Anima'*, tr. Robert Pasnau (Yale University Press: New Haven, Conn., and London, 1999).

—— *The Literal Exposition on Job*, tr. Anthony Damico (Scholars Press: Atlanta, 1989).

—— *On Being and Essence*, tr. Joseph Bobik (University of Notre Dame Press: Notre Dame, Ind., 1965).

—— *On Evil*, ed. Brian Davies, tr. Richard Regan (Oxford University Press: Oxford and New York, 2003).

—— *Summa Contra Gentiles*, tr. Anton Pegis, James F. Anderson, Vernon J. Bourke and Charles J. O'Neil (University of Notre Dame Press: Notre Dame, Ind., 1975).

—— *Summa Theologiae*, Blackfriars Edition, 61 vols (Eyre and Spottiswoode: London and McGraw-Hill: New York, 1964–80).

Ballantine, Samuel, *The Hidden God: The Hiding of the Face of God in the Old Testament* (Oxford University Press: Oxford, 1983).

Barton, John, and Muddiman, John, *The Oxford Bible Commentary* (Oxford University Press: Oxford, 2001).

Brown, Raymond E., Fitzmeyer, Joseph, and Murphy, Roland E. (eds), *The Jerome Biblical Commentary* (Geoffrey Chapman: London, 1968).

Cicovacki, Predrag (ed.), *Destined for Evil? The Twentieth Century Responses* (University of Rochester Press: Rochester, NY, 2005).

Bibliography

Copan, Paul, and Craig, William Lane, *Creation out of Nothing* (Baker Academic: Grand Rapids, Mich., and Apollos: Leicester, 2004).

Crenshaw, James L., *Theodicy in the New Testament* (Fortress Press: Philadelphia and SPCK: London, 1983).

Davies, Brian, *Aquinas* (Continuum: London and New York, 2002).

—— 'Aquinas on What God is Not', *Revue Internationale de Philosophie* 52 (1998).

—— *An Introduction to the Philosophy of Religion*, 3rd edn (Oxford University Press: Oxford, 2004).

—— 'Kenny on Aquinas on Being', *Modern Schoolman* 82 (2005).

—— *The Thought of Thomas Aquinas* (Clarendon Press: Oxford, 1992).

Davies, Brian, and Leftow, Brian (eds), *Thomas Aquinas, 'Summa Theologiae', Questions on God* (Cambridge University Press: Cambridge, 2005).

Davis, Stephen T., *Logic and the Nature of God* (Macmillan: London, 1983).

Delaney, C. F. (ed.), *Rationality and Religious Belief* (University of Notre Dame Press: Notre Dame, Ind. and London, 1979).

Dixon, Philip, *Nice and Hot Disputes: The Doctrine of the Trinity in the 17th Century* (T&T Clark: Edinburgh, 2003).

Dodd, C. H., *The Johannine Epistles* (Harper: New York, 1946).

Eddy, Mary Baker, *Science and Health with Key to the Scriptures* (Christian Science Board of Directors: Boston, 1971).

Eichrodt, Walther, *Theology of the Old Testament*, tr. J. A. Baker, vol. 1 (Westminster Press: Philadelphia, 1961).

Flew, Antony, *The Presumption of Atheism and Other Essays* (Elek/Pemberton: London, 1976).

—— 'Theology and Falsification', in Antony Flew and Alasdair MacIntyre (eds), *New Essays in Philosophical Theology* (SCM Press: London, 1955).

Geach, P. T., *God and the Soul* (Routledge & Kegan Paul: London, 1969).

—— 'Good and Evil', *Analysis* 17 (1956).

—— *Logic Matters* (Basil Blackwell: Oxford, 1972).

—— *Providence and Evil* (Cambridge University Press: Cambridge, 1977).

Hart, William, *Evil: A Primer* (St Martin's Press: New York, 2004).

Hawthorne, Gerald F., and Martin, Ralph P. (eds), *Dictionary of Paul and his Letters* (InterVarsity Press: Downers Grove, Ill., 1993).

Helm, Paul, *The Providence of God* (Inter-Varsity Press: Leicester, 1993).

Hick, John, *Evil and the God of Love*, 2nd edn (Macmillan: London, 1977).

Holland, R. F., *Against Empiricism* (Barnes and Noble: Totowa, NJ, 1980).

Howard-Snyder, Daniel (ed.), *The Evidential Argument from Evil* (Indiana University Press: Bloomington, Ind. and Indianapolis, 1996).

Hume, David, *Dialogues Concerning Natural Religion*, ed. Stanley Tweyman (Routledge: London and New York, 1991).

—— *An Inquiry Concerning Human Understanding*, ed. Tom L. Beauchamp (Clarendon Press: Oxford, 2000).

Jacob, Edmond, *Theology of the Old Testament*, tr. Arthur W. Heathcote and Philip J. Alcock (Harper and Brothers: New York, 1958).

Bibliography

Johnson, Luke Timothy, *The Gospel of Luke* (Liturgical Press: Collegeville, Minn., 1991).

Kant, Immanuel, *Critique of Pure Reason*, ed. and tr. Paul Guyer and Allen W. Wood (Cambridge University Press: Cambridge, 1997).

—— 'Toward Perpetual Peace', in Immanuel Kant, *Practical Philosophy*, ed. and tr. Mary J. Gregor (Cambridge University Press: Cambridge, 1996).

Kenny, Anthony, *Aquinas on Being* (Clarendon Press: Oxford, 2002).

Kremer, Elmar J., and Latzer, Michael J., *The Problem of Evil in Early Modern Philosophy* (University of Toronto Press: Toronto and London, 2001).

Larrimore, Mark (ed.), *The Problem of Evil: A Reader* (Blackwell Publishers: Oxford, 2001).

Leaman, Oliver, *Evil and Suffering in Jewish Philosophy* (Cambridge University Press: Cambridge, 1995).

Leibniz, G. W., *Theodicy*, ed. Austin Farrer, tr. E. M. Huggard (Yale University Press: New Haven, Conn., 1952).

Lewis, C. S., *The Problem of Pain* (Macmillan: New York, 1962).

Lewis, H.D., *Philosophy of Religion* (English Universities Press: London, 1965).

Mackie, John, *The Miracle of Theism* (Clarendon Press: Oxford, 1982).

Madden, Edward H., and Hare, Peter H., *Evil and the Concept of God* (Charles C. Thomas: Springfield, Ill., 1969).

Marshall, I. Howard, *The Gospel of Luke* (Paternoster Press: Exeter, 1979).

Martin, C. F. J., *Thomas Aquinas: God and Explanations* (Edinburgh University Press: Edinburgh, 1997).

Mathewes, Charles T., *Evil and the Augustinian Tradition* (Cambridge University Press: Cambridge, 2001).

McCabe, Herbert, *God, Christ and Us* (Continuum: London and New York, 2003).

—— *God Matters* (Geoffrey Chapman: London, 1987).

—— *God Still Matters* (Continuum: London and New York, 2002).

Midgley, Mary, *Wickedness* (Routledge & Kegan Paul: London, 1984).

Miller, Barry, *A Most Unlikely God* (University of Notre Dame Press: Notre Dame, Ind. and London, 1996).

Moltmann, Jürgen, *The Crucified God*, tr. R. A. Wilson and John Bowden (SCM Press: London, 1974).

Moore, Gareth, *Believing in God* (T. & T. Clark: Edinburgh, 1988).

Morris, Thomas V., *Our Idea of God: An Introduction to Philosophical Theology* (University of Notre Dame Press: Notre Dame, Ind. and London, 1991).

Morton, Adam, *On Evil* (Routledge: New York and London, 2004).

O'Connor, David, *God and Inscrutable Evil* (Rowan and Littlefield: Lanham, Md and Oxford, 1998).

Peterson, Michael L., *God and Evil: An Introduction to the Issues* (Westview Press: Oxford, 1998).

Phillips, D. Z., *The Problem of Evil and the Problem of God* (SCM Press: London, 2004).

Phillips, D. Z. (ed.), *Religion and Morality* (St Martin's Press: New York, 1996).

Pike, Nelson (ed.), *God and Evil* (Prentice-Hall: Englewood Cliffs, NJ, 1964).

Plantinga, Alvin, *God, Freedom and Evil* (George Allen & Unwin: London, 1975).

—— *The Nature of Necessity* (Clarendon Press: Oxford, 1974).

—— 'Is Theism Really a Miracle?', *Faith and Philosophy* 3 (1986).

Plantinga, Theodore, *Learning to Live with Evil* (Eerdmans: Grand Rapids, Mich., 1982).

Powell, Mark Allen, *Jesus as a Figure in History* (Westminster John Knox Press: Louisville, Ky, 1998).

Quinn, Philip P., 'Divine Conservation, Continuous Creation, and Human Action', in Alfred J. Freddoso (ed.), *The Existence and Nature of God* (University of Notre Dame Press: Notre Dame, Ind. and London, 1983).

Reichenbach, Bruce R., *Evil and a Good God* (Fordham University Press: New York, 1982).

Rice, Hugh, *God and Goodness* (Oxford University Press: Oxford, 2000).

Rocca, Gregory P., *Speaking the Incomprehensible God* (Catholic University of America Press: Washington, DC, 2004).

Ross, James F., 'Creation II', in Alfred J. Freddoso (ed.), *The Existence and Nature of God* (University of Notre Dame Press: Notre Dame, Ind. and London, 1983).

Rowe, William L., *Philosophy of Religion: An Introduction*, 3rd edn (Wadsworth: Belmont, Calif., 2001).

Rudiger, Bittner, *Doing Things for Reasons* (Oxford University Press: Oxford, 2001).

Rundle, Bede, *Why there is Something Rather than Nothing* (Clarendon Press: Oxford, 2004).

Schlesinger, George N., *New Perspectives on Old-Time Religion* (Clarendon Press: Oxford, 1988).

Shanley, Brian, *The Thomistic Tradition* (Kluwer Academic Publishers: Dordrecht and London, 2002).

Singer, Mark G., 'The Concept of Evil', *Philosophy* 79 (2004).

Sobrino, Jon, *Christology at the Crossroads* (SCM Press: London, 1978).

Stump, Eleonore, 'Aquinas on the Sufferings of Job', in Eleonore Stump (ed.), *Reasoned Faith* (Cornell University: Ithaca, NY and London, 1993).

—— *Faith and the Problem of Evil* (Calvin College: Grand Rapids, Mich., 1999).

Surin, Kenneth, *Theology and the Problem of Evil* (Basil Blackwell: Oxford, 1986).

Swinburne, Richard, *The Coherence of Theism*, revd edn (Clarendon Press: Oxford, 1993).

—— *The Existence of God*, 2nd edn (Clarendon Press: Oxford, 2004).

—— *Is There a God?* (Oxford University Press: Oxford and New York, 1996).

—— *Providence and the Problem of Evil* (Clarendon Press: Oxford, 1998).

Taliaferro, Charles, *Evidence and Faith: Philosophy and Religion since the*

Seventeenth Century (Cambridge University Press: Cambridge, 2005).

Tanner, Kathryn, *God and Creation in Christian Theology* (Basil Blackwell: Oxford, 1988).

Trethowan, Illtyd, *Absolute Value: A Study in Christian Theism* (George Allen & Unwin: London, 1970).

van Inwagen, Peter, 'The Argument from Particular Horrendous Evils', *American Catholic Philosophical Quarterly* 74 (2000).

—— *God, Knowledge, and Mystery* (Cornell University Press: Ithaca, NY and London, 1995).

—— *Metaphysics* (Westview Press: Boulder, Col., 1993).

van Inwagen, Peter (ed.), *Christian Faith and the Problem of Evil* (Eerdmans: Grand Rapids, Mich., 2004).

Vardy, Peter, *The Puzzle of Evil* (Fount: London, 1992).

Weinandy, Thomas G., *Does God Change?* (St Bede's Publications: Still River, Mass., 1985).

Welbourne, Michael, *The Community of Knowledge* (Aberdeen University Press: Aberdeen, 1986).

—— *Knowledge* (McGill-Queen's University Press: Montreal and London, 2001).

Whitney, Barry L., *Theodicy: An Annotated Bibliography on the Problem of Evil 1960–1991* (Philosophy Documentation Center: Bowling Green, Oh., 1998).

—— *What are they Saying about God and Evil?* (Paulist Press: Mahwah, NY, 1989).

Wierenga, Edward R., *The Nature of God: An Inquiry into Divine Attributes* (Cornell University Press: Ithaca, NY and London, 1989).

Williams, Bernard, *Morality: An Introduction to Ethics* (Cambridge University Press: Cambridge, 1972).

Williams, C. J. F., 'Being', in Philip L. Quinn and Charles Taliaferro (eds), *A Companion to Philosophy of Religion* (Blackwell Publishers: Oxford, 1997).

—— *Being, Identity, and Truth* (Clarendon Press: Oxford, 1992).

—— 'Knowing Good and Evil', *Philosophy* 66 (1991).

—— *What Is Existence?* (Clarendon Press: Oxford, 1981).

Williams, Rowan, 'Redeeming Sorrows', in D. Z. Phillips (ed.), *Religion and Morality* (St Martin's Press: New York, 1996).

Wippel, John F., 'Thomas Aquinas on Our Knowledge of God and the Axiom that Every Agent Produces Something Like Itself', *American Catholic Philosophical Quarterly* 74 (2000).

Wittgenstein, Ludwig, *Philosophical Investigations*, 2nd edn, tr. G. E. M. Anscombe (Basil Blackwell: Oxford, 1968).

Index